FONDREN LIBRARY

S0-CMV-965

Withdrawn SMU Libraries

THE INCORPORATED WIFE

The Perfect Wife Audrey Blackman, 1983.

THE INCORPORATED WIFE

EDITED BY HILARY CALLAN
& SHIRLEY ARDENER

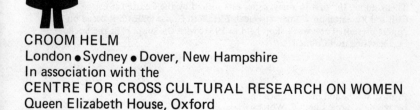

CROOM HELM
London ● Sydney ● Dover, New Hampshire
In association with the
CENTRE FOR CROSS CULTURAL RESEARCH ON WOMEN
Queen Elizabeth House, Oxford

© 1984 Shirley Ardener, Janice Brownfoot, Hilary Callen, Isobel Clark,
Beverley Gartrell, Deborah Kirkwood, Mona Macmillan, Lidia Sciama,
Soraya Tremayne, Malcolm Young.

Croom Helm Ltd, Provident House, Burrell Row,
Beckenham, Kent BR3 1AT

Croom Helm Australia Pty Ltd, First Floor, 139 King St.,
Sydney, NSW 2001, Australia

Croom Helm, 51 Washington Street, Dover,
New Hampshire 03820, USA

Library of Congress Cataloguing in Publication Data

Main entry under title:
The Incorporated wife.
    Bibliography: p.
    Includes index ,
    1. Wives – Great Britain – Effect of husband's employment
on. 2. Wives – Effect of husband's employment on.
3. Wives – Great Britain – Social conditions. 4. Wives –
Social conditions. I. Ardener, Shirley. II. Callan,
Hilary.
HQ759.I47   1984   306.8'72   84-12743
ISBN 0-7099-0521-1

British Library Cataloguing in Publication Data

The Incorporated wife.
    1. Husbands–Employment 2. Wives
I. Ardener, Shirley II. Callen, Hilary
306.8'72   HD4901
ISBN 0-7099-0521-1

This volume, the first in a new series established by the Centre for Cross-
Cultural Research on Women at Queen Elizabeth House Oxford, is based on
papers presented at a work shop held in 1981, with the support of the Social
Science Research Council.

Printed and bound in Great Britain
by Billing & Sons Limited, Worcester.

CONTENTS

B840448

Illustrations

Frontispiece: *The Perfect Wife*, 1983. Audrey Blackman, FSD-C.;
    20 cms.; porcelain bisque.

Facing p. 36: *A Man's World*, 1962. Audrey Blackman, FSD-C.;
    20 cms.; slip-decorated earthenware.

PREFACE

This preface briefly notes the genesis of this volume and welcomes readers among whom, we hope will be those whose inclinations, and perhaps whose 'incorporation', have led them to a personal interest in the experiences of wives, as well as those with purely practical or scholarly concerns in this field of study. The latter may include industrial anthropologists, sociologists and business managers. Historians of the Commonwealth will find some common ground also. We hope that all may find something here which will amuse, dismay, or perhaps provide new ideas for reflection or further research.

We present a range of case studies relating to the 'incorporation' of wives within the institutional and moral frameworks associated with their husbands' occupations. We start 'at home' by considering wives married to academic members of two ancient English institutions, Oxford and Cambridge Universities, then consider women married to members of the British civil and armed forces. Following studies of wives who regularly move between 'home' in the United Kingdom and 'abroad', we end with historical accounts of women living overseas, in Africa and Malaya, as wives of settlers, traders and colonial officials.

Details in some of these papers are often usefully corroborated or echoed in others, while sometimes variations or different structures and practices are revealed. Some years ago I discussed the interesting problem of how one can deal with sets of information on different groups which, like these, are not identical but in which there are enough similar elements to suggest that they might be expressions of a common underlying pattern, only partially discernible through the 'screens' of any particular case (1975: xix). Although at the level of the 'surface of events' there may be differences in the way these features appear, due to differences in circumstances, an analyst might nevertheless try to construct a general picture, or an abstract model, from them: a model containing, perhaps, more elements than can be found in any particular case. The English language contains more words than most English speakers are likely to use, or even know of, just as grammars may record more verbal forms than some speakers have recourse to. Nevertheless, a dictionary and a grammar may still be of use in understanding a particular individual's discourse. Similarly, an embracing model constructed from elements drawn from different social formations may help us to understand better just one of them. In a recent paper (1983) I discussed this question again and attempted to find a common pattern of elements relating to the iconography of gender. The material in this present book provides another tempting opportunity for a similar exercise, although the scale of the task and the inevitable gaps in our data make this, as always, a hazardous and tentative enterprise.

The studies here clearly illuminate the relationships between, and the expectations of, husbands and wives and augment the work already undertaken by others on the institution of marriage in western society. The papers are not, however, primarily directed towards these aspects. They present new ethnographic and historical data to add to the descriptions of business and other occupational institutions already available (a selection of which is noted in the bibliography). Much of the data is collected from women, frequently being enriched by the personal experiences of the writers themselves. The style of analysis here focuses more particularly on the articulation of institutions as they embody systems of values, of purposes, having their own aesthetics, symbols and modes of being. In particular, in their various ways, the introductory essay and the following studies show the part played by certain occupational structures in constructing the personal identities of the wives of employees. The degree of co-operation given by wives is not everywhere the same. For some, avoidance or resistance is attempted; often the strategy of acceptance is adopted as the best option; sometimes the identity generated may be valued, even eagerly sought by the wife who fulfills her ambition or gains her satisfaction by assisting her husband's climb up an occupational hierarchy or by her participation in the success of a cherished cause.

The studies here do not take a judgmental attitude, preferring to report some of the various options open to wives and a range of their responses to them. These may offer opportunities for creativity as well as moments of frustration. This is neither 'knocking' nor approving copy. It reveals the humour, as well as the boredom and anxiety, in the situations it describes. Wives too are at times amused by the absurdity of the circumstances in which they find themselves, and by the games which men and institutions play, as the two illustrations show. Some of the explorations here more sombrely reveal or hint at the difficulties wives face when the games are over, as a result of their husbands' unemployment or retirement, of their changes of job, of long periods of separation or, finally, because of divorce or widowhood. Some of the skills wives have acquired will be transferrable, some will not be – or can no longer be – exercised. The hard choices that some wives must make, for example between their own careers and those of their husbands, between parents and husbands, husbands and children, are often shown to be even more poignant where overseas travel is involved.

The volume is the first in a new series sponsored by the Centre for Cross-Cultural Research on Women based at Queen Elizabeth House, Oxford. This House has been the locus for such research at least since 1973 when a group of women social anthropologists began to hold a regular weekly seminar, which still continues. All but two of the contributors here

(Malcolm Young and Beverley Gartrell) have, at one time or another, participated in this seminar, which, over the years, has kept an interest in women as wives on its academic agenda. Some of the ideas in this book were first bruited there. *Perceiving Women* (ed. S. Ardener, 1975), which is owed in part to it, included an influential paper by Hilary Callan on the wives of diplomats. In 1980 and 1981, with the helpful support of the Social Science Research Council, I convened three two-day workshops at Queen Elizabeth House on the general theme 'The Social Anthropology of Women'. While the majority of those present were trained in social anthropology, this was not the case for other participants, all of whom were nevertheless familiar with its concerns. The approach, like that of this volume, was interdisciplinary. The topics of the workshops were 'The Education of Women', 'The Study of Groups of Wives' and 'Life Trajectories'. I invited Hilary Callan to come from Canada to act as rapporteur of the second workshop, envisaging that we might jointly edit a volume based on the papers presented there. Hilary Callan gave an introductory paper, while various points raised in the other papers and in comments were embodied in her final summary, from which her present splendid introductory essay grew. She has picked up some of the threads which have been variously teased out and has woven them together in her introduction. I would like to record here the pleasure and profit I have gained from the many long discussions we have had while editing this volume.

Of the ten authors of the papers here, although our interests overlap, six (Callan, Young, Sciama, Tremayne, Gartrell and I) are social anthropologists, three are historians (Macmillan, Kirkwood and Brownfoot) while one (Clark) is concerned with history and literature. Ellan Derow gave a talk at the workshop on 'The Classification of Wives in Policy Making' and Mary Bouquet spoke about her research on 'Farmers' Wives'; unfortunately previous commitments have prevented them from presenting papers here. Others at the workshop who chaired sessions or who otherwise contributed to the discussions were Jane Khatib-Chahidi, Maryon Macdonald, Helen Callaway, Edwin Ardener, Pat Holden, Susan Wright, Alison Smith and Rosemary Ridd. We are grateful to them for their largely unacknowledged ideas and appraisals. Audrey Blackman has kindly allowed us to use her ironical figurines for illustrations. The editors would like to thank Mike Clarke and Jan Tagg, who so expertly set our manuscript in type on the Oxford University Lasercomp machine and also, of course, our publisher.

Queen Elizabeth House, Oxford   Shirley Ardener

INTRODUCTION

Hilary Callan

> An organization can ... be viewed as a place for generating assumptions about identity ... Every organization ... involves a discipline of activity, but ... every organization also involves a discipline of being - an obligation to be of a given character and to dwell in a given world. (Goffman 1961: 170-1)

'Incorporation': constituting the problem

This collection of papers seeks to explore the condition of *wifehood* in a range of settings where the social character ascribed to a woman is an intimate function of her husband's occupational identity and culture. The housewife's provision of general domestic support to the male breadwinner, and the implications of her economic dependence, have been abundantly researched and debated elsewhere. Here, we are more narrowly concerned with what it means for a woman - who may or may not be dependent and may or may not be a housewife - to be socially identified as 'wife of' a particular kind of worker: policeman, colonial official or colonist, soldier or sailor, corporate executive, professional scholar. To come to our attention as incorporated wives, of course, women have already had to undergo the 'silencing' or under-recognition of the rest of their personhood which allows them to be so designated. An analytic acquiescence in this process cannot be avoided, and is indeed a necessary condition for understanding the forces which create and sustain it.

The idea of incorporation resonates with others - *corporateness, corporation, corporeality* - all pertinent to our theme. It points also to a set of issues which concern all the book's contributors: the nature of institutional boundaries, mechanisms of inclusion and exclusion, and the structural dilemma that arises when, because of marriage, women have to be given a location in, on or outside the boundary of an organization or institution. Often, as we shall see, this location is equivocal in ways that may be advantageous to the organization, but may also pose a threat to it. Such concerns, even if they appear here in relatively novel guise, are familiar ones in anthropology: the 'stranger wife' with her ambiguous status is herself no stranger to the ethnographer. In most societies, needless to say, married women are in many ways asymmetrically drawn into the 'social person' of their husbands. In industrial society, this is reflected and reinforced by powerful economic, legal and administrative practices. The approach to be adopted in this book focuses equally on the concrete circumstancess and the consciousness of incorporated wives. Incorporation, in other words, is to be viewed as a material and simultaneously as a moral condition.

Who is an incorporated wife? The concept of incorporation is necessarily indeterminate at present; it points to an area of inquiry but does not fully specify it. At the level of institutions, questions arise about the power of an organization's instrumental objectives, its values, its formal and informal procedures, rewards and control systems, to flow across the conjugal link and so gain effective jurisdiction over the wives of its members. Other questions concern the resource value of wives to the organization, and the recognizability of this to the parties concerned. Investigation of this area often displays interlocking but contradictory realities, as several of the papers reveal. At the level of the personal the questions concern the refractions within the wives' own consciousness of the character of their association with an incorporating organization, their sense of partnership in, or exclusion from, their husbands' work, and how far the latter may create for them a distinct universe of experience and judgment.

This ground cannot be definitively marked out in advance. There is as yet no theory of organizations, nor indeed of marriage, that would do justice to the assumptions organizations have about marriage, and the load they place upon it. Moreover, as we shall see, the situation of wives *vis-à-vis* organizations is intimately moulded by context: by shifting perceptions, permeable boundaries, the creative manipulation of ambiguities. Thus the phrase 'incorporated wife' points to an *available*, rather than an *empirical*, category: one that cannot be populated by mechanical criteria of inclusion and exclusion alone. At the Oxford workshop at which plans for this book were first laid, someone remarked 'But to whom would you *say* that you were the wife of a such-and-such?' and there is no mistaking the power of language itself in setting up the category and controlling access to it. Words reflect reality, and reconstitute it. At the heart of Lidia Sciama's paper is the verbal designation *academic wife*. The wives in her sample are sensitive, with reason, to the use of the phrase, and to whether they are themselves included in its scope. As she shows, its ambiguity is far from accidental. We can say the same of other 'innocently' ambiguous labels such as 'political wife', 'military wife', 'diplomatic wife'. In each case the adjectival form (compare 'wife of a politician', for example) invites a reading which pre-emptively ascribes to the wife something of the character of the institution.

Mona Macmillan gives an excellent example of language acting as an instrument of incorporation in its own right. Her description of the use of Army slang by wives in India in the last century has a distinctly tribal ring to the modern ear, but present-day equivalents are not hard to find: witness Malcolm Young's account of 'the job' as a phrase constantly on the lips of police wives as of their husbands. The converse power of words to exclude is well illustrated in Soraya Tremayne's observation of 'shop-talk' carried on by male Shell company executives at social gatherings where wives are present. Here, pointedly it seems, the language sets up a boundary within the system, so creating an inner circle and a 'periphery' to which wives can be assigned. I shall suggest below that this may have a dramatic purpose of its own, but it clearly occurs in a limited range of contexts. In other settings the internal barrier dissolves, and executives and their wives declare in unison that 'we are Shell'. Oxford wives similarly may on occasion think or speak of themselves 'as' Balliol, or St John's, but conversely again, as Shirley Ardener shows, the words 'academic wife' supply a label which can be rejected. Thus the very phrase brings into existence a person for a woman to refuse to be.[1]

Until recently there have been few attempts to look systematically at the impact on wives of the society and culture of their husbands' occupations. Isolated studies have been made in the setting of particular organizations (see e.g. Kanter 1977, Finch 1980, Callan 1975). But it has not so far been possible to deal with incorporation comparatively: to consider where and why it occurs, which parts of the pattern are constant and which variable across organizations, and what the implications are now and for the future.[2] This relative neglect is not hard to explain, given the legitimate priorities of academic feminism and the undeniably bourgeois character of most situations of incorporation. While there may well be counterparts in other social systems, the cases here examined seem to be products of a European social form in which the enabling institutions exist, and where, since labour itself is thought of as contractually based, the 'patrimonial' aspects of wives' relations with their husbands' employers show up in contrast. The clearest examples are likely to be found among wives of men in occupations which are historically and predominantly male, and whose cultures have evolved alongside parallel conceptions of what constitutes a proper wife for their members. For example, Sciama's material suggests an association in the history of Cambridge between the emergence of the 'don' as professional, and his acquisition of an 'academic wife' of appropriate character. In the case of newer occupations, perhaps the creation of incorporated wives is similarly connected with the invention of 'professional' identities. Young's and Macmillan's accounts of police and Armed Service wives indicate that incorporation is not intrinsically confined to middle-class life; it is in any case unlikely to be sharply bounded and further research will doubtless reveal many kinds of marginal case. But for the most part, the incorporated wives discussed here are by anybody's standards materially privileged women. They are not easily seen, nor do they readily see themselves, as victims. Nor do they carry conviction as figures of tragedy in a world of mass unemployment, cohabitation rules and domestic violence.[3]

The women's movement has, of course, brought rising expectations to women in the industrial world, and a corresponding recruitment problem for the employers of husbands of career women, who are under increasing pressure to give recognition to these women's independent aspirations. No longer, it may seem, can employers unreflectingly count on a wife's willingness to provide unpaid and unrecognized services ('two for the price of one'). The growing visibility of symmetrical marriages, female executives and men in the position of 'spouse' has undermined many of the symbolic associations, as well as the concrete expectations, derived from the paired concepts *man* and *wife*.[4]

But it would be quite wrong to conclude that the incorporated wife is on the brink of extinction, her situation therefore unworthy of serious study. Incorporation has been and is a dominating force in the lives of significant numbers of women. The cases mount up, when one puts together the examples from past and present that we have collected in this book, and the many others that we have not - alas - been able to include (see Finch 1980 and 1983). In some cases (notably those of expatriate organizations) there is cause for much concern about the stresses to which wives are rendered particularly vulnerable by unrecognized features of their situation. The incorporation of wives also has implications for more established areas of social theory: the formal and informal workings of organizations, the position of women and of men in the family and the labour market, the conditions governing the treatment of classes of people as dependent or as socially adult. Moreover, organizations themselves have a legitimate and practical interest in understanding their own processes. Most have been able to take wives for granted in the past, because a folk theory of marriage easily allowed incorporation to be seen as a 'natural' and inevitable condition. They become aware of the 'hidden services' of wives only when these are, or threaten to be, withdrawn. Or (as Tremayne points out) it is only in the face of 'deviance' that they can articulate a concept of what a wife 'should' be. In diplomacy, for example, the status of spouses is a matter over which consciousness has been well and truly raised in recent years throughout the industrial world. People nevertheless do not know what to think or do: there is much genuine agonizing among both liberals and conservatives over what, if anything, can be fairly expected of a wife. There is some recognition that (ignoring the cultural and intellectual resources which wives may contribute) the budgetary consequences of including the value of their labour in the accounting system would be formidable. But the critical issues have not, to my knowledge, been formulated by management in a clear way (some administrations have, naturally, made more efforts than others); certainly no global policy options have emerged.[5]

Finally, the impact of social change on the incorporation of wives has not so far been as profound as might appear. The treatment of wives has become controversial in many organizations, piecemeal changes have taken place, and formal restrictions now widely viewed as indefensible (such as prohibitions on wives' having independent jobs) have, where they existed, sometimes been relaxed. Some of the changes are described in these papers. But I suggest that what has often not changed is the person-defining power of organizations. Their ability to gain acceptance for their own assumptions about the essential and inward character of wives and women is remarkably resistant to change. As we might expect, and as the papers reveal, institutions differ greatly in the use they make of the powers they seem to have over the organization of consciousness. Wives too differ individually in their response to incorporation, and in the salience that it has for them. But to the extent that incorporation does involve the 'subordination' of wives, openly coercive techniques of control (although they exist) are hardly needed. Control can be as effectively gained, and discipline exercised, through a system of definitions which sustains an intact and unchallengeable world-view.

Wives as fiction: wives in fiction
If little is systematically known about the incorporation of wives, much is 'known' about it in the form of stereotype, anecdote and folk-belief. Folk images of incorporated wives (the 'Colonel's lady' and the like) are worthy of study in their own right, both as an important part of popular culture and for the reflexive influence they surely have on the situation and consciousness of actual wives. Stories are told of the open or tacit 'vetting' of the wives of candidates for corporate or political office. Tremayne hints in her paper that such vetting may take place; Young attests to its reality for police wives. Belief in it is widespread, and implies shared conceptions of the kind of woman who is a 'suitable' wife in each case. To understand incorporation we need to consider not only how and why such evaluations take place, but how the expectation of them influences the thought and conduct of the women concerned and of their husbands.

The stereotypes are powerful, and many of them are unattractive. The mythology of the British Empire, for example, seems to contain the idea that colonists and 'natives' were able to live happily together until *memsahibs* appeared and insisted upon racial and social separation. Thus may a post-colonial generation unload a little of its moral discomfort at the expense of its mothers and grandmothers. In this book we present three essays with a colonial theme. In none of them, significantly, is this particular stereotype of the colonial wife straightforwardly endorsed, although all the authors allow that parts of it sometimes corresponded to reality. From the accounts of white-ruled Rhodesia, Malaya and Uganda given by Deborah Kirkwood, Janice Brownfoot and Beverley Gartrell respectively, it is clear that while details varied according to locale, the relations of white wives with one another, with the expatriate community and with the 'natives' were always complex and often problematic.

Colonial societies were, indeed, themselves many-stranded cultures; they cannot be reduced to one-dimensional models of political and racial subordination. In Brownfoot's account the *mems* appear as locked into contradictory perceptions of their own role and function; they are routinely disparaged by men (and observers) for limitations of outlook which men have largely forced upon them. Yet, she argues convincingly, they were not mere shadows of their men, nor passive ciphers in a system of racial values and theories of Empire, but played a distinctive part in both the colonial order and its demise. Her painstaking work in capturing this special role from the few records and the recollections of survivors is an impressive example of 'rescue work' in the history of women; the material presented here is only a part of a larger work in which she is engaged.

Gartrell's paper is a natural complement to Brownfoot's, although she, writing specifically of officials' wives, is most concerned with the part they played in political control in colonial Uganda. A particular virtue of her treatment is that, while allowing some factual basis to the commonly-held belief in wives' obsessive interest in social differentials and protocol, it also describes the very limited and largely symbolic rewards available to wives in return for their efforts; in this context such an obsession becomes intelligible. On the sensitive question of race, too, Gartrell offers a measure of support to the prevailing view while rejecting its cruder variants. But once again she places the supposed racial exclusivity of wives in the context of a web of restrictions on knowledge and entrenched anxieties about health and sex which they were in no position to challenge, and within which it made a kind of sense. There were, surely, exceptions to the pattern, and if wives did contribute to racial exclusiveness they evidently did so passively by providing a self-contained society for white men, as much as actively through their behaviour towards colonized peoples.

Colonial wives, then, were indeed sometimes looked upon as bearers of a special *civilizing mission* to both the colonized and their own men. But they could also be, through their relations with 'native' women, wittingly or unwittingly subversive to the colonial social order itself. Brownfoot's analysis of the situation in Malaya brings out this dual potential in a particularly clear way, and Kirkwood gives it a special twist for Rhodesia to which I shall return. Unfortunately we lack enough information on wives in other systems of colonial rule to offer any comment on the Britishness of either the stereotype or the reality, although all three of our present contributors make suggestive points which would repay further study. The evidence now available, however, seems to support current moves for the restoration of the colonial wife to visibility and also for some rehabilitation of her memory, notwithstanding the morally indefensible aspects of colonialism itself.

There is not always a clear line to be drawn between culturally available stereotypes of incorporated wives, and fictional portrayals of them. Gartrell's ethnography indicates, for example, that the fictional 'horror' may correspond to one of a number of distinct types that were recognized and judged within the complex social field of 'real life'. The common perception of any social 'reality' must contain an element of stereotype. Fictional portrayals of incorporated wives draw on both the 'stereotype' and the 'perceived reality', while feeding back into both. They are therefore doubly useful and doubly difficult to use in the study of incorporation. Fiction first alerted several of our contributors to the real-life anthropological interest of the incorporated wife, as they have recorded; others have drawn substantially on fiction in their arguments. The difficulties and implications of this cannot be fully discussed here, but any definitive analysis of incorporation must allow for the influence of imaginative fiction, since it, like the 'stereotype', is part of a common culture that moulds the perceptions of observer and observed alike.

Conversely, the concept of incorporation may be of service in studying the representation of women in fiction. Mona Macmillan in her paper singles out Thackeray's Mrs O'Dowd as a portrait of the military wife; she could equally have taken the naval case of Mrs Croft in Jane Austen's *Persuasion*. Mrs Croft offers an intriguing example of what we could reasonably call incorporation, used for a very exact artistic purpose. In depicting the Croft marriage as a *naval* partnership, its happiness giving us a foretaste of the happiness Anne Elliott deserves and will get as a sailor's wife, Jane Austen was (we may assume) appealing to a common understanding of naval virtues which in 'real life' she knew and admired. At the same time, the architecture of the novel as a whole designates the naval figure as repository and sign for the humane liberality which stands in formal opposition to the moral deficiency of the characters who compose the Sir Walter Elliott grouping. So in moving from the one camp to the other - in becoming a *naval wife* - Anne achieves happiness and gets her man according to genre. But as a character she does more than this: she gives her author the means of making a complex and elegant moral statement about marriage, society and human responsibility, and the ground for all this has been carefully and economically prepared for us in advance by a progression of unforgettable glimpses into the happy and successful *naval marriage*.

> 'And I do assure you, ma'am,' pursued Mrs Croft, 'that nothing can exceed the accommodations of a man of war; I speak, you know, of the higher rates When you come to a frigate, of course, you are more confined - though any reasonable woman may be perfectly happy in one of them; and I can safely say, that the happiest part of my life has been spent on board a ship. While we were together, you know, there was nothing to be feared ... nothing ever ailed me, and I never met with the smallest inconvenience.' (*Persuasion*, O.U.P. edn: 79)

In an unpublished paper on the treatment of wives in fiction, Isobel Clark has noted that in a writer such as Somerset Maugham, 'reality' and 'truth' are elements to be bent for a paramount narrative purpose. Wives are accordingly given a character which allows their function in the machinery of Maugham's plots: a flawed and destructive 'human nature' which is inimical to the values of friendship, loyalty and honour as defined by male expatriate society. Clark contrasts this with the intent behind the depiction of a projected marriage in Forster's *A Passage to India*. Here, she observes, the relationship between the two central English characters is a field on which are deployed conflicting attitudes to, and perceptions of, India. Clark writes:

> The conflict is counterpointed in the consciousness of other characters, such as the English wives of the community, one of whom knows Urdu verbs 'only in the imperative mood'. Adela's feelings about her possible marriage to Ronnie vary with her orientation to his values. She oscillates between a defence of liberalism against the intolerant expatriate attitudes he shares, and a sense of common culture with him in face of the alienness of India. But she sees, and we see, that their marriage if it takes place will be not just a coming together of two people but an overwhelming of her principles and world-view by his.

Thus where Jane Austen succeeded in using incorporation as a way of talking about marriage, marriage itself becomes, in Forster's hands, a metaphor for incorporation.

Private and public spheres again

Dissatisfaction with the private/public opposition has become widespread in anthropology of late; Atkinson writes for example (1982) that it 'has, for many, outgrown its usefulness as anything more than an ideological distinction that often disguises more than it illuminates.' The case of incorporated wives seems paradoxically to turn this objection on its head, since the private/public contrast is of interest here precisely as an ideological, not an analytical, opposition. Sir Edmund Leach has recently observed (1982: 164) that in contemporary society, alongside the ranking system in which 'honour' attaches to the acquisition and control of money, there exists a counterpart system within the sphere designated as 'domestic', in which honour accrues from the offering of gifts and services to the very extent that they are divorced from monetary recognition. The conception is of a balanced opposition between the home and the marketplace as regards the conditions under which honour is earned and dispensed: ' ... the coding of behaviour presupposes a sharp division between what goes on within the household and transactions which link the household to the rest of society.'

Leach is surely right to locate this 'sharp division' in the domain of particular world-views rather than that of absolute categories of analysis. His approach makes it possible for us to see the incorporation of wives as one area of social life in which the 'sharp division' undergoes some subtle transformations. In an earlier publication, Lidia Sciama (1981) drew attention to the contextual character of the opposition between private and public spheres; in situations of incorporation this very relativity seems to render the domain of the 'private' available to the incorporating institution and, simultaneously, to give it a special force. The village policeman's wife described by Young is, like many incorporated wives, on permanent display on the organization's behalf. The whole of her personal life must be an affirmation to the community of police concepts of an orderly and proper life, and is open to inspection and criticism because (according to the logic in force) it is indeed relevant to her and her husband's 'public' credentials. *Because* home and family life are culturally marked as 'private' space they are powerful when projected 'outwards' by a police force or an embassy as vehicle for the dissemination of civic or national virtues. (In diplomatic entertaining, important messages may be conveyed by the mere choice of a format of 'domestic intimacy' instead of 'formality'.) *Because* Christmas, birthdays and other feasts are occasions of 'private' celebration they can be the more effectively harnessed by a company such as Shell for the 'public' affirmation of corporate values. In a colonial or settler society, a properly managed home is more than a precondition of the *civilizing mission*: it is a part of it. At the same time, some suppression of perception may be needed if the opposition of ideas is to be kept clear and preserve its force. 'Knickers' on girls must not be visible to 'natives' (Kirkwood); the actual visibility of knickers in the wash and of whites' visits to the lavatory can be (with difficulty, one assumes) ignored.

If play can be made locally on the dialectics of private and public, the opposition can at the same moment be re-mapped on a global scale. For the expatriate wife, as we see from Soraya Tremayne's and Isobel Clark's accounts, *abroad* is in an important sense a public sphere and *home* (in these cases the U.K.) a private one. Once she returns to the latter's 'dimlight' (to borrow Tremayne's haunting expression) the organization's claims on her and also its supports are dramatically attenuated. A different private and public then come, no doubt, to the fore; her private and public will again differ from her husband's, but with a different difference.

It is tempting to classify these cases with others in which the institution benefits at the expense of the individual. Certainly the unpaid labour of women is involved, especially where the wife is the recognized manager of the family's consumption, and where 'the job' carries with it an expected level and style of consumption which is subject to surveillance and criticism. But the truth seems to be, not that the organization 'appropriates' the private times and spaces of its members and their families, but rather that it is often able to turn to advantage an indeterminacy which is already present in the private/public opposition itself. Shirley Ardener has noted (1981: 14) that 'The notion of 'private' as opposed to 'public' is seen as a criterion for 'mapping' metaphysical space ... *regardless* of the fact that some 'private places' can really be walked into.' Incorporation seems to belong to a class of situations where the 'metaphysical map' *first* identifies a private and a public sphere, *then* picks up the first and inserts it 'into' the second.

In some cases, it seems, the spotlight of 'public' witness falls on children rather than wives. Shirley Ardener, for example, has material which vividly documents the pressure for academic success placed on children in some Oxford families. Concepts of success in lives dedicated to scholarship may indeed turn children into an available means of sustaining the self-definition of the *intellectual family.*[6] In ways largely unexplored, it is clear, wives, children and the inner life of the family can be transfigured into 'goods for speech'; accessories of 'public' discourse. Thus political conventions in North America accord a marked ritual role to the wives of candidates. Kisses, hugs, brave smiles of disappointment and becoming tears of triumph are dramatically choreographed before the TV cameras between husband and wife, between wives, and between each rival and the other's wife. These public maulings seem essential to the psychodrama of the political duel; they assert the men's sexuality, while demonstrating its proper orientation and containment. The bedroom, obliquely invoked, is a political resource. Is it perverse of me to see a thematic connection between this and the male scholar's traditional acknowledgment to his wife for typing and indexing the great work? He is thanking her, of course; but is he not also telling the world that he has an appropriately constituted 'private' space, and a wife who will do these things for him?

The transposition of sexuality into the sphere of social action and communication is very imperfectly understood. Our present symbolic matrices may indeed be such that while the physical nature of men translates readily into metaphors of power and effectiveness, that of women does not. Other times and other cultures may of course be quite different in this respect, and the discrepancy is addressed in much current feminist art and iconography. (For relevant discussions see Ardener 1983 and Blair 1981). Popular ethology assumes a simple relationship between bodily assertiveness and social power, and this seems to hold in some circumstances, as Tremayne's description of the licence for gallantry accorded to senior Shell men indicates. Yet Ardener's observation (citing Mayer) that hierarchy can demand a 'tight handling' of the body points to a negative relation between social power and physical demonstrativeness. As in other contexts we are brought up against the variety of symbolic association between assertion of potency and title to power, and the profound implications of this for the political anthropology of gender.

The proper recognition of the personal
Examination of the personal as a construct for manipulation within social structures leads inevitably to consideration of its role in fieldwork itself. Several of the papers in this book are, alongside their other qualities, explorations in 'personal anthropology' (Pocock 1973); Young offers the most explicit discussion of the issues of method involved. To say this is not of course to disclaim the authors' other credentials in any way. It is rather

to invite attention to the fact that in several of the papers personal experience has an immediacy which honestly reflects its role in the formation of intellectual judgment, and which may also convey something of the mixture of comedy and pain that can be involved. For some contributors neither the decision to participate nor the exercise itself has been easy. They have had to find ways around a range of technical and personal problems that are special to being 'in' the situation one seeks to analyze.[7] Incorporation itself generates problems of loyalty and confidence which are not resolved even by recognition that they are artefacts of the very structures under investigation. Such situations supply poignant documentation for the running debate on the ethics of fieldwork. (See for example Dingwall 1980, and the exchanges to which this refers.)

But the game is worth the candle. Leach (1982: 124) expresses distrust of reflexive fieldwork (studying 'one's own society': he is not explicit about the inclusiveness of this phrase) on the grounds that 'When anthropologists study facets of their own society their vision seems to become distorted by prejudices which derive from private rather than public experience'. *Mais, au contraire*: the use of 'otherness' as a technical aid, a trick of the trade, a shelter behind which to cultivate academic rigour, can be another kind of limitation. There are some chronic disorders – diabetes is a good example – whose management demands of the patient a realignment of consciousness to space and time, food and activity: to every detail of daily existence. Consequently, every diabetic learns very quickly that he must 'be his own doctor'. Likewise, there are structures within the social order that reveal themselves most clearly through the disciplined monitoring of personal and common life. In seeking to understand these by reflexive inquiry and to communicate understanding, each of us is necessarily her/his own recording instrument *and record*. To acknowledge this is not to offer any excuse for amateurism or for loss of rigour. It is rather to make a case for the exploration of forms of rigour which both include the personal and recognize its intervention as analytically necessary.

Hierarchy and representation

Organizations differ in many respects, not least in their central values or theories of being. For a University such as Cambridge, according to Sciama's informants, the dominating value is that of the good society or 'centre of civilization'; for the British Council it is perhaps the promotion of that concept and those ideals. For the police it is that of the ordered society, the proper life as lived within the dualistic moral universe which Young elegantly dissects for our benefit. Other institutions have their own, perhaps more circumscribed, organizing belief or 'project' (to borrow an existentialist term). In this section we ask how an organization's project, its arrangement of its resources and its formal structure, are refracted in the lives of its incorporated wives.

The police case seems to show direct replication of a hierarchy, with each wife taking a position that accords with her husband's in the chain of command. Comparable patterns clearly prevail in the Armed Services, in international business and formerly in colonial settings. Yet, as Young's analysis shows, we cannot read the whole pattern in any one segment of it. Wives in one-man village stations are (or were) inspected for their conformity to police concepts of an ordered domestic life: a well-patrolled inner space. On police-owned estates they are conscious (sometimes resentfully) of the administration's intervention in all details of personal life, from wallpaper patterns to approved conduct at the 'kneepad ball'. The owner-occupier wives in their private houses seem on the surface to be leading lives indistinguishable from those of other middle-class married women. They may have no knowledge of village-station or police-estate life. Yet only in the context of these can we see that they also are living in a manner responsive to police modes of thought. There is, it seems, a special kind of orderliness in the arrangement of their lives, detectable only in the frame of the 'total structure', of which they have an implicit knowledge and of which their actions are a condensed and intermittent realization.

On a broader scale, it appears that incorporation creates for organizations a range of possibilities regarding the treatment of wives, and that these are selectively manifested in organizations of different kinds and purposes, and on different occasions. Thus in a University, where hierarchy is (comparatively speaking) not emphasized, we should not expect rank to be a prominent daily force for wives. Yet, because there is seniority and juniority even in a University, we can expect the hierarchical principle to be 'there' for wives in some shadowy or latent form, and to make itself obliquely visible on occasion. This indeed is what we find in Sciama's account of the relation of rank to hospitality in Cambridge: a relation we can the more richly comprehend in the context of other, more patent, hierarchies described in this book and elsewhere.

The position of *senior lady* is, it seems, always a special one. Even in an Oxford college, where much of the formal machinery of incorporation found elsewhere is absent, this position remains visible and is, apparently, ceremonially marked. In diplomacy, as I have shown elsewhere (1975), the role of an Ambassadress or Doyenne transcends the indeterminacies characteristic of lower levels, and her rights and duties are formally recognized. As a result she becomes a representative figure in her 'own' right. It seems that this pattern is common, at least in outline, to some of the organizations described in this book: to corporations (see also Kanter 1977), to colonial administration and to the British Council.

But the wife who becomes a *senior lady* may quickly encounter new conflicts peculiar to that position. Because of the measure of formal recognition accorded her, she is likely to feel that whoever else declines to provide the services expected of a wife, she may not. By the logic of incorporation she has attained the rewards of office, and she owes something in return. Other women's campaigns against the constraints of incorporation may merely strengthen them for her. The social transformations of the women's movement, limited as has been their effect on the more traditional organizations, have frequently left her holding responsibility without power - and without a working theory of either. In the 1960s she could call automatically on 'junior' wives to help make (say) a hundred canapés for an official party. In the 1980s, still convinced that the canapés 'have' to be made, she may well make them herself. Moreover, although the high status is not 'truly' hers, it can have the equivalent effect in isolating her from intimacy with other women. She cannot have close friendships within the organization for exactly the same reason that prevents any person actually doing a top job from having favourites among subordinates.

We have already given attention to stereotypes as perceptions from outside the system. But from the perspective of those inside it, husbands as well as wives, the *senior lady* position may render a woman particularly vulnerable to evaluations which flatten her individuality and assimilate her to an expected type. In the case of an Ambassador's wife, as Eric Miller noted in a perceptive study (1981), the mystique of the role itself seems to be connected with her being held personally to account for the morale of her husband's Mission. Her performance is judged starkly in polar opposites. She must be an angel or a 'horror': either '"very, very nice" or else "ghastly" ... it is relatively rare to hear the performance of an Ambassador's wife described in middling terms, such as "quite good", "not too bad", "good in some ways, not so good in others"' (Miller, op. cit.).

The *senior lady* position clearly exposes one connection between the refraction in wives of a system's formal structure, and wives' part in representing the system to a world outside. In some of the cases at least, 'representation' is deeply woven into the organization of seniority and role-division, and touches individuals selectively according to their place in it. A *senior lady* is more likely than others to find that expressions of personal opinion, however informally delivered, are taken as having something of the stamp of policy. Misunderstandings are especially likely where the wife is herself well qualified in a field which coincides with her husband's brief. From the organization's point of view, the ambiguous authenticity of a wife's words can be valuable, because (as Tremayne shows for both corporate life and diplomacy) it can allow things to be both 'said' and 'unsaid'. But setting aside the special circumstances of the *senior lady*, do wives in general have a part to play in the image-work of organizations? Is their part the same as their husbands', or different? On this point the papers reveal some interesting variations and reversals.

Marriage itself can be given many different meanings; in the present context, crudely, it can be seen as *complementary* or *antithetical* in varying degrees to the 'project' of an organization. We can imagine a continuum on which organizations would be placed according to the degree to which marriage of their members is seen as necessary to (or compatible with) their central purposes and values. Towards one end would be the British military units of the nineteenth century and earlier, described by Macmillan. Here, it seems, wives were present on the battlefield and on the march *in despite of* the wishes and intentions of the authorities. Clearly, conjugal ties were seen as antithetical to the military life: a necessary evil, to be tolerated and made use of in small ways, but hardly to be encouraged. The battle for recognition of wives' claim on the Armed Services has evidently been a long one, and is perhaps not over. (With some cynicism, we may speculate that concessions have been achieved down the years as much through changing conceptions of men's needs - sexual, domestic, parental - as of those of women and children.) Macmillan's account suggests, interestingly, that the sustained antithesis between conjugal and military values helped to turn the women into signifiers of the former *to their men*, both through their own conduct and as focus for the rhetoric of 'hearth and home'.

Towards the other end of the continuum would be found the settler wives in Rhodesia (now Zimbabwe) described by Kirkwood. Here, as she shows, marriage was conceptually integral to the settler commitment and the presence of wives - both in themselves and as potential mothers - was a powerful symbol of that commitment. (In Malaya by contrast, it seems, white wives were in some manner to 'stand for' the *absence* of long-term commitment to the land and its people.) Kirkwood's paper throws important light on the special ways in which women's experience is given shape through the reconstitution of the social order in everyday time and space (see Ardener ed. 1981). In addition, her work contains valuable insights into the wives' position as both *women* understandably attached to the homes they had created, and *symbols* of settler tenacity, available to the rhetoric of both sides of the independence conflict. It is, therefore, a significant contribution to the history of decolonization.

If Kirkwood's and Macmillan's papers mark out a rough continuum for us, other essays in the book, notwithstanding their diversity, can be seen to fall somewhere within it. Clark's note on British Council wives shows how a variety of social mechanisms combine to promote an identity for wives as members of a cultural elite and effective supporters of the Council's efforts in cultural representation. That there is ambivalence in the system is, however, evident from the wives' disposition to look to diplomatic practices as reference point for both identification and differentiation. Clark comments perceptively on what happens when an organization which must effectively control wives' movements also has values which go against any formal definition of their roles and relationships: a timely reminder that formal structures are not necessarily the source of all discomfort. The Shell Company wife seems to face more difficult problems of image management than most. While her husband furthers the Company's interests through the conduct of business, she (it seems) is given the task of 'representing' the multinationality and corporate patriotism of Shell - a task in which the instrument of communication must be her own life and conduct. An intangible reality must be disseminated by implicit means, and the rules change every time you move.

Within our continuum also we can place Ardener's and Sciama's accounts of the history of marriage in Oxford and Cambridge, and its influence on the situation of 'academic wives' today. The two Universities have so much shared history that the differences of fact and interpretation stand out as especially interesting. To my mind the most intriguing contrast is in the two authors' views of how, when celibacy rules were abolished, the concept of the married state came to be accommodated to that of the community of scholars. Sciama presents for Cambridge a tripartite edifice of the University, the family and the Church. Monasticism has of course long ceased to be a formally dominant force in the University. Yet its historical shadow could still be felt throughout the period covered by Sciama's essay, one of whose major themes is a suspicion of marriage as inimical to scholarship, and a concern among conservative dons to 'protect' the essential character of the Cambridge college from the polluting force of domesticity. Ardener's interpretation for Oxford is subtly different. She also recognizes an association between the physical life of the family and ideas of pollution. But for her, the Colleges with their valued tradition of commensality and common residence do not stand in total ideological opposition to the home. Rather, they afford the male don an *alternative domesticity* against which wives, in the changing conditions of the twentieth century, have been increasingly unable to compete. Hence, it may be, the progressive exclusion of wives from academic discourse and College affairs by comparison with the 'great ladies' of Victorian Oxford. Only recently, perhaps, has this been put into partial reverse through wives' increased access to College spaces and occasions - and indeed by a 'retreat to the home' on the part of some husbands.

Young judges that the police wife's representational task is a copy of her husband's: to hold up to the community a model of proper living according to police concepts of order and control. Yet parts of his analysis suggest a more differentiated underlying structure. There seems to be a mirror-image relationship between the village and the estate-dwelling wife, in which important aspects of the police-wife *persona* are directed outside the organization in the one case and inside it in the other. For the village wife, the police station is the family home, and police work and family life are run together. (We are generously treated to the comic potential of this.) The estate wife also lives by, and 'represents', police modes of thought. But her posture is negative in relation to non-police society, amounting as it does to the reciprocal maintenance of social distance. Its positive components appear on a different stage: that of police society itself. Is this opposition mediated anywhere else in the system? Young's account of urban detectives' wives suggests a partial answer. The 'representative' function of these women is both inward- and outward-facing. The police operate, it seems, within a cosmology dominated by polarities of good and evil; they are taught to see themselves as upholders of social virtue in an imperfect world. But where police work is mainly crime-solving and thief-catching rather than broad community supervision, this perception is constantly undermined and the oppositions blurred by the need to associate with crime and criminals. In this situation, we learn, wives are kept rigidly apart from police work and are denied all knowledge of its details. This surely enables them to sustain *for their husbands* the clear distinctions which are basic to police thought but are inevitably strained in practice. Young's ethnography is, I suggest, compatible with the interpretation that these wives are tacitly given the specialized task of 'representing' the system of thought *to itself*: of preserving its integrity in the eyes of a public which importantly includes themselves and their own men. We may look, then, for other situations in which incorporated wives, being 'of' an organization but not fully 'in' it, may be well placed to 'represent' its accredited values both inside and outside itself, in a condensed or idealized form.[8] Organizations other than the police may benefit from the symbolic services of wives as mediators of the chronic tensions between theory and practice; ignorance too has its uses.

The boundaries of the system

The police case is one of several in which issues of power and control are explicit. Gartrell, for example, alerts us to the political force of wives' presence in an organization where government itself is the 'project'; she and Brownfoot comment valuably on the political significance of dignity. The white wife must not only be a defence against 'poor-whitism' or 'going troppo'; she must play her part in the ceremonies of rule, gloves, calling cards and all. Like the police Inspector's wife, she no doubt must never be seen to be in debt, because indebtedness is a relationship between individuals which subverts that between groups. Shirley Ardener has noted in discussion that the political hazard of sexual liaisons between colonizers and colonized is not intrinsically a problem of race but one of rule; in this respect, of course, sex and debt are akin. There is however an issue about boundaries here as well as one about power. Wherever organizations need to project a consistent 'image' towards an outside public, sexual, romantic or merely social liaisons with members of the target group are suspect because of the competing associations they create. Hence courtship between policemen and members of the public is highly sensitive for the police, and is accordingly closely supervised. Marriage and the incorporation of wives effectively re-seal the breach and restore the integrity of the system's boundaries. It is ironical that wives should be in a position to defend the metaphysical wholeness of the system, while they themselves remain in so many ways spectral to it. And to compound the irony, wives have an opposite capacity to compromise the boundaries; we see this in the case of Cambridge, where they constitute a threat to the character of colleges as 'elective' societies; of Oxford, where they present a reminder of common physical humanity in logical opposition to differentials of status and function; and of colonial Malaya where their friendships with Asian women were recognized by white men as subversive to the political order. Looking, then, across the array of incorporating institutions, we can understand that one reason why wives are a problematic category is that they both breach the system's defences, and re-seal them: they pose a political problem, and are a part of its solution.

Becoming and being

It is by marriage most obviously that one becomes an incorporated wife. Yet the social order itself contains controls, selectors, filters of experience, teaching and learning devices which ensure, albeit haphazardly and imperfectly, that the 'discipline of being' which may come from the organization acts on structures of awareness already pre-adapted to receive it. This issue is addressed by Kirkwood in her brief paper on the preparation of girls for 'suitable' marriages. Many have noted a curious hesitancy, a drawing back from commitment to personally chosen projects and identities, in the education of British girls (especially those of the middle and upper classes) in the past. Implicit training for incorporation may, however, have necessitated a subtle balance between general and specific skills. Girls had perhaps to be given a broad preparation for the incorporated state, but 'space' had to be left for them to acquire the special character of the military, corporate, colonial, academic, diplomatic, police or other wife, according to the dictates activated by a particular marriage. We cannot argue of course that the production of incorporated wives has been the sole or even a major aim of British girls' education, although that of 'good wives' has apparently sometimes been envisaged (cf. Blackstone 1976). Even where this has been an important objective – as it clearly was in the classes of institution brought to life for us by Kirkwood – it seems always to have been an implicit rather than a recognized one in Britain. It required Kirkwood's anthropologically informed recollection, sharpened no doubt by the perceptiveness she gained from her 'colonial' status at the time, to make the connection. In other parts of the education system, those very schools which were explicitly teaching a few girls to become autonomous women have perhaps implicitly prepared others to be the incorporated wives of the men their counterparts in the boys' schools were being groomed to become (compare Okeley 1978). The 'hidden curriculum', too, has channelled girls into female occupations such as nursing: an honourable pursuit in its own right, of course, but also (as

Young observes) a thoroughly appropriate background for a woman who will become a police wife. Something like a total structure begins to reveal itself, if crudely and fitfully.

Formal education may play its part, then, recognized or not, in preselecting and predisposing women to be incorporated wives. But, clearly, the 'well-trained wife' must become so mainly on the job; the discipline of being is closely calibrated to the culture of particular organizations and the views of life that they find acceptable. At the same time, there are surely other forces external to organizations but important for an understanding of how incorporated wives are produced. Many strands, we must assume, are woven together to create the material from which 'performances' are put together and the social self constructed (see also Finch 1980.) For example, the fact already noted that wives are frequently the designated managers of approved levels and styles of consumption should encourage us to look at the ethnography of consumption itself – and indeed at the anthropology of advertising – for ways in which it can be demonstrated to women what a 'good' incorporated wife looks like and how to be one. As Sciama suggests, the consumer cult of the 1960s translated readily into an imagery of incorporation. At that moment of history at least, the interests of advertisers and of organizations in moulding an appropriate culture for wives could well coincide.[9] Other papers in the present book also document the emblematic force of 'lifestyle'.

'Wives talk'
The above heading is intentionally ambiguous. 'Wives talk!', says Young, is a succinct warning that 'any detective' will understand, as will many another husband. This sounds like a threat to the system, calling for, say, the witholding of sensitive knowledge from wives. But there is also 'wives' talk': the modes of self-expression available to them as wives, which may sometimes be more specialized than those available to them as women. This could be an asset to the system, whatever limitations it may place on the wives themselves. How are these opposing tendencies accommodated?

We noted earlier that language can itself set up and dissolve the territories over which incorporation and exclusion take place, and we used the case of 'shop-talk' to illustrate. Ardener attests to the 'finesse and great self-control' that an Oxford wife must exercise in speech, lest she appear to intrude on confidential business or on male intellectual preserves. It is perhaps not surprising that wives' speech should be a delicate matter for a community whose 'project' is discourse itself. Yet we may surmise that rules govern the speech of wives at gatherings 'internal' to other organizations; and further that the task of sustaining the differentials is not left entirely to 'shop-talk' but is partly entrusted to the wives themselves. Wives may not simply be excluded by 'shop-talk' from the centre of action. To the extent that they are excluded, they may be tacitly counted upon to control and direct their speech in ways that mark, even dramatize, their own exclusion.[10] Thus wives may learn to collaborate in sustaining a segregated speech system, and this skill will in turn be used against them when pollution fears hinder their admission to centres of discourse ('nappy talk at High Table').

The 'wives' talk!' problem, on the other hand, mainly affects wives' relations and conduct outside the organization – although there is always the possibility that it may be a recognized weapon against a husband's interests inside it. The problem arises not only because wives may ignorantly betray privileged information, but because (as noted earlier) by the logic of incorporation itself they may at any time be taken to speak 'for' the organization, or indeed 'for' the marriage. This can be turned to advantage, as we saw; but the inherent ambiguity of the situation makes it a difficult one for organizations or individuals to control. What counts may be not what a wife may *say*, but what others may choose to *hear*. Hence, incidentally, a common protective strategy: the legendary 'banality and triviality' of wives' talk. Where, therefore, the conversation of wives is conspicuously anodyne, we may well suppose that this is no accident or deficiency but the result of a careful discipline.[11]

In the setting Kirkwood describes, it is clear that learning to be an incorporated wife included negative as well as positive accomplishments; how *not* to do things, what *not* to talk about at dinner. These tacit restraints may be fairly widespread, may be consonant over several areas of life and may pertain to wifehood in ways more specialized than the forms of 'silencing' recorded by many as the daily experience of women. Diplomatic life, for example, offers inducements for wives to interest themselves in pursuits such as flower-arranging, doll-dressing, embroidery and internationalized versions of local crafts. Although (needless to say) excellent and beautiful work is often produced, as art forms these are essentially decorative rather than disturbing. Social comment and penetrating wit in art such as Audrey Blackman's (illustrated) exist, but are rare. Naturally, not all wives accept this proffered pattern. Many have quite other concerns, and many are committed individuals whose projects it would be merely impertinent to examine in any terms but their own. But for those who are at ease with it, the system of meanings generated by incorporation seems to make readily available a matching aesthetic: one of decoration, accommodation and acquiescence. This, I suggest, is structurally consonant with other markers of incorporation which recur in the papers: with *cuisine* (which is a challenging art but hard to think of as an art of challenge), and with the unspoken rules of speech and conduct which frequently seem to hold sway over wives at social functions.[12] In the final section of this essay I shall argue that some parts of this pattern are best regarded as a condition of wifehood overlaid on that of womanhood; and shall consider it in the context of the 'bargain' in force between organization, husband and wife.

The moral transaction: implications for a theory of marriage

There is no need to catalogue the benefits that wives can confer on an organization: a few will suffice. The resource value to the employer of wives' material services requires no emphasis and is amply documented in the papers and elsewhere. The administration of sociability may count as a material service, but it is significant (as Sciama observes) that men and women may disagree about this in ways that protect their own sense of worth. 'Taking the strain' can be seen as a service to the organization rather than to the husband, especially in high-pressure occupations, since it allows the level of stress to be raised to a point approaching the tolerance limit of the couple rather than that of the man alone. Non-material services may include wives' role in 'representation' discussed above: they often seem to be the appointed guardians of an occupational culture and ideology. Their presence may bind the husband's interests more securely in with those of the organization; most obviously through long-term financial commitments such as mortgages, but also through beliefs in their negative power to damage a career, which can supply a husband with an alibi for failure without undermining his sense of common cause with the organization. (Similarly, 'withdrawing from public life to devote more time to his wife and family' becomes a stock retreat for a man whose ambitions have suffered a setback.)

The 'segregated system' of speech and demeanour mentioned earlier can have important functions at social gatherings where business is transacted. As part of the drama of occasions, it can provide a basis for tightly constructed 'performances' which complement and balance one another. It may thus heighten the protagonists' sense of their own centrality through the contrasting presence of wives who, if *well-trained*, will be offering counter-portrayals of 'non-centrality' as noted above.[13] At the same time it may reinforce the governing idiom of sociability-for-its-own-sake, into which protagonists are able to retreat whenever it suits them. A diplomatic example is taken from a dispatch, leaked to me by an accomplice:

> Mr X, as usual, and especially when he is the host, failed to reveal his instructions, or indeed whether he had any, and diverted the conversation by pulling in some adjacent ladies to join us.

Segregated discourse can be seen as a property of the culture of wives rather than that of women; and as an outcome, in turn, of properties of organizations and of occasions. Once, no doubt, it coincided effortlessly with the sexual division and with received concepts of appropriate masculine and feminine demeanour. Now, however, wives may find themselves marked off by it in the very presence of other women who are newly enjoying the fruits of opportunity.[14] Hence, perhaps, a tendency (hinted at by Clark and Tremayne) to tension in the relations between wives and women professionals.[15] As Sciama notes for Cambridge at an earlier time, each group may be sharply aware of what is actually and ritually negated in itself *vis-à-vis* the other.

In return for all this, ceremonial rewards are often available, especially for the 'successful'. But, intended or not, there can be some manipulation of illusion in what is offered to a wife as the organization's side of the bargain. She may discover to her cost that its commitment to her is very conditional indeed. Macmillan mentions the sense of being gradually shut out that Service widows may have, and the recurring controversies over financial provision for them. The divorced wife of a diplomat wrote to the wives' magazine of her pain when she discovered on separation that (understandably) the first concern of the very institution of which she had been urged for years to suppose herself a valued member, was to put her husband in the hands of a solicitor who would best represent his interests against hers. There is growing concern at the plight of deserted clergy wives, who apparently may lose a role, an income and a home without adequate compensation (Report by Frank Field to the Church of England Synod on divorced and separated clergy wives, cited by David May in *The Times*, 5 December 1982.) Against this however we must set the testimony of Clark and Ardener to the concern shown by the British Council and at least one Oxford college for divorced wives and widows. Clearly, organizations differ in the extent to which the incorporated state can survive the marriage which occasioned it.

We saw earlier that for some organizations wives present – and in part solve – a political problem. For others, such as Shell, they pose appropriately enough a management problem. These perceptions suggest that there is a fundamental dilemma in the very presence of wives 'in' organizations: in the accommodation of relations based theoretically on contract with those based theoretically on sentiment. Wives are in truth Janus-faced creatures from the viewpoint of organizations. Through wives, the long-range commitment of members can be both evoked and advertised. But the opposite is also true: wife-and-family can signify a rival commitment which limits that of the member to the organization. As several papers indicate, organizations can be fully cognizant of this dual potential. What means of resolving the paradox are available to the parties concerned?

Inevitably, the organization seems to hold most of the high cards. It may discipline marriages by controlling the circumstances under which they are made; as in real or reputed wife-vetting (which will surely influence the marital choices of the ambitious), and in the rationing of access to marriage by age and seniority. By this means marriage itself becomes a scarce good, an earned privilege dispensed by the organization, for which both husband and wife may feel beholden. It may control in large measure the concept people have of marriage: a task made easier in some of the cases described by its control over the physical conditions in which the relationship is experienced. Institutional provision of (say) bedroom furniture can be remarkably influential in conveying assumptions about how a marital relationship 'should' be conducted. Several of the papers suggest that the 'premiss of dedication' (Callan 1975) is common to the moral structure of a number of situations of incorporation; in this way the sentiments which are culturally allocated to marriage can be harnessed in a relation of ethical overspill between the wife and the organization. Propaganda directed to wives, often by other wives, may clothe the organization in an exaggerated glamour or sense of mission which may call on idealized images of an earlier period. Thus any failure of reality to measure up is easily seen as personal failure. Finally, as Tremayne points out, organizations are often able to resort to forms of 'strategic leniency' in the face of deviance and dissent: this too is an effective technique of containment.

These powers of discipline are remarkably successful, as we can appreciate by glancing at the single though critical area of information control. A general assumption seems to exist of community of information within marriage. Notwithstanding the occasional cultivation of ignorance noted earlier, wives are characteristically trusted with a great deal of knowledge which the organization considers confidential. They are likely custodians of a valued good, but their stewardship is not easily called to account since the forms of command to which they are subject are rarely articulated. Responses to this dilemma seem to vary. Wives may be brought into the system of formal sanctions, and rulings issued about what they may and may not be told. More typically, organizations place an unspoken reliance on marriage itself to guarantee the trustworthiness of wives. (This is one reason why they have trouble with non-marital partnerships; how do you know how far you can trust a man's 'keep' (Brownfoot) or his live-in girlfriend or boyfriend?) The evidence suggests that the confidence placed in marriage is generally well-founded. A startling degree of trust can be quite casually accorded to wives, and their discretion regarding the organization's vital interests can more often than not be successfully taken for granted. As noted earlier in a different context, both the problem – in this case one of trust – and its solution flow from understandings about marriage within the social order which are seldom consciously examined. But they surely derive much of their stability and serviceability from the disciplines of consciousness that we have been considering.

A dilemma of social control – of government – seems then to be broadly common to several incorporating institutions: control of their operations and information, government of their members as needed for their 'project', and, sometimes, government of others such as 'natives', students or civil society. A paradox of incorporation is that it can turn wives into ambiguous subversives who are at once reconstituted as ambiguous guardians. Such ambiguity is structurally disturbing to organizations, which must act, it seems, *as if* they had a stable theory of human nature and human needs, even where, in fact, the theory in question shifts according to operational circumstance. Thus in colonial Malaya and white-ruled Rhodesia the reputed special physical needs of white women were salient, while for Shell company the concerns of 'wives' are perceptually collapsed into those of 'families'. The British diplomatic service is reluctant similarly to accommodate competing loyalties in wives other than loyalties to children; but both it and the Armed Services have available an alternative view of wives as people who can be called on to subordinate the claims of motherhood to those of wifehood. In assembling their own performances, individuals may be expected to be highly responsive to these perceptions. For some no doubt this responsiveness is unquestioning; for others tactical.

Organizations also conduct their affairs as if they had a theory of marriage; often, as we have seen, with considerable sophistication and success. Marriages too must be conducted with some regard to such implicit theories, which husband and wife may of course fully share. Not all of the cards are stacked on one side: what Young calls the 'power of the margins' may, at the cost of ambition, give individuals the protected status of the licenced dissident, eccentric or joker. The exact bargain struck between the organization and the wife will naturally depend on the personal contract in force between her and her husband (which he may effectively control through his willingness to trust and include her, and to sub-contract to the organization his moral claim on her services). But not only is the personal contract in large measure itself a social product, but forces outside the control of either husband or wife as individuals strongly influence the form that incorporation takes and the way it is experienced. In the 'negotiation of reality', for example (cf. Berger and Kellner 1964), the world-view that comes to be taken for granted in the marriage is likely to be the one shared by the husband and the organization (which can easily override employer–employee differences). While this is true for all wives whose access to the world is through their husbands, it is intensely true for incorporated wives. As Young and Tremayne suggest, the reality that is experienced comes to be the only reality that can be imagined. This creation and preservation of a taken-for-granted world enables all manner of troubles (unhappiness in children, for example, as well as in wives) to be represented as failures of 'adjustment' calling for ever more strenuous efforts at accommodation, rather than as consequences of institutional practices that could be changed. Thus, to varying degrees and in a number of ways, do incorporating institutions gain acceptance for their own conception of what marriage is and what a wife is 'for'.

In several of the papers the question of community is raised: to what extent does the system allow wives a 'corporate' experience of their own lives? The formal associations generated by and for wives (Wives' Clubs and the like) appear in the papers both as sources of genuine support and as reinforcers of the taken-for-granted world just mentioned. Community of situation can certainly modify the structural isolation of the housewife that has been well analyzed, by Marxist writers in particular. Yet (although there are exceptions) the organization's penetrating control over material and moral life makes it overwhelmingly likely that the solidarity that emerges will be of a kind to affirm rather than to resist the structures which are its source. It should not surprise us, then, if wives themselves are more enthusiastic than anyone in patrolling the territories of incorporation.

Taken together, the papers in this book seem to me to demonstrate two things. The first is that as anthropologists and historians of the contemporary social order and its antecedents, we need to examine even more minutely than is commonly recognized the moral interpenetrance of institutional with conjugal structures and theories of being. The second is that as analysts of women's experience we can perhaps make the best sense of some aspects of that experience by referring it to the special conditions of wifehood that such study reveals, rather than to general ones of womanhood. The papers that follow are testimony that the designation 'incorporated wife', while not as yet fully clarified, nevertheless renders visible a social reality which merits examination.

Acknowledgments
Among the many who have helped me in preparing this Introduction, I owe a special debt to the other contributors to this book (especially Shirley Ardener), to seminar audiences at the Universities of Ottawa and Trent, and to Dorothy Johnston and the Foreign Service Community Association of Canada. I thank Helen Yardley, too, for valuable criticism of parts of the draft. Responsibility for the result is, of course, mine.

Notes
1. In any organization, of course, all manner of demarcations are linguistically encoded. Linguistic markers are wonderfully responsive to both static and moving systems: to boundaries and boundary-crossings. My own sensitivity to words as a tracking device was raised during fieldwork among student nurses, for whom delicate processes fixed the moment before which it was too soon to use certain technical language, abbreviations and colloquialisms, and after which it was too late not to. Mistakes were easily made and worth avoiding. Once I was present in class when a beginning student used the words 'cardiac arrest'. The instructor's response was: 'My, aren't we using long words already!' The language had been technically correct; the put-down was for laying claim to it too early.

2. Janet Finch's book *Married to the Job* (1983) appeared when the present volume was in its final stages, and too late to be taken properly into account herein, although some references to it have been included. We hope that the present book (written entirely independently) will add useful additional ethnography to Finch's excellent work as well as considering aspects of incorporation not dealt with therein.

3. This is not to deny that incorporated wives may be deprived and abused for causes unrelated to incorporation.

4. With the partial exception of Malcolm Young's tantalizingly brief account of

the transformation of policewomen into police wives, this book makes no attempt to consider dual-worker marriages or the relations of organizations with their members' husbands. We are painfully aware of this gap, and of the significance of the intervention of these newer social formations into established structures of thought and action.

5. It may take dramatic events to bring wives a good press. During the Iranian hostage crisis of 1979-81, six fugitives from the U.S. Embassy were sheltered for three months in the homes of Canadian diplomats in Tehran. While the two Canadian officers involved were awarded the Order of Canada, their wives initially received no personal recognition, although not only had the burden of care fallen directly on them, but (since the success of the whole exercise depended on their husbands' keeping up the appearance of normal working life) it was they who had braved alone the physical dangers of the concealment. In the face of public opinion and internal pressure, technical difficulties were overcome and it was announced from Government House that the two wives were to receive the Order of Canada in their own right. A plaque now stands in Ottawa to honour the 'heroic action' of those involved: it names the two officers and other Embassy personnel but not the wives. At the time, gossip focused on the puzzling 'invisibility' of the women's personal heroism. But public honours, surely, are given in our culture *either* for outstanding devotion to 'duty', *or* for heroism beyond its call. Yet the 'premiss of dedication' (Callan 1975) allows no stable conception of what a wife's duties are or where they end. Under its logic, anything a wife is called on to do can be represented as 'duty' and simultaneously as an expression of her intrinsic wifehood or womanhood. Small wonder that a wife who is seen to have acted *as* a wife (no matter what she may have actually done) is not easily recognized as a candidate for public honour. British diplomats' wives are in fact occasionally decorated; but where the domain of 'duty' is itself structurally indeterminate, wives will not readily receive forms of public credit that are conceptually bound to that domain.

6. Other trade-offs are available between incorporated wives and incorporated children, which space makes it impossible to explore here. Thus Prime Minister Trudeau of Canada, in default of a wife, has delegated some aspects of her ceremonial role to his three young sons. In general, demonstrated success in personal life seems able to stand as a claim to credit and competence in spheres designated as 'public'. What counts *as* success will be subject to change; single parenthood has clearly 'arrived', and only time will tell what new cues and standards (gay partnerships for example) may emerge and become accepted.

7. For this reason also the papers vary widely in ambition and scale. Some contributors have preferred to confine themselves to brief and descriptive ethnography, while others have offered more extended theoretical discussion. The policy of the editors has been that the widest possible range of voices should be given a hearing.

8. Compare Dorothy Smith's valuable insight (1973), within a very different analytical frame, that the wife acts for the corporation as its agent of 'the external moral order' in relation to her husband. An interesting comparison can be made between Smith's analysis of the role in the social order of goods surplus to subsistence, and that of Mary Douglas (1978 and 1982). For Smith, the home is a dead-end where such goods become 'display' and pass out of the matrix of social relations. Douglas in contrast asks why people want goods: for her, consequently, the sociological problem does not end but rather begins at this point.

9. Stuart Ewen (1976), writing of the growth of advertising as a cultural force in America in the 1920s, stresses its success in coupling the new market requirements of the productive process to new, commercially appropriate concepts of the 'good wife and mother'. His concerns are not ours, but his work suggests that the 1920s also may have been a point at which significant parts of the broad structure of

incorporation were laid down, possibly on a pre-existing Victorian base. The emergence of woman as trained consumer, her social self both product and instrument in market-like transactions, may have contributed to the value that wives can have for organizations through special ways in which they may be schooled to 'live and move and have their being'.

10. I still remember with regret my own anger and rudeness when, as an undergraduate, I worked one summer as a research assistant in Italy. I was the only girl in the group, but this was quite usual and I was not made to feel unduly conscious of my gender until an evening we all spent in a bar with one other woman present, a professor's wife. No sooner had we begun an argument about the project than this lady pointedly drew me aside and began a conversation about clothes. I was (perhaps prophetically) alarmed and responded impatiently; I was too young at the time to summon a proper tolerance for her predicament.

11. I take no position here in the controversies over whether 'women's language' is a reality or an artefact of 'patriarchal bias' in the evaluation of women's speech (see e.g. Spender 1980). The possibility exists however of a 'wives' language' which would call for separate examination. The debate might benefit from further refinement of its categories and more micro-perspectives. What counts may be not the speech patterns imposed on 'women' by 'men', but those prescribed for (say) 'junior wives' at coffee parties, or secretaries at lunch; and what happens when these groups are called on to 'explain themselves' to superordinates. The novelist Barbara Pym understood this very well.

12. In diplomacy, amazingly, departure from these norms can be cumulatively misread as sexual provocation. This is an institution where a chaste and domesticated sexuality - charm, fashionable dressing and social kissing - is itself a prime vehicle of meta-discourse!

13. Lee Comer writes comparably of housewives that 'real events are defined by her non-participation in them.' (1974: 100) The point here is that the creation of a 'penumbra' to be inhabited by wives may be an effective way of marking out a 'reality' from the viewpoint of *that reality itself*, as well as of those who are excluded from it.

14. The arrangement of complementary performances linked to gender is no doubt undergoing steady erosion through the presence at work-related social gatherings of women protagonists and of male 'wives', for whom a place in it has yet to be found. Whether it will collapse or, because of its usefulness, find new forms in which to survive, only time will tell.

15. Tensions to which even a modern feminist may not be immune. Witness Germaine Greer: 'As a female lecturer at a provincial university I have to tolerate the antics of faculty wives, but they are fairly easy to ignore ... ' (1970: 132).

INCORPORATION AND EXCLUSION: OXFORD ACADEMICS' WIVES

Shirley Ardener

Introduction

This paper takes a preliminary look at the experience of some Oxford academics' wives in relation to the University and considers some of the changes which have taken place during the University's history.[1] Oxford University may loosely be described as a federation of colleges (compare Sciama on Cambridge University, this volume). The colleges, permanent, autonomous foundations with their own royal charters and finances, jealously guard their independence. Each is governed by its head and Fellows.[2] College heads are known variously as President, Master, Rector, Provost, Principal, Dean or Warden; collectively they are Heads of Houses. The majority of the teaching staff at Oxford hold college Fellowships, and it is usually to their colleges that they owe their deepest allegiance. Each college has its own special features, making it difficult to generalize about them. They choose and are responsible for teaching their own undergraduates. The University provides facilities which individual colleges cannot (laboratories, libraries and other specialist institutions) and it matriculates, sets syllabuses, examines and awards degrees to students presented by the colleges.

Until the nineteenth century teaching at Oxford was in the hands of celibate clerics. Any college Fellow who married resigned his Fellowship automatically. The rule of celibacy was, however, waived for Heads of Houses. Increasingly after the Reformation the semi-monastic structure of many of the early colleges included a domestic enclosure of no mean proportions housing the Head's large family, with visiting relatives, as well as servants. It was not until the middle of the nineteenth century, when many features of Oxford University were considered to be in need of reform, that the 700-year-old rules governing the celibacy of Fellows were seriously questioned. A Royal Commission was set up, but when it reported in April 1852, no change concerning celibacy for Fellows was recommended although professors were now to be exempted from this obligation like Heads of Houses. Pressure grew to extend the new liberalization, but it was only after another Government Commission of 1877 that a formal recommendation was made to remove the requirement of celibacy for Fellows. Colleges were nevertheless left to make their own decisions. Some had even anticipated the recommendation; thus Thomas Humphrey Ward of Brasenose College was married on April 6, 1872, and A.G.Butler of Oriel married Miss Edgeworth in 1877. Some colleges moved cautiously. For example in 1898 a liberalizing amendment of Lincoln College statutes provided that:

> any fellow marrying within seven years of his election should vacate his fellowship, but allowed a fellow after seven years to marry if 2/3rds of the Rector and fellows, voting by secret ballot at a special meeting, gave their assent. Sixteen years after, a further amendment, dated 14 May 1914, allowed a fellow to marry without the time restriction if there was a 2/3rds majority; though a fellow who married without the assent of the College was held to have vacated his fellowship. (Green 1979: 525-26)

In 1891 in St John's College, Ball's Fellowship was in jeopardy:

> They are uncertain about my position – whether I may not claim to retain my Fellowship. In equity I ought to, as I am allowed by statute to marry after seven years' tenure. I have been a Fellow over eight years, but they tried to prevent my availing myself of the permission under the statute by interposing a day between the lapse of the first seven years of my Fellowship, and my re-election, so as to be able to say I am elected in a new Fellowship – a very unworthy dodge, to put it mildly ... (Ball 1923: 50)

The College found other grounds to disqualify Ball when he married and he did lose his Fellowship until 1902 (op. cit. pp.88-9). Even when Lane Poole married just after the First World War, he temporarily resigned his Fellowship at St John's College.

The Nineteenth Century

Documentation on the earliest wives of Heads of Houses is thin compared to that available for the nineteenth century when we begin to meet richer material, including some useful accounts by Oxford wives themselves. This latter evidence presents a generally positive view of Oxford life, but we must be wary of assuming that this would be shared by all wives. Those who wrote their memoirs may have been unusually well able to cope with their situations (which may have enabled them to move in particularly interesting circles), and they may have had unusually helpful husbands. Unfortunately those who feel that they and their lives are dull rarely leave records. As many wives know, to admit unhappiness is to admit failure; suppression may have occurred, even in diaries. And how would a book of discontent get published then? But there are clues hinting at less happy experiences for women. Some of these are to be found in writings by their children or their husbands' biographers.

Margaret Dyre Jeune came to Oxford in 1843 at the age of 25 when her husband was elected master of Pembroke College. Her excitement at the prospect is evident from her diary. Margaret was a woman of spirit who regularly dined out and followed all the affairs of her husband's college and the University controversies of the day. Her house was filled with undergraduates (who played games with her five children), and her dinner table seated the scholars of her husband's circle, their sisters and the wives and daughters[3] of other Heads of Houses. When in 1833 the College Visitor (Lord Derby) came, she reports that

> As Mrs Cotton had hardly received any ladies to see Lady Derby I thought many would be gratified by having an opportunity of seeing her and hearing the speeches. So we invited about 40 who all seemed highly delighted with the occasion. I received them in the Drawing-room and then we adjourned to the Hall, being summoned by two Knights when the speeches were beginning - Lord Derby spoke very well - but how rare is the gift. The *entertainment*[4] was very handsome. (Gifford 1932: 36)

In November 1851 Margaret began a course of lectures, which included one on geology by Mr Strickland. 'The class', she notes, 'is chiefly composed of women - enough to frighten the Professors from opening their lecture rooms to the fair sex' (Gifford: 18). Clearly the prevailing exclusion of women as undergraduates was already on her mind.

The description given by Mary Humphrey Ward of Mrs Pattison, wife of the Rector of Lincoln College, gives another happy picture of what Victorian Oxford could offer a woman endowed with youth, beauty and wit:

> It was in '68 or '69 - I think I was seventeen - that I remember my first sight of a college garden lying cool and shaded between grey college walls, and on the grass a figure that held me fascinated - a lady in a green brocade dress, with a belt and chatelaine of Russian silver, who was playing croquet, then a novelty in Oxford, and seemed to me, as I watched her, a perfect model of grace and vivacity ... a handful of undergraduates made an amused and admiring court round the lady ...

She speaks of her

> gaiety, her picturesqueness, her impatience of the Oxford solemnities and decorums, her sharp restless wit, her determination *not* to be academic, to hold on to the greater world of affairs outside ... (Humphrey Ward 1918: 102-3).

Later, for personal and health reasons, Francis Pattison withdrew from Oxford society (which she came to dislike) to the South of France,[5] though she returned in 1884 to nurse her dying husband.

Unlike wives of Heads of Houses, Fellows and their wives were not usually accommodated within college walls. Housing was hard to find (see Oona H. Ball 1923: 61ff, and Butler MS). Mary Oman was able to secure a central town house next door to the Ashmolean Museum. Many settled into houses just north of the Parks in the newest part of town. William Spooner of New College (known for his 'Spoonerisms'), no doubt anxious to show that marriage did not conflict with his college duties, describes his early life in North Oxford:

> In settling our plans we attached importance to being as reasonably near College as circumstances would permit ... [This made it] possible to begin work in good time and to treat College as something more than an office where business had to be transacted ... I gave the same number of lectures and had almost as many men [undergraduates] as I did while I was still resident in College ... Besides our undergraduate dinner parties I dined two evenings a

week at High Table in College so keeping up with my colleagues resident
there. (Hayter 1977: 67-8)

Two evenings seem rather few for then. For Mary Humphrey Ward, the
nine years she lived in Oxford with her husband were:

> for both of us, of great happiness and incessant activity ... Nobody under the
> rank of a Head of a College, except a very few privileged Professors,
> possessed as much as a thousand a year. The average income of the new race
> of married tutors was not much more than half that sum. Yet we all gave
> dinner-parties and furnished our houses with Morris papers, old chests and
> cabinets, and blue pots. The dinner-parties were simple and short. At our
> own early efforts of the kind, there certainly was not enough to eat ... our
> fashion was not that of Belgravia or Mayfair, which indeed we scorned!
> (Humphrey Ward 1918: 119-20)

When invited to dine with the Warden of All Souls or the
Vice-Chancellor Mary Oman (like Mrs Humphrey Ward) was tugged in
her bath-chair by 'a Shakespearian looking character', one of the
'chairmen of old Oxford', while her husband would walk beside her in
full evening dress and cap and gown (Oman and Humphrey Ward).
Because new brides were given the place of honour 'she would seldom sit
next to a host of less than seventy, for the first year, and always on his
right hand'. The Warden himself had a footman in powder until 1914!
(Oman 1976: 29-30)

In the Victorian period Oxford University wives frequently went to
lectures, balls and other functions. Their rounds of dinner parties were
attended not only by the male establishment of the day, but often by
distinguished women such as the writer George Eliot, and Mme Blaise de
Bury, said to be the cleverest woman in Europe (Gifford 1932: 127). Mrs
Ball's log of guests soon ran to three volumes. The organization of such
entertainment was not necessarily a burden. Mrs Oman, when at Frewin
Hall, had only to inform her excellent cook and order on a little slate for
her dinner parties to be taken care of. An 'ordinary mid-Term dinner' for
sixteen, 'not anything like those given for the Vice-Chancellor when
everyone had to come in cap and gown', would have seven courses, served
by college waiters (Oman: 108-9). Carola Oman, daughter of Mary, saw
her home as lying 'in the centre of thrilling pulsating Oxford' (op.cit.
p.100).

The demands of rearing children, running large households,
entertaining undergraduates and dons and participating in such Oxford
public life as was permitted, and of maintaining considerable family
connections by going on and receiving visits,[7] would seem likely to have
left wives little time or energy to do other things. Nevertheless many did
have outside interests. Catherine Spooner was a pioneer of a scheme for
the rehabilitation of long-term hospital patients suffering from depression
and boredom (Hayter, op. cit: 66-7). In 1866 Eleanor Smith, Professor
H.Smith's sister, had organized lectures and classes for women (Mallet
1927: 431); Mary Humphrey Ward later got involved in similar work:

Mrs Creighton and I, with Mrs Max Muller, were the secretaries and founders of the first organised series of lectures for women in the University town; I was the first secretary of Somerville Hall, and it fell to me, by chance, to suggest the name of the future college. My friends and I were all on fire for women's education, including women's medical education, and very emulous of Cambridge, where the movement was already far advanced.[8] (Humphrey Ward 1918: 153).

Mitchison noted (1979: 31) that 'Oxford society did not give much scope in academic matters for the wives of dons, and the University has never treated them with courtesy and attention'. Nevertheless, some wives (like many dons' wives to come) were themselves involved in scholarship in their own right. Francis Pattison, for example, published *The Renaissance of Art in France* (1879) and *Claude Lorraine. Sa vie et ses oeuvres* (1884) and eight other works. Mary Humphrey Ward herself noted:

I twice examined – in 1882 and 1888 – for the Taylorian scholarship in Spanish in Oxford; our old friend, Dr Kitchin, afterwards Dean of Durham, writing to me with glee that I should be 'making history', as 'the first woman examiner of men at either University'. (p. 191)

She also became a successful novelist. There were other activities familiar to many academics' wives today. Charles Oman took his wife abroad on holiday; when it rained all day,

Mary was given a new occupation – 'Made Index'. It was her first job in this for her husband. He told her she had an unerring eye for misprints and promoted her to proof-reading.[9] (Oman 1976: 41)

The overall picture presented by the nineteenth-century wives quoted is a romantic one, emphasizing the beauty, gaiety and elegance of Oxford and the intellectual excitement in which they felt involved. Mrs A.E.Butler noted: 'Oxford had always been the city of my dreams, but I had not set eyes on her ... till a month before my marriage. It was wonderful to find myself living in Oriel ... '. Some wives, like Mary Oman and Mrs A.L.Smith, appear to have accepted that they would be excluded from many spheres of their husbands' professional lives, and Mary would probably have agreed with the latter's phrase 'the masculine is the worthier gender' (quoted in Mitchison 1979: 32). Margaret Jeune, Mary Oman, Mary Humphrey Ward and Oona Ball experienced the sweeter side of Oxford life. But was there not a sour side too? We can glean details of a less attractive picture. The dinner parties, for example, were not always liked. In 1810 a 13-year-old girl, Elizabeth Grant, stayed with her uncle, the Master of University College. Rather snobbishly she writes of Doctors of Divinity who:

brought ladies of inferior manners to grace what appeared to them so dignified a station. It was not a good style; there was little talent and less polish and no sort of knowledge of the world ... (Strachey 1898; 1928 ed.: 131).

The girl may not be an unbiased or well-informed witness. She certainly found the 'restraint in fashion in the University' very irksome. But later, in the 1880s, although Mrs Butler enjoyed the 'circle of highly cultured scholars, full of educational ideas and academic interests', she also found that 'they spoke a cautious unemotional language' quite new to her since she was used 'to very clear expressions of opinion and pretty strong prejudices' (Butler MS). The Oman children spoke of the 'fusty-musties'. As we have seen, for Mrs Pattison (who had special problems) Oxford eventually became distasteful. Not all hosts were skilled in social affairs. Mrs Humphrey Ward remembered an occasion in Jowett's drawing-room at Balliol 'full of rather tongue-tied embarrassed guests, some Oxford residents, some Londoners; and the Master among them, as a stimulating – but disintegrating! – force, of whom everyone was uneasily conscious' (Humphrey Ward: 127). The 'sofa-mothers' referred to in Carola Oman's childhood reminiscences may well represent those academics' wives who were frustrated or unhappy, or who for some other reason withdrew from social life.[10] There were also humiliations to mar the delights; after her marriage, for Oona Ball:

> The most serious bar to happiness was the taking away of Sidney's Fellowship. It was like him to say that he 'preferred the New Fellowship' with me and the money value was made up to him by the College, which was anxious to retain his services, but he had no seat on the Governing Body of the College and was unable, except indirectly, to control its policy and debarred from any voice in the election of new Fellows. This was a difficult as well as a humiliating position for [him]. (Ball 1923: 72; cf. Sciama, this volume)

The Early Twentieth Century

At the beginning of the twentieth century life for wives of Heads of Houses could still continue in a grand style. When Spooner became Warden of New College in 1904, such was her new station, Mrs Spooner could then use the front entrance to Elliston & Cavell, the principal Oxford drapers (now Debenham's department store), a prerogative reserved for wives of Heads of Houses and of Canons of Christ Church; other customers had to use the side entrance (Hayter 1977: 110). No doubt her new position demanded much skill and application in return. After the renovation of the Warden's Lodgings Catherine Spooner managed 'an almost princely mansion' (Hayter 1977: 105) with sixteen bedrooms and an indoor staff of eleven servants. This was a management task comparable to that of many a small hotel or business today.

Mrs A.L.Smith's family lived relatively frugally. When her husband was a Fellow of Balliol College she had a number of young men waiting to enter college actually boarding with her. Indeed her house was treated by her husband and his college 'as an outstation of Balliol. College affairs flowed into it, college people came to meals ... her house became part of the Balliol system of education' (Mitchison 1979). Nevertheless as

Harrison (1976: 47) notes she still found time for community work, being one of the 'quartet of dons' wives ... who presided over Oxford's world of social work' at the beginning of the twentieth century (Harrison, p.64). This band was 'not a collection of mere well-meaning philanthropists, but were ladies endowed with inexhaustible energy, experience, and above all, tact', according to the local Medical Officer of Health when praising their efforts to reduce local infant mortality (Harrison p.65). It seems there were sometimes more volunteers than preferred charity work to go around (Mrs Butler MS). Of the other members of the 'quartet', Mrs Fisher had won a first in history and taught economics as one of the University's earliest tutors in the subject. Mrs Wells had won a first in history too, and Mrs Pritchard a first in Greats.[11]

After World War I

Although as already noted, there was considerable social stratification within the University in the nineteenth century, after the First World War Oxford increasingly drew in people from a wider range of social backgrounds and diversity of experience. For some who came having little acquaintance with University circles, the society could be intimidating. Edith Tolkien, to take one example, lived in Oxford from 1918 to 1920, and (after her husband was elected to a Chair) from 1926 until 1968 (nine years after he retired). Both Edith and her husband, J.R.R.Tolkien, were effectively from one-parent families, and orphaned in adolescence; neither had a conventional middle-class upbringing. Edith was an only child, inclined to be shy, and the University seemed to her to be:

> an almost impenetrable fortress, a phalanx of imposing buildings where important-looking men passed to and fro in gowns. Her husband's friends often 'did not know how to talk to women' and she could think of nothing to say to them 'for their worlds simply did not overlap'. Worse still, the visitors might be dons' wives, such as the terrifying Mrs Farnell, wife of the Rector of Exeter, whose presence even frightened Ronald [Tolkien]. These women only confirmed Edith in her belief that the University was unapproachable in its eminence. They came from their awesome college lodgings or their turreted mansions in North Oxford to coo condescendingly at baby John in his cot, and when they departed they would leave their calling cards on the hall tray [*one* card bearing their own name, *two* (smaller) cards bearing their husband's] to indicate that Mrs Tolkien was of course expected to *return* the call after a short interval. But Edith's nerve failed her. What could she say to these people if she went to their imposing houses? What possible conversation could she have with these stately women, whose talk was of people of whom she had never heard, of professor's daughters and titled cousins and other Oxford hostesses? Soon it became known that Mr Tolkien's wife *did not call* and must therefore be quietly excluded from the round of dinner parties and At Homes. (Carpenter 1977: 157-158)

Although Oxford society was gradually becoming less rigid, Alison Smith, who in her childhood lived two doors from Edith Tolkien, remembers exclusive bridge-playing circles where social distinctions were rigid and gossip was rife (personal communication). Edith Tolkien made few friends among other dons' wives. She did not continue her interests in music (in which she was trained) except within her own home, although there were musical circles in Oxford. She suffered from migraines.

A different picture of postwar Oxford emerges from Dorothy Allen's exuberant autobiography. Active in many spheres, she describes the life of a young bride of a college Fellow in 1922:

> now I was a don's wife, who must prepare to be called on and to return calls; to go to dinner-parties and sit on the right of the host as a bride and be ready to be the first to leave the party; to entertain undergraduates to tea as their tutor's wife ... For one who enjoyed people and good talk, college dinner-parties to which we were constantly invited were a great pleasure. It was exciting too being a bride and allotted the place of honoured guest. All the brides wore their wedding-dresses during that period for dinner-parties, and felt very special persons. (Allen 1960: 18)

While Edith Tolkien and others withdrew from Oxford society, in 1930 Dorothy Allen was finding life so congenial that when her husband was being considered for the Wardenship of Rhodes House she was far from enthusiastic.[12] However, she accompanied her husband to London for luncheon with the Trustees. When she had a long talk in private with Lady Beit, wife of the Chairman, she felt that she herself was being interviewed:

> I [later] reflected ruefully that if I had been a little more anxious about the job, and a little less happily at ease, perhaps we should not have got it! (op.cit. p.45)

The use of the plural *we* indicates an awareness of her 'incorporation' into Rhodes House, one of Oxford's prestigious institutions. Dorothy Allen threw her prodigious energies and abilities into the affairs of Rhodes House, attending and giving various functions almost non-stop, with the help of a team of eight servants. Unusually, when her husband retired in 1952 the University awarded Dorothy an honorary M.A.[13]

The Second World War and After
Dorothy Allen gives a vivid account of the dramatic changes which the Second World War brought to Oxford, including the reduction of domestic help, shortages of food and other necessities, and the influx of evacuees and others who arrived in wave after wave needing help. The colleges were deeply involved; college wives were recruited into war work of various kinds. Alison Smith recalls this as being a period of great liberation for some of them; Mrs Sherwin-White remembers the war as a 'watershed' (personal communications). From the middle of the century changes in the social fabric of England greatly altered the circumstances of both college Fellows and their wives; but of the two, wives were probably the more affected. Indeed, so difficult was life after the war compared to before it that Dorothy Allen prepared what she called a 'misery pamphlet' which was sent to the wives of all Rhodes Scholars coming from abroad to prepare them for the conditions they would meet.

By then the household of the average Oxford academic was lucky if it had part-time help with the cleaning. In the 1950s and 1960s, Kirkwood noted (1977), many wives lived in vast, sometimes magnificent houses, hardly able to keep them moderately tidy, let alone clean and warm. (Most of the larger 'North Oxford houses' to which she referred have since been either taken over by University institutions or divided into flats.) But despite the reduced scale of living, entertaining at home a husband's colleagues and distinguished visitors and their wives remained the ideal. Formal dinner parties were, however, becoming more a pleasure for wives to attend than to give: Fellows increasingly used their colleges when they had speakers to dine. This, of course, had the effect of excluding wives from their discourse. Employing an American expression, Muriel Beadle, whose husband was Eastman Visiting Professor at Balliol College in 1958, concludes:

> One thing I *did* learn; you can't beat City Hall. The colleges set a better table than any woman can, and the after-dinner conversation of fellow-scholars in a senior common room is likely to be more interesting than the domestic trivia of a wife's day. So the successful Oxford wife is the one who early accepts her husband's college as his mistress. (Beadle 1961: 100)

Indeed, Deborah Kirkwood noted twenty years later (1977) that for some men the college becomes 'their *alter ego*'; 'some wives feel during term that for their husbands the college is the reality and the home the shadow'.

Beadle also learnt (as Oxford wives still do today) to study invitation cards with care to avoid embarrassingly appearing at a function uninvited. She recounts the story of a new official at the American Embassy in London who arrived at a college with his wife not noticing that she was not included on the invitation:

> Anyway, there they were - the invited guest and his uninvited wife. Faced by such a *fait accompli*, it never occurred to the head of the college to have an extra place set for the lady. He simply parked her at his lodgings with his wife. Having gotten all dolled up and driven out from London for a black-tie dinner at one of the famous Oxford colleges with all those fascinating dons, the American wife was doubtless tickled pink to find herself sharing a family dinner with another woman and four small children. Women do not dine in Hall, and that's that. (Beadle 1961: 98)

A 'well-trained' or thoughtful Oxford wife today often anticipates such a situation by independently inviting wives of college guests to her home.

Beadle reveals her irritation at being omitted from the various formal dinners to which her husband, as a special visitor of scholarly eminence, was automatically invited, and draws a dispiriting if comical picture of the contrast between her experience and his. She sits at home mending or letter writing, before going early to bed with a book:

> Just as you are getting drowsy, Himself comes home. And *then* things hum! He bounds up the stairs and into the bedroom. He flings his top-coat onto a chair. He bounces his shoes into the closet. He smells of Corona Coronas. The port was vintage, he says. It is obvious that he has done it more than justice.

The roast beef was jolly good. The Brie was admirable. Old Barclay was in top form tonight. Good chap, Old Barclay, listen to this ... (1961: 98-99).

We are now clearly entering a period when a developing awareness of the disparity in status and rewards between dons and their wives (as wives) is being made public: for example by Audrey Blackman with subtle irony through her art (see plates), and Muriel Beadle more rebelliously and directly in writing.

Beadle's sometimes amusing picture of the excluded wife was resented by some of her former acquaintances. It does seem, however, that in the twentieth century, and in particular after the Second World War, wives no longer listened almost daily to discussions of University affairs and intellectual debates around their own dinner tables; and when they did entertain it was not with the freedom that servants could provide. Some like Beadle probably longed to be included in the presumed excitements of academic conversation within college walls. Many others, perhaps, who had developed their own interests, either did not care about, or even resented being involved in, college matters.

Colleges, however, *pace* Beadle, were by no means entirely closed to women, albeit the spaces within them open to wives were strictly circumscribed. Let us now give further consideration to those areas within the colleges and University into which women have gained admittance, and demarcate those from which they have been excluded.

College Spaces

College gardens and quadrangles. These have long been open to wives. Indeed, many old engravings of colleges show women and children strolling about. Mary Oman went for daily walks in the college gardens near her home. Today these liminal areas are regularly opened to the public as well as to wives, except when members of the college may be distracted from ·their studies. Wives might also be invited to college garden parties, the grandest of which is that given by the Vice-Chancellor on Encaenia day - 'surely one of the few social occasions in the West when men regularly outshine women in appearance' (Kirkwood 1977). Beadle (pp. 752-3) describes a ceramic sculpture depicting two figures:

> The dominant one was a lion of a man in academic regalia, his gown falling in massive folds from his shoulders to his firmly planted feet. Head back, chin up, paunch rounding gently forward, this was a man with the universe in the palm of his hand. He was unmistakably an Oxford don. A step behind him a dowdy little woman. There was a shapeless hat on her meekly bowed head, a shapeless jacket drooping from her slightly stooped shoulders, the hint of a wrinkle in her stockings. Equally unmistakably, she was the don's wife. The title of the figurine was, *It's a Man's World.*

This is an ironical study made in 1962 by an Oxford wife and professional artist, Audrey Blackman, of the Vice-Chancellor's annual garden party. Later a wife told Blackman that having seen this piece she always hesitated when choosing a dress for this party. Blackman responded by producing a

A Man's World Audrey Blackman, 1962.

new study of a more formidable woman equalling if not dominating the figure of her husband, reflecting the changes which had taken place by then. She entitled the piece *A Man's World No Longer*. Her most recent comment is *The Perfect Wife* (see plate).

Private apartments. Entertaining within college walls in the Head of House's Lodgings, or in Fellows' or undergraduates' rooms, has often included women - and even children, who were frequent visitors at teatime in the nineteenth century. Unmarried women would, of course, once have been chaperoned.

College Common Rooms. Some colleges admitted wives to Common Rooms in the nineteenth century. In the delightful 'factional', virtually documentary, account of Oxford as it was at the turn of this century Barbara Burke, pen name for Oona H. Ball, describes a luncheon party in Pembroke College Common Room for two unmarried women who were accompanied 'for the proprieties' by a Fellow's wife (Burke 1907: 180-1). But one of the oldest Common Rooms, at St John's, was then still 'kept sacred to its original use, no flippant female can come to luncheon here'. Even in St John's, however, there were 'two other and less ancient rooms: one in which women may be entertained, and one for smokers' (Burke 1907: 221). In the late 1960s the Fellows of St John's College instituted an 'academic ladies' night' held occasionally on a Sunday, at which lady guests were in fact entertained in the 'sacred' Common Room. This function became defunct when women guests were admitted to the College on the same basis as men visitors.

Hall. Hall has always been different from the Common Room. It is usually presided over by the President, or in his absence the Vice-President or senior Fellow. In the Senior Common Room, in contrast, the President is only a guest.[14] Until the 1950s, for many Fellows' wives the great (and for some almost the only) occasion they attended in a College Hall was the 'Ladies' Christmas Dinner'. In St John's College, for example, this was introduced in 1953, and was the first occasion for most wives on which they had dined in this Hall; nowadays Fellows' wives are also included on other special occasions, such as when a dinner is given for a Fellow leaving.

The extension of access for Fellows' wives in St John's was, perhaps, as much a result of pressure from below as of initiative from the top. It was 'other women' who broke the mould. Undergraduates obtained the right to invite female coevals to dine in Hall. The younger bachelor Fellows also began to invite their female friends to High Table. Thereafter married Fellows would have suffered from discrimination if debarred from bringing their wives. Eventually all distinctions were dropped: women guests, like other visitors, could be invited on any occasion not specifically set aside for College business.[15] Wives who are themselves academics sometimes wear gowns in Hall like other University guests, but usually decide to go un-gowned when they appear with other wives not entitled to wear one. One reason for the freer admission of wives to colleges parallels the permitting of marriage for Fellows in the nineteenth century: the Fellows might otherwise increasingly withdraw from the community life of the colleges.

Other colleges have other practices; some are 'much less friendly' places than St John's. The new 'graduate colleges' – only five in number – have probably become the most liberal towards spouses (of both sexes), although Linacre College has only recently dropped the rule that a Fellow could invite any guest other than a spouse. This rule clearly distinguished attitudes to the role of wife from attitudes to gender. This distinction is maintained in practice if not by prescription in many colleges. In all colleges the frequency of a particular wife's attendance will depend very much on her relationship with her husband and on her own range of choices and inclinations; even those who would resent a prohibition usually do not attend often, some never.

Church and Chapel. It is not uncommon to hear references to the 'monastic' origins or traditions of the University (see also Sciama). In a society where each group has its special bounded territory (where, for instance, college members congregate separately in 'Junior', 'Middle' and 'Senior' Common Rooms, and where one table in Hall is 'High' in contrast to the rest) we may expect wives to have their separate places in spiritual territories: Church and Chapel. Mrs Humphrey Ward recalled how in the nineteenth century she looked

> out from those dark seats under the undergraduates' gallery – where sat the wives of the Masters of Arts (Humphrey Ward 1918: 139).

Oona Ball entered the same University Church of St Mary around 1900, and found that inside

> the church has a very odd appearance ... On the right and left of the Vice-Chancellor sit the Doctors, on each side under the pulpit are seats for the Masters and Bachelors. There are large galleries for the undergraduates, tucked away under these galleries there are pews for women, on the one hand for the 'Doctors' Ladies', and on the other for the 'Masters' Ladies'. (Burke 1907: 251)

The older College chapels, of course, were built for celibates. In 1958 when Muriel Beadle entered Christ Church Cathedral:

> the verger had indicated that we were to go left, into the lower pews. But he had detained George long enough to say that *he* might go right, if he cared to, closer to the altar. It seems that in Christ Church chapel women may not sit above the Bible. (Beadle 1961: 153)

At St John's College, in order that the President's wife and daughters could attend services without being seen, a special annexe with direct access to his Lodgings enabled them to watch proceedings through openings. Sheila Southern, in 1969, was the first President's wife to sit, not in this 'hen pen', but next to her husband in one of a special pair of stalls. Women have only regularly used the Chapel since the 1970s; nowadays

Fellows' wives and widows sit in the Fellows' stalls.

Any Fellow's wife who resents college claims on her husband may well
ponder the provision that a Fellow of St John's has the recently acquired
right for his ashes to be buried before the altar; she, of course, has not.
Even in death ...

'A Life of their own'

If some wives have felt themselves to be on the outside of Oxford
academic life looking in and have retreated into further isolation, others
have set about generating their own institutions - wives' groups and
associations - to meet the new needs. The rights some women have to be
members of such groups are clearly dependent on the connections
between their husbands, but such associations do not simply mirror the
interactions between the latter. It is not uncommon, for example, for pairs
of wives to know each other more intimately than do their spouses. This
can require delicacy should the husbands ever be in dispute, say over an
educational policy, or if both are candidates for an elected post. There
exist in Oxford various 'Town and Gown' groups, a '53 Club' (named
after the year of its foundation), a highly successful University
Newcomers Club, and various college wives' groups. All of these
organizations deserve attention, but for reasons of space I shall only
consider here examples of the last, before looking briefly at special
conditions affecting wives' independent work.

College Wives' Groups. At the beginning of this paper we noted that it is
difficult to speak of a typical college. In some colleges wives become
acquainted primarily through special hospitality offered by the wife of the
head of the college. In Pembroke College, for example, between 1969 and
1974 Mrs Pickering (herself an academic) would entertain Fellows' wives
in the Lodgings twice a year while their husbands were attending feasts in
Hall. Not all wives enjoyed such parties. Beadle quotes one:

> 'Once a year ... we wives were privileged to go to the Master's Lodge, were
> given an ersatz cup of coffee and a bun, and were allowed to look through a
> peephole at our husbands in Hall below, feasting on the fat of the land.'
> (Beadle 1961: 99).

Possibly she is referring here to the viewing slits so carefully built into his
New College study by Warden Spooner. But when a bachelor heads a
college even this entertaining is not possible. In some Oxford colleges,
therefore, associations have evolved specifically for Fellows' wives; here
we will consider one of them.

The 'St John's Wives Luncheon' started in 1967. In the last few years of
the then President's time he and his wife did not live in College owing to
her ill-health, and she had largely given up attending or organizing
functions for wives. Consequently when wives did rarely meet interaction
was superficial. The Vice-President's wife was therefore persuaded that a
luncheon club would be worth trying. From then on the St John's Wives

has met at least once a term for sandwiches or a light meal (which they pay for themselves). Invitations to the St John's Wives' luncheons are sent not only to all Fellows' wives but also to all widows of Fellows who retired in office. Currently invitations go also to the unmarried consort of one Fellow, to the separated wife of another, and to the only husband so far of a senior member of this college, a political scientist who in fact enjoys the occasion and likes to be asked. The contingency of a divorced Fellow remarrying, so that his second wife would be invited as well as his former wife, has not yet had to be considered. (At one time divorce would have led an Oxford College Fellow to resign; later it at least stigmatized him, though probably no longer).

Not long after the event was established, invitations for the second luncheon in term were extended to *all* St John's wives (that is, also to wives of undergraduates and graduate students). But most did not even bother to reply; generally attendance was so disappointing to the Fellows' wives that these invitations are no longer sent. For a number of years in the 1970s a small art circle was formed by wives of Fellows and graduate students at St John's: it met at least once a term and wives brought with them a piece of their own work.

Wives of Heads of Houses. Deborah Kirkwood has noted that 'Apart from the hierarchy of age there is not much sense of position and seniority among Oxford women. Professors' wives count for very little. But the wives of Heads of Houses have recognizable status. One is conscious of a slight but real social distance between Them and the rest of Us' (Kirkwood 1977). They may take their responsibilities very seriously, for example by trying to memorize the faces and names of some 300 students! Responding, perhaps, to a need created by these responsibilities, some Heads of Houses' wives formed themselves into an informal luncheon group, and a gathering of wives of retired Heads of Houses once met following an initiative by Lady Cairncross.

Wives at Work. Many Oxford wives today still engage in various forms of unpaid community work. Many, of course, do paid work. But if a wife (like her husband) has been trained as a specialist it may be difficult for her to find employment locally. The competition at Oxford is considerable and specialist posts are by definition few. It can be frustrating for those who have to stand down, or take a job that does not use all their hard-won qualifications. One wife explained how difficult it was after her marriage, until she found a suitable position in a prestigious local commercial house, to see her own career petering out while her husband (who got his doctorate when she did) was steadily gaining an international reputation. Such feelings can lead some women to see the roots of their distress in the very institution of marriage and the word 'wife' becomes distasteful. They may refuse, for instance, to join college wives' associations or attend Christmas dinners. Nowadays they may signify their attitude by retaining their own names, or by cohabiting without getting married.

But if a wife does create 'a life of her own', one particular academic institution can have an especially upsetting effect. Thus Deborah Kirkwood (1977) has commented on how sabbatical leave, 'a perquisite greatly valued by the don - which may indeed be an enriching and rewarding experience for both him and his wife - can sometimes instead be a nightmare for a wife. Either she stays at home, while he goes away for 6-9 months, or she interrupts the pattern of her own life, makes complicated plans for the children, and goes too. When she gets wherever it is, she may feel uprooted and disoriented. His work and contacts with colleagues ensure his identity, while she feels hers threatened'.

Small Talk

When Mrs Fisher died in 1956 her obituary in *The Times* was headed *A Great Oxford Hostess*. The skills needed to maintain social discourse and provide hospitality have not therefore always been undervalued. Indeed, in the nineteenth century the witty dinner-table conversation of women was often noted. We should however remember the role of women in 'servicing' the conversation of men, as discussed by, for example, Dale Spender (1980) and it is difficult to assess now the character of those women's wit. For wives to participate in general conversation without appearing to exert unwelcome influence on college matters or to intervene in University politics requires finesse and great self-control, even today. That the problem is not a new one can be seen from Margaret Jeune's note dated 24 June 1854:

> Mr. Liddell too told us that Lady Theresa Lewis said to somebody 'What! going to vote against Cradock's scheme. That'll never do!' This may have an awkward effect on matters sometimes. (Gifford 1932: 41)

On certain topics Fellows jealously guard access to information. Dissimulation is often required. Once when Margaret Jeune's husband summoned friends to vote against a new bill, the vote in the House gave, Margaret said,

> a majority of 2 - a victory in fact for *our* party ... Met and walked in the High Street with Mrs. Cardwell - amused at her caution in pretending ignorance of her husband's vote (p.44, her own emphasis)

A few years ago a Balliol wife confided to Kirkwood that she actually dreaded the Christmas dinner because she couldn't believe anything she said could be of the slightest interest to 'all those clever men'. Such lack of confidence may be entirely misplaced; the wife of a Visiting Fellow at Magdalen College once told me that she always felt tongue-tied in her husband's college *despite* the fact that she was herself an academic. It is probable in such situations that wives have commonly 'filtered' from their speech all but banalities lest they introduce into the conversation an opinion or exhibit an attitude liable to disturb relations between a husband and his colleagues. Since wives may be relatively uninformed about these, they may face a mind-boggling task! Further, a wife might occasionally have to resist being gently 'pumped' for information which her interlocutor might hesitate to ask directly from her husband! (see also Tremayne, this volume). Most wives prudently profess to be ignorant of college or other secrets.

Conversation at events like a college wives' gathering has depended very much on familiarity. Some years ago one newcomer noted that three questions were typically put to her to start a conversation. First, she was asked her husband's academic subject; then she was asked where she lived and if in a college house; thereafter the conversation was likely to move straight on to whether she had children. If the subject was an unusual one and if she did not live in a college house (a 'tied cottage' which could make a wife vulnerable if divorced or widowed), or have children, the ground was quickly covered. In recent years wives may try to elicit whether a new wife has her own professional interests while avoiding the solecism 'Do you do anything?', or 'What are you?' or even 'Do you work?'. One Fellow's wife said some years ago that she kept a teaching job which really bored her because, when asked solicitously 'And what do you do?', she couldn't bear to answer 'I am a housewife'. At an academic party a man did once turn to me and ask disconcertingly: 'And are you somebody's wife?'. The modern shame at 'doing nothing' (with its implication of 'being nothing') has, I suspect, led to a narrowing of conversation with women. Sensitive men and women may avoid probing for topics of common intellectual interest with a woman lest she be 'exposed' as having none, and resort is often taken to discussions of holidays or domestic matters. This 'muting' only reinforces any prejudicial views among misogynist dons that the presence of wives lowers the level of discourse.[16]

Since one of the acceptable topics among wives is their children, special mention must be made of the latters' role among the academic families of Oxford. For an indication of the domination of male interests, we may consider the Oman children. The eldest girl was called Dulce after the Winchester Boys' School hymn *Dulce Dulce Domum*[17] (Oman, p.46). Carola Oman – whose layette had been prepared with the monogram 'C' in the hope that the *boy* could be called Charles after his father – was baptized in All Souls' Chapel (in a punchbowl, since fonts are, of course, not provided in college chapels built on the assumption of male celibacy).[18] As the congregation filed out, the Regius Professor of Civil Law said:

> 'I have been thinking that as this is the first time that a child has been baptized in the chapel, you might have named her Anima.' The parents almost shouted at him, 'Oh, Professor Goudy, why on earth did you not mention this before? We should have loved to have called her Anima for All Souls' ... Well, it was too late, but the parents looked into the possibilities and in 1914 I was duly confirmed as Carola Mary Anima.

When Charles Chichele Oman was eventually born (in 1901) his second name anticipated his father's election as the Chichele Professor of Modern History by four years! (Oman, pp. 57, 87)[19]

In a profession where a scholarly reputation is crucial in determining success among colleagues as well as in relationships with students, the apparent intelligence passed on to offspring and the success of their socialization will be a source of pride or shame for parents, and will inevitably be monitored by others.[20] Mary Humphrey Ward recalled an incident which probably took place in the 1870s in the Master's drawing-room at Balliol, and which was burned into the minds of some visiting parents and their son:

> On a high chair against the wall, sat a small boy of ten - we will call him Arthur - oppressed by his surroundings. The talk languished and dropped. From one side of the large room, the Master, raising his voice, addressed the small boy on the other side. 'Well, Arthur, so I hear you've begun Greek. How are you getting on?' To the small boy looking round the room it seemed as though twenty awful grown-ups were waiting in a dead silence to eat him up. He rushed upon his answer.
> 'I-I'm reading the Anabāsis,' he said desperately.
> The false quantity sent a shock through the room. Nobody laughed, out of sympathy with the boy, who already knew that something dreadful had happened. The boy's miserable parents, Londoners, who were among the twenty, wished themselves under the floor. The Master smiled.
> 'Anábasis, Arthur,' he said cheerfully. 'You'll get it right next time'.
> And he went across to the boy, evidently feeling for him, and wishing to put him at ease. But after thirty years, the boy and his parents still remember the incident with a shiver. (Humphrey Ward, pp. 127-8)

Times are not entirely different today, as one Oxford preparatory school, the Dragon School, illustrates. It was established in 1877 after the Commission had recommended that Fellows should be allowed to marry (Jacques 1977). The school publishes a magazine each term, its name *Draconian* being well chosen in at least one respect. At the back can be found tables recording each pupil's exact age and class placing, subject by subject. Kirkwood notes that no mother could really resist looking and comparing the performance of her own and her friends' children; 'nor could they resist helping with Latin prep, etc. (mothers phoned each other to find out the assignments)'. Worse, she recalls, some mothers disliked attending coffee parties when their sons were at the bottom of the 'baby school', the lowest form!

Preoccupation with the quality of discourse is to be expected in an academic milieu where the privilege of a seat at High Table, a scarce resource, can only be justified by the supposed contributions made to thought, to discussion of the enabling mechanisms (such as University and college regulations and syllabuses and students' welfare) and to the college's social health.[21] A wariness towards the prospect of change which might threaten these instrumental functions is perhaps not surprising. Lidia Sciama has recorded elsewhere (1981: 108, and see this volume) the attitude of some Cambridge academics who thought that 'if the colleges were freely open to wives "The level of conversation would be lowered and the character of intercourse changed for the worse'". She writes that there was 'the fear of pollution in the often repeated commonplace "they will speak of nothing but nappies and babies!"' (1981: 111) The unpleasing expectation that some wives if invited might discuss nappies at High Table was volunteered to me in Oxford as recently as 30th October 1982, when I was dining as a guest in a college Hall.

In 1981 in the Oxford Dragon School the ratio of boys to girls was 601:23. Younger boys may refer to girls as 'hags'. To be touched by an eight-year-old 'hag' is to be 'haggalized' and the ritual of being 'dehaggalized' then becomes necessary for boys. A special stick kept locked in a cupboard in the music room (a baton?), was said to be used for rubbing the pollution away.[22] We may see here a parallel attempt to justify the isolation of an 'intrusive' minority by calling upon fear of pollution which seems to echo concerns in their fathers' colleges. Since Mary Douglas's classic *Purity and Danger* (1966), attitudes to 'pollution' and 'dirt' have been clearly shown to be linked to notions of *order* in the sense of boundary maintenance. 'Dirt' is matter *out of place* - rather than 'bad' in itself.

In an interesting study of family relationships among the Gusii of Kenya Iona Mayer, following up ideas derived from Douglas, has speculated on the need for 'traditionalists' to construct 'hard-edged' categories where sharp contrasts are 'drawn between the social *personae* for the different kinds of people ... '. Taking a lead also from Goffman's works, Mayer writes:

> In principle traditionalists are neither humanists nor individualists. They are categorists instead. They are seeing their fellow men primarily in terms of a number of fixed different categories or kinds, each with its own social uniform, its specific limits, its own nature and essential quality; and not primarily as unique individuals, or as humankind all sharing a common nature. (Mayer 1975: 260)

And there's the rub. Not only can babies and bodily emissions present a threat by breaking the boundaries between nature and culture, between the inside of the body and the outside, and thus introduce conceptually threatening anomalies into the classifying process, they may also be reminders of the 'common nature' of mankind which is logically opposed to many ideas of social stratification justifying privileged access to scarce resources.

Mayer shows how the privileges of Gusii elites are maintained by their 'distancing' themselves from young men and women and children. Prudery, like distance, seems built into many hierarchical institutions; they illustrate, Mayer concludes:

> the wider principle, that any assertion of status distinction demands a tight handling of the body. Every manifestation of the physical body simply as such will tend to draw attention to the common animal nature, or if not that, the personal peculiarities, which are both inimical to the discriminating sense

of 'who is who' in strictly social terms.

We may remember Mayer's thesis when we consider not only 'nappy talk', but also the long tradition of denying the body represented in the old rules of celibacy in Oxford colleges.

Final Remarks

Various papers in this book indicate that many occupational structures affect the wives of those working in them and pervade the family. Oxford college life does, however, introduce special features which some other employing institutions do not. Colleges are seen essentially as communities in which people not only work together but also regularly break bread together – after dark as well as in the daytime. As Spooner said, a college is regarded as 'something more than an office where business is transacted'. Any who may resent the demands of her husband's college and its exclusive dinner-table would probably not have the same expectations of, and hence feelings of resentment towards, an impersonal company luncheon room or factory canteen, unless similar claims were made for it. In practice in the 1980s pressure of work, the reduced representation of bachelors and the increased involvement of husbands in the daily concerns of the home and children, especially if their wives are employed, have resulted in a shift of focus such that some colleges barely maintain the 'common table' except at lunchtime or on special evenings. Living far from College exacerbates this tendency. The domesticity of home has gained at the expense of the domesticity of college. Nevertheless the ideal of the latter persists: the term '*Domus*' is in regular use.

Moreover, the tradition of Oxford, as in Cambridge (see Sciama), is that Fellows not only eat in college but sleep within the embrace of its walls: colleges are still full of beds. When in 1925 Dorothy Allen's husband became responsible for undergraduate discipline and welfare he had to move into college during term (Allen, 1960: 24). Indeed, even when some of today's wives were first married their husbands, if junior Fellows, were still required to sleep in college every night of term. Mrs Sherwin-White recalls how her husband left through the gates of St John's each morning to breakfast with her.

It is probably the overlapping (for husbands but not for their wives) of the conceptual categories of the domestic (and sexual) sphere of the family home and the ambiguous domestic (but non-sexual) sphere of college that makes some wives particularly sensitive to the claims of colleges on their husbands.

How far do wives feel incorporated in the University, their husbands' colleges and their careers? It seems that in the reign of Queen Elizabeth Katherine Hovenden, wife of the Warden of All Souls', was safe from prosecution 'as a lady at All Souls' (Batey 1982: 21). One of the few early wives of Heads of Houses to gain a place in popular history was Mrs Fell, who demonstrated her commitment to Christ Church, of which her

husband was Dean (head), by defiantly refusing to quit her home in
college when he was evicted by Roundheads in the Civil War, finally
being carried out into the quadrangle with her children on planks 'like so
many Pyes to the Oven' (Mallet 1924 (2): 376, quoting a royalist skit).
That formerly some women did feel set apart by their husbands'
University connections is attested by the gentle Mary Oman's reluctance
to associate with non-University families. Her daughter's best friend at
school was at first barred from the house because her father was not
University. Christina Colvin remembers asking Nellie, the daughter of
Bartholomew Price, Master of Pembroke College, whether she
remembered meeting Christina's maternal grandmother at a school they
shared. Nellie responded: 'Was she town ? - Then I wouldn't have known
her'. But not all maintained this boundary so sharply, and indeed many
'town' and 'gown' families intermarried.

Nowadays it is still not unknown for wives to be asked: 'Are you
St John's ?' or 'Are you Balliol ?' or the like, and some wives even
occasionally refer to themselves that way. That a college recognizes a
specific responsibility to wives as such, and to some extent 'incorporates'
them in their own right, is perhaps indicated when it invites Fellows'
widows to college functions. This may be, coincidentally, prudent since
widows might well have the disposal of their husbands' estates, from
which a college might hope to gain ! But probably few, if any, colleges
feel that wives are *necessary* for their success and well-being, even though
they do not undervalue the contributions they may make. Wives are not
normally interviewed when Fellows are appointed, and neither are wives
of prospective Heads of Houses, though the latter may be informally
discussed since there is a definite expectation that they will take an interest
in members of the college at all levels. Bachelors or widowers still become
Heads of Houses.

This preliminary study of Oxford academics' wives has revealed two
clear stereotypes or models. On the one hand there is the 'involved wife'
participating in heady intellectual discussions in elegant social settings at
home or in college and busily making a modest but real contribution
towards community life and the aims of scholarship. On the other hand
we have the 'excluded wife', frustrated, isolated, eating her (proverbial)
scrambled eggs alone while waiting for her husband to return from
stimulating talks across a laden college table or from poring over his books
as he adds to knowledge. Probably most Oxford academics' wives would
be able to identify with both these models ocassionally, although they may
generally be too engrossed in their own work or interests to be greatly
preoccupied by either of them. It is difficult to get a truly balanced picture
of mundane reality; further documentary research (including if possible on
unpublished correspondence written by wives themselves) and further
interviews must be undertaken.

In practice, the extent to which wives feel 'incorporated' in their husbands' work and career will depend very much on individual circumstances. There are wives who feel uncomfortable in or who distance themselves from their husbands' colleges, rarely appearing except on a few formal occasions, and some not even then. They are nevertheless exposed to the alternating rhythm of term and vacation, which pervades their lives. A wife cannot normally contribute directly to a Fellow's main responsibilities for administration, tutoring, lecturing and examining (demands which have a much more pressing and constant impact on his household than his occasional evening in Hall) – except as an unofficial secretary. But wives may expend considerable time and family money providing occasions when problems can be discussed in an informal atmosphere, seeing this (as one widow put it) as 'part of the job'. Many help their husbands with their research, seeking out references, typing manuscripts and preparing indexes. The commitment to research which has to be done in the evenings or at weekends can also bear heavily on wives' patience. Indeed, some wives today might be tempted to echo the wife of Sir Henry Saville (a sixteenth-century Warden of Merton who disliked being interrupted at his studies), who cried out

> I would I were a book too and then you would a little more respect me.
> (Mallet 1924: 125)

The straining after 'excellence' and the long hours worked, especially during term time, can cause great stress within the home. Nevertheless, probably many wives, even if not themselves academics, respect the scholarly endeavour (at least as an ideal) and are pleased to be able to make a contribution to it, considering that they are doing so not just for the sake of their husbands but for learning itself, thereby becoming part of the historical traditions of scholarship at Oxford. Referring to her future husband's 'unique qualities of heart, mind and brain,' Oona Ball saw herself as 'helping to take care of an unusually delicate and precious instrument'. One wife told Helen Callaway that she was happy to forgo her own career and assist her husband, since one very good scholar in the family was better than two second-rate ones. Finch has written that 'wives of men who undertake noble endeavours (or perhaps more accurately men with wives who *believe* that they are engaged in noble endeavours) may find that the potential competition between work and family, far from being expressed in conflict between husband and wife, results in the husband being given *more* space to get on with the great work' (1983: 28). She associates this statement with clergy wives; it could apply equally to wives of academics.

The duties, constraints and privileges which Oxford University entails upon the wives of its academics cannot easily be summed up, because of the autonomy and diversity of its components and its long history. Perhaps we may end this paper, however, by quoting the advice which Oona Ball (through a fictional character) ironically tendered to a newcomer at the turn of this century, giving 'Three simple rules by which to guide her life in Oxford as the wife of a highly respected don':

> Know your proper place and keep in it. Honour the Vice-Chancellor.
> Revere the Head of your own college. Let the chief business of your life ... be
> to see that your husband's body gets its sop and holds its noise and leaves his
> soul free a little ... (Burke 1907: 281)

Notes

1. This interim paper on Oxford academics' wives merely touches the surface of
the topic; it draws upon a longer work still in progress which deals more
comprehensively with topics alluded to here and others not included. I am greatly
indebted for help to many Oxford wives. Audrey Blackman, Christina Colvin and
Christine Martin are but a few of those who have passed on their experiences. I am
grateful to Deborah Kirkwood for allowing me to quote from some notes from
her perceptive paper 'North Oxford Wives' given at the Oxford Women's Social
Anthropology Seminar in 1977. As always, I owe much also to all the other
members of this seminar. Keith Thomas is among those who kindly lent me
books, not all of which are referred to here; David Hawke valuably helped with
proof reading. This paper does not discuss the implications of the institution of
marriage itself, on which much work has already been done by others, but
concentrates on the peculiar relationship of the University to its senior members'
wives. The common usage for women married to academics is 'academic wives'.
Here I use the term 'academics' wives' since we are not concerned only with wives
who are themselves academics. This slight change has, interestingly, had the
incidental and unintended effect of stressing the dependence of wives on husbands
(see also Sciama, this volume). Conventions relating to husbands of academic
women are omitted; practices at women's colleges are mainly 'calqued' on those
already established in colleges which were, and the one which still is, all-male.

2. Not all Heads of Houses are, strictly speaking, scholars; some are chosen for
their administrative skills, personal contacts and knowledge of public affairs. With
few exceptions (e.g. some bursars) Fellows are academics.

3. Unmarried sisters and daughters seem to have played significant parts in
Oxford social life in the nineteenth century.

4. 'Entertainment' seems to have meant refreshments.

5. Francis Pattison became the subject of gossip among Oxford wives: 'people
talked. But on the whole I don't think there was much ill-natured gossip' (Butler
MS). Mark Pattison was a model for Casaubon in George Eliot's *Middlemarch*.

6. At the time of the abolition of the celibacy rule, official Fellowships in New
College were raised to £300 per annum, which secured an income when
combined with their Lectureship and possibly some other payments for College
offices, enough to 'enable them to maintain a frugal family life' (Spooner's Diary
MS). No doubt 'frugal' is here a relative term.

7. Mary Oman, for example, had 60 first cousins.

8. She goes on, however, 'But hardly any of us were at all on fire for woman
suffrage, wherein the Oxford educational movement differed greatly from the
Cambridge movement. The majority, certainly, of the group to which I belonged
at Oxford were at that time persuaded that the development of women's power in
the State - or rather, in such a state as England, with its far-reaching and Imperial
obligations, resting ultimately on the sanction of war - should be on lines of its
own. We believed that growth through Local Government, and perhaps through
some special machinery for bringing the wishes and influence of women of all
classes to bear on Parliament, other than the Parliamentary vote, was the real line
of progress.' Mary Oman attended her first Anti-Women's Suffrage Meeting in
1905 (Oman 1976: 90).

9. For an amusing paper on acknowledgements to anthropologists' wives see 'GERTRUDE' 1978.

10. 'Her mother was a sofa-mother, like those of a great many of our friends' (Oman 1976: 146). Childbirth was considered to be, and probably was, a considerable health risk then. But at some periods it was also fashionable for women to have delicate health (see Agatha Christie's autobiography, for example) and this may have obscured the truth. For a good general discussion see Duffin 1978.

11. Women students were not full members of the University in their day.

12. The Rhodes Trust is a foundation which provides prestigious scholarships open to citizens of the Commonwealth and the United States and Germany, tenable at Oxford colleges.

13. ' ... her greatest title to praise' was for suddenly coping with 80 wives and 50 children when, after 1946, certain Rhodes Scholars could be accompanied by their wives (Allen 1960: 140ff, 184). Dorothy also undertook youth work for city boys.

14. He marks his 'stranger' status by wearing his gown in the Common Room, while Fellows do not.

15. One wife only went once, feeling that since she (conspicuously the only woman present) must be placed on the President's right, to continue to attend would be to impose on him.

16. For a discussion on 'muting' see e.g. Ardener, S. 1975, 1978.

17. It was only when sorting her papers after Mary Oman's death in 1917 that her son discovered that Dulce had been registered as 'Dulcie'.

18. In St John's College a rose bowl is used.

19. Chichele was a founder member of All Souls' College.

20. Edwin Ardener, in a discussion on the transmission of minority mother tongues, recently remarked that whereas the majority of the UK population seemed to accord autonomy to small children, the middle classes regard them, to a considerable degree, as dependents who are malleable by, and therefore reflect directly upon, their parents.

21. Conviviality is regarded as a duty which many men find irksome and increasingly avoid (regular evening attendance in Hall is losing to the more hasty luncheon).

22. While the effect on girls can be debated, one former Dragon schoolgirl, now of middle age, told me that the abhorrence of girls could carry over into the home; she herself had been acutely affected by her brother's attitude, which probably has had a lasting effect, and thought that sisters of other Dragon boys had also suffered in the same way.

AMBIVALENCE AND DEDICATION: ACADEMIC WIVES IN CAMBRIDGE UNIVERSITY
1870 - 1970

Lidia Sciama

> This new bill permitting the fellows of colleges to marry makes a great matrimonial rush among those beings ... I only hope it won't quite spoil the charm of the place by filling it with paupers! (Bobbit 1960: 173)

Introduction: The Background

My task in this paper is to illustrate some of the connotations of the phrase 'academic wife' in the ethnographic setting of Cambridge University, Great Britain. To reach a full and satisfactory description of the realities of marriage at the English universities, and to recapture women's experiences as 'academic wives', requires far more extended and detailed historical research than is possible here. Stone has suggested that

> The university, like the family and the church, is one of the most poorly integrated of institutions, and again and again has been obstinately resistant to changes which were clearly demanded by changing conditions around it. (1975: v)

Our theme here is that of the relations between marriage and the University. Stone's third institution, the Church, is however not irrelevant, since during the nineteenth century the monastic tradition of Cambridge (like that of Oxford) caused the more conservative elements and their supporters in the University to take a position of uncompromising resistance to change. The history of Oxford and Cambridge is the result of a complex and sometimes elusive interplay of numerous factors. All their changes of constitution and policy seem to have occurred through successful compromise between deep-seated and often conflicting interests, as well as through the continuous presence of different conceptions of the nature of the ancient Universities, not to mention competing intellectual, ethical and religious ambitions. Given this paper's necessary brevity, however, only the barest historical outline can be introduced here.

Unlike the earliest European universities, such as that of Bologna (which had its origins as a guild of students) the English universities could be described as primarily guilds of masters or 'dons'. From the outset, they were structured around authority - and authority was, for six or seven centuries, that of the Church. But although Cambridge University had Royal Charters and Statutes, and, by the thirteenth century, had acquired some of its administrative features - a Chancellor, two Houses or Councils and Proctors - after the Reformation its status as a *locus* of authority became somewhat vestigial, since most power now lay with the Heads and senior Fellows of colleges.

Between the Reformation and its own reform in the second half of the nineteenth century, Cambridge University (like Oxford) was largely conceived of as an institution for the education of clergymen. All entrants had to belong to the Church of England, and Fellows of colleges were required to subscribe to the Church's thirty-nine articles. Fellowships would be given to the most diligent and successful students, while the more usual outcome for a young man who had attended college, and who had no other expectation of a career in medicine, in politics, in the army or in the law, was to get a 'living' and to pursue a clergyman's career. Since Elizabethan days Anglican clergy have been allowed to marry and share the care of their parish with their wives; but those who wished to remain in Cambridge as Fellows of colleges and dedicate their lives to learning took celibacy vows for the duration of their Fellowship, which could vary between ten years and 'life'.

Thus, paradoxically, the old Roman Catholic ordinance stating that '*socios collegiorum maritos esse non permittimus*' was kept most effectively in Anglican Cambridge and Oxford, through the colleges' interest in maintaining their own character as communities of celibate - or, at least, single - scholars. As Michael Grant writes, 'after the Reformation, Masters - alone among members of colleges - were allowed to marry; a prohibition by Elizabeth I remained a dead letter' (1966: 80). No such freedom, however, was granted to other members of the University for three more centuries; not until the nineteenth century did some lecturers, professors and holders of lay Fellowships obtain dispensation to marry.

The long controversy over marriage of Fellows must have put to a very hard test their years of courtship and their determination that it should end in matrimony. At the same time it must have been a source of unease for those young women who, if unintentionally, were the primary cause of disagreement. Yet, except for those few individuals whose letters or biographies have been rescued from oblivion, we have little knowledge about those women who married Fellows during the period of transition (about 1850-1882) when marriage was still not universally allowed. It must surely have been at that time, however, that the married state started to become very heavily laden with negative associations. Vigorously opposed by those who viewed it as incompatible with teaching and scholarly pursuits, and who saw the marriage of their junior colleagues as a loss to their college, it must have been regarded with a great deal of apprehension by those young men for whom it might involve the loss of a

Fellowship and a livelihood (cf. Butler 1903). This penalty meant removal from all college society and (except for those few fortunate individuals who had independent means or were lucky enough to fall in love with a rich woman) the uncertainties of a 'coaching' career. Indeed in the eighteenth century, as G.M. Trevelyan writes, some Fellows 'kept their wives hidden away in neighbouring towns like Huntingdon. Some were otherwise accommodated' (1972: 74).

For some of the women involved, therefore, marriage to a Cambridge don at that time must have been not unlike that of hypergamous and unwanted brides, who might cause their husbands to be disinherited (impecunious as they might be, dons certainly carried their *noblesse de robe* proudly!). As we shall see, all this was to change radically during the latter part of the nineteenth century. The celibacy rule, perceived as an obstacle to the development of truly secular and scientific learning, was finally abolished in 1882 (Winstanley 1947: 335; Rothblatt 1968: 242; see also 1852 *Parliamentary Report*: 80-81, 156) but ambivalence towards the married state continued to preoccupy Cambridge dons to a larger extent than it did men and women in other occupational groups and in other areas of English middle-class society. In summary, Cambridge nineteenth-century history was marked by a long process of secularization, and this polarized opinion on the marriage issue no less than it did on a number of other problems: above all, that of the admission of dissenters and non-believers - and of a few brave women - to the University. In the following part of this paper, we shall attempt to understand some of the reasons why attitudes and styles of life in Cambridge were so much slower to change than formally stated rules and legislation.

Women as Scholars and Women as Wives

An important element of change in the overall structure of Cambridge's academic society was the development of women's education, which, coinciding with the removal of the celibacy rule, gained momentum during the 1870s. Paradoxically, however, the pressure of a few persevering women and of those few liberal dons who were their early allies, and its eventual success in the founding of the first women's colleges (Girton and Newnham) made very little positive difference to those who were in the position of 'academic wives'. On the contrary, the presence of women students threw into sharp relief within Cambridge some of the more general problems of Victorian society, and laid bare a number of difficulties and contradictions related to changing notions of individual rights and of marital roles (see Rivière 1971: 57ff).

The presence of a few more enterprising or more fortunate women than themselves acted as a reminder for the wives of their own lack of formal education and of the very sporadic and haphazard nature of women's access to professional opportunities; it tended to be a divisive element rather than a token of optimism. Relations between wives and women academics were closely influenced by those of the latter with the all-male Cambridge establishment. Sadly, as we learn from Rita McWilliams' admirable book on the history of women's education at Cambridge (1975: 102), after the first two decades (1870-1890) during which liberal academics such as Sidgwick, Marshall and Fawcett struggled alongside their wives to see Newnham and Girton established, 'the resentment of women competing with men begins to grow' - and such resentment was often expressed or echoed by the dons' wives. When (because of the University's stubborn refusal to grant women degrees and full academic status) disagreement arose even among earlier supporters of women's education, wives and women scholars came to be seen as fundamentally different, and opposed, kinds of women. This view - mostly created and upheld by men as a deterrent against too large an influx of aspiring girls to the University - could not fail to exercise in turn a strong divisive influence between the two groups of women. This was all the more damaging to women's confidence, since Girton and Newnham graduates and tutors frequently married Cambridge dons, so that 'scholars' and 'wives' were, in fact, overlapping categories: the same individuals (occasionally, as some confessed, not without embarrassment) could at the same time belong to both. But at that time - and indeed well into the 1960s - *professionalism* and *wifehood* were commonly held to be different and incompatible identities. Thus the two categories remained ideologically opposed, while some of the actual women involved were induced by an old undercurrent of vested interest and prejudice to regard one another with little confidence and sometimes little friendliness.

Strange as this may seem it is nonetheless understandable if we consider briefly both the wives' and the scholars' problems and points of view. Some women academics, especially those dedicated to the cause of 'emancipation', regarded marriage itself as a betrayal of that cause. In the first place it usually implied the abandonment of a full career, but, even more dauntingly from the point of view of many an intelligent woman, it was feared as a surrender of all independent will and judgment.[1] Women scholars tended to look down on wives both because of the latters' supposed ignorance and vanity and because, even when they were not openly hostile, time often showed them to be the most uncertain and easily swayed of allies.

For their part, married women, accustomed as they were to look upon the social world around them through the lens of a Victorian double sexual standard, sometimes considered those girls who struggled to go to university to be 'not very nice'. Some of them accepted the relentless outpouring of negative representations, ridicule and outright moral condemnation of female academics, and became very anxious to dissociate themselves from any suspicion of professional ambition or of devotion to feminist causes.[2] Foremost among such negative myths were those concerning the supposed gaucheness, social ineptitude and lack of femininity of Girton and Newnham students. Indeed (as Henry Sidgwick clearly foresaw with an amazing sense of reality when he referred to the girls' youthful beauty as 'their unfortunate appearance' (Marshall 1947: 12), physical attractiveness could constitute a considerable handicap to those with intellectual ambitions.[3] For the opponents of women's university education, images of female academics as plain and undesirable would then serve a double purpose: firstly, that of dissuading large numbers of girls from seeking places at university by the threat of male contempt and neglect, and secondly, that of protecting wives from fear that the presence of women scholars might become a threat to their own peace of mind and marital security.[4]

As Mary Paley Marshall recalls, 'some of the Cambridge ladies did not approve of women students and kept an eye on our dress' (1947: 12). Whenever evidence clearly belied those collective misrepresentations, the fear of sexual rivalry (whether real or imagined) could indeed turn some of the wives into the strongest of all opponents of women's education. Above all, the perception of 'wives' and 'women academics' as constituting two mutually exclusive, or even opposed, categories[5] - a perception strongly propounded by men - succeeded in preventing each group of women from fully trusting and identifying with the other. Since, clearly, both scholars and wives had to adjust to somewhat disadvantaged positions in relation to their male colleagues or husbands, each group was perhaps painfully reminded by the other of freedoms and aspirations it had had to forego.

From Clerics to Professional Academics:
the Transformation of the Don

The most important and far-reaching factor in the history of Cambridge marriage was perhaps the transformation of dons from urbane sinecured *dilettanti* into hard-working and dedicated *professionals*. In the second half of the nineteenth century, success in scientific research brought a new sense of purpose to the Universities, and a need was accordingly felt to reform University statutes and to create new appointments. It is ironical that, as soon as the rule forbidding Fellows to marry was withdrawn, the perceived need to improve standards of teaching for Cambridge's constantly rising student body led colleges to impose residence requirements and time demands which were often quite incompatible with married life as ordinarily conceived in Victorian - or even in present-day - England. In the Governing Council of Trinity, for example, 'it was proposed that the tutor sleep in college at least three nights per week' (Rothblatt 1968: 243), and a general rule was established that married Fellows should reside in the immediate vicinity of the University in order to carry out their teaching and supervisory duties. Ardener (this volume) discusses some responses to corresponding expectations at Oxford.

Thus professionalism took over exactly where monasticism had left off as a force antithetical to marriage, and its demands provided grounds for a new, and sometimes far more rigid, organization of time - and often of sentiment - than that of earlier monastic tradition. Indeed the ancient association of asceticism with intellectual power provided dons with a strong ideological basis and moral justification for even extreme neglect of families and wives. Thus, although by the late nineteenth century colleges had largely shed their religious aims, they were still believed to be ideally constituted for their new function as an optimum *milieu* for teaching and research. Consequently every effort was made to keep them as far as possible unchanged and to retain their character as 'total institutions', with which the institution of marriage was often regarded as competing for Fellows' loyalty and time (cf. Ayer 1977: 126).

The uncertainties and the reluctance with which the celibacy rule was finally removed are clearly documented in Winstanley's *Later Victorian Cambridge*. On the one hand, as he writes,

> it was detrimental to the efficiency of academic instruction that so many of
> the fellows were unable to marry ... (1947: 236)

On the other hand:

> These restrictions upon marriage ... were not based on a belief in the moral or
> spiritual value of the celibate life: they had their roots in a more worldly soil.
> It was held that married Fellows could not possibly have the same devotion to
> the college, or take the same interests in its affairs, as men who were free from
> the distraction of family life. (op.cit: 256)

Fair-minded liberal that he was, Winstanley concedes that 'the claims of the past were subordinated to the needs of the future', even though that meant 'recasting the life of the colleges into another mould and losing something in the process'. As he concludes:

> It was well that the bar on matrimony should be completely removed ... but
> these changes brought new problems in their train.
> That passionate and exclusive affection which the Fellows of the past felt for
> 'the House' often had unfortunate consequences; but it was not entirely an
> evil; and their successors of the present day, having other and competing
> interests, have not infrequently to undergo the stern ordeal of a conflict of
> loyalties. (op.cit: 346).

Such conflict between devotion to family and involvement in the wider community, be this the place of work or of recreation, seems to have been experienced with increasing keenness in the Cambridge of the recent past. Noel Annan, for example, speaks of a 'conscience' in respect to wives (1966: 21); while wives themselves, in my experience, have often discussed their place in Cambridge social life with a mixture of indulgence and resentment, and a clear awareness of anomaly. A general tendency (which no doubt started in late Victorian days when marriage of Fellows became generally accepted) was for colleges to emphasize the desirability of their members' participation in their numerous, and convivial, social functions (cf. Goody 1982: 141-142), while wives would be invited from time to time, but with such formality as to underline their status as 'guests'. As anthropologists have learned through cross-cultural study, to accord this status is formally equivalent to classifying the persons involved as *strangers* - albeit friendly ones, or ones to be appeased.[6]

Wives, then, often unbeknown to themselves, constituted a threat to the colleges' nature as 'elective' societies. The same Fellows who were fully trusted to serve on electoral boards and to choose their new colleagues were often highly suspect in their choice of a wife. True, college elections of Fellows usually involved collective rather than individual choices. Another basic difference between professional and marital selection, however, is that the first is usually based purely on criteria of competence and is ideally reducible to *agape*, a sentiment greatly valued and deeply understood by the devotees of common-room traditions (see Faber 1933: 215-232). On the other hand marital choices, inevitably individual, are suspect as being governed largely by *eros*, a sentiment which seems to fill a number of dons with the kind of embarrassment often observed in highly pollution-conscious groups when some hallowed taboo is broken (Sciama 1981: 111).[7]

Although at the time of my arrival in Cambridge (in 1960) the celibacy rule had been abolished for almost a century, the monastic tradition so deeply encoded in the colleges' architecture, as well as in their customs, was still spoken of by a number of people as a heavy burden. According to some of my informants, both male and female, many wives suffered a great deal of loneliness and disorientation. There was a widespread feeling that, even when they did share in their husbands' social activities, their sense of personal identity was undermined by the men's adoption of social and conversational mannerisms which emphasized the women's position as outsiders, or heavily underlined their primary commitment to children and home. Dons, too, often found conversation with the wives of their colleagues a great trial. Paradoxically, some of their least fortunate efforts were their well-intentioned attempts to bridge a supposed intellectual gap which they, cloistered in their rooms, sometimes thought greater than they might have found had they had the skill and good nature to seek to know the wives in any serious way.

Despite its great intrinsic interest and despite the availability of the most various and plentiful material, the social history of marriage in Cambridge remains to be written. References to the 'married Fellows problem' appear frequently in personal memoirs as well as in parliamentary reports and in many a college or University history, but marriage itself was never the topic of enquiry. When it was acknowledged, it was often treated as a peripheral embarrassment and a potential threat to academic dedication. Consequently, life in the homes dotted around Cambridge's compact city centre seems never to have aroused the historian's interest as an alternative and a complement to life in the colleges.

The most informative accounts still remain in the letters and memoirs of a number of Cambridge wives or daughters. Foremost among these are a collection of letters by Lady Jebb, a vivacious American widow who, having come to Cambridge in the eighteen-seventies, 'took the place by storm ... till ... in the end she married the shy and reserved Professor Richard Jebb' (Marshall 1947: 47). Another invaluable source is *Period Piece*, an admirable book based on her childhood recollections by Lady Jebb's great-niece, Gwenn Raverat. Raverat's narrative presents a very full and detailed picture, as well as containing a great deal of amused critical insight into Cambridge's day-to-day life and customs. Yet, while it remains a treasure-house of valued information, it cannot be considered representative, since it mainly describes one (albeit prominent and extended) academic family.

Lady Jebb's letters too contain some acute observations on the characters and idiosyncracies of Cambridge dons. At the same time they offer us some glimpses into the development of Cambridge's fascinating group of inter-related families - possibly the only social structure which could provide women with some companionship and solidarity in the shade of their husbands' colleges (Annan, 1955). With her innocent materialism and her unabated admiration for English aristocrats, intellectuals and gentry, Lady Jebb describes a period of change and of enthusiasm for marriage, courting, women's education and mixed social life. True Victorian as she fundamentally was, however, she never questions or even comments on her position as a don's wife. Her life emerges as a constant round of social activities: benevolent, complacent and just a trifle smug.

Both her letters and Gwenn Raverat's book, however, convey a sense of delight and warmth for acquaintances and friends. This gives a very different picture from that of Cambridge in the 1960s, when social change, academic competitiveness and the ever-increasing and often frustrated desire of women to have careers of their own, generated a feeling that (at least as far as women were concerned) the University had not sufficiently kept up with the times and had not quite fulfilled its promise as a 'liberal society'. Some evidence of this unease is in the notes I have collected, but much further and more up-to-date work is necessary to complete a picture which is as yet partial and statistically narrow.

Cambridge 1960-1970

The following observations are based on notes collected over a number of years in Cambridge. Although this part of my paper may be construed as an exercise in 'personal anthropology' (Pocock 1975; Okely 1978), some of the experiences it relates are analogous to those reported by more traditional ethnographers in the field. Since I had moved to England from abroad in 1959, my very first attempts to understand social life at Cambridge went hand in hand with, or, I should say, 'developed out of' my language learning. My first - and blundering - attempts to come to terms with a new and entirely foreign way of life were certainly such as to bear out Edwin Ardener's observations about the importance of linguistic

awareness in anthropological fieldwork, as well as his more particular
dictum that 'The anthropological experience derives from the
apprehension of a critical lack of fit of (at least) two entire world views
one to another' (1971: xviii). For, if I already had some command of
literary English, only in Cambridge did I truly *experience* the language in
one of its living social contexts. Understanding then changed; bits of
insight, often piecemeal and inevitably belated, led to the formulation of
new questions. Although in the course of time I may have formed some
picture of 'academic wives' and may have attempted some translation of
that phrase and of the social reality it conveyed into my native language, I
have never felt, as some do or say they do, that I had fully become one of
them. Solidary feelings and some perception of common problems could
not fail to produce a sense of belonging, but I don't think I would call
myself an 'academic wife' - any more than, for instance, Evans-Pritchard
would have called himself a Nuer or Leach a Kachin although they lived
and worked among these peoples. Some of the questions I had dimly
formulated in the early sixties seemed to compel re-thinking under the
stimulus of copious work on women, both descriptive and analytical. This
paper was written as a first attempt (1981) to place past experiences into
some orderly perspective, particularly in response to questions about what
it means in terms of women's moral, as well as material or time
commitments, to be wives to men in professions which may themselves
imply a calling or a commitment to a special social setting or way of life.

Theoretical questions related to work on wives are well known from
earlier discussions, particularly those of S. Ardener (1975, 1978, 1981) and
Callan (1975). To mention only the most pertinent of these, the first is: do
'academic wives' form a social group or class of persons with sufficiently
well-defined features to justify anthropological study? The second
question (in fact an extension of the first) could be stated as follows: since
'wifehood' is only one personal attribute or 'relational quality', how far
does it go in determining the social identity of the persons involved? How
far do other aspects of their lives, such as being 'daughters', 'mothers',
'professional women', and the like constitute alternative or competing
sources of identification which may strongly modify or render
insignificant the fact of their being 'academic wives'?

The first time I came across the notion of 'academic wives' as a social
type sufficiently distinctive to form a category was when I told a friend -
the daughter of an Oxford head of house, whom I had known before
coming to England - that I was about to marry a Cambridge scientist.
After the usual offer of courtesies and congratulations, she concluded with
a laugh 'So you will become an academic wife!' I must have looked
puzzled, so she added by way of explanation, 'Oh, they are *so* dowdy and
grim, they really hate one another. Mother had a terrible time of it ... ' At
that time I did not pay too much attention to my friend's description, but
I was impressed both by the fact that she had referred to 'academic wives'

collectively as if they had themselves been members of an institution, and by the fact that she had characterized them in terms of negative reciprocity.

After moving to Cambridge I heard people refer to academic wives in a number of different ways. At first I had not concerned myself much with the ambiguity contained in the phrase, which could designate 'the academically trained wives of academic husbands', or 'the academic wives of non-academic husbands', or, as it did most frequently (but not always) 'the wives of academics'. As it later turned out, the ambiguity was no mere looseness of speech on the part of many who can use language only too well. On the contrary, the phrase seemed to provide a useful polysemic expression, which could be applied to different effects on a variety of social occasions.

One curious feature of my early encounter with the phrase 'academic wife' is that when this was used (as it frequently was) in negative or ironic terms, the fact that I myself was one of these people was ignored or suppressed. A number of male dons, especially single ones, asked me with some solicitude how I was getting on with the 'other wives', while female dons or research students referred to the wives as frumpish, intractable, hostile or frightening. I probably owed my exemption from the category to the fact that I was foreign, or possibly (but was that wishful thinking?) to that of being myself engaged in academic work. When my having become an 'academic wife' was acknowledged, it was often discussed with apprehension: 'academic wives' were almost invariably experienced as an uncomfortable category.

Thus for some Cambridge men, as well as for women who were themselves professional academics, wives taken collectively were a source of embarrassment, while women discussed their own role as 'academic wives' with some concern and awareness that it could generate stress and frustration. So a partial answer to our first question - 'do academic wives form a category?' - is that most people in Cambridge would use that expression to designate a well-defined and understood social reality. Wives were in fact treated collectively, as a category, both through self-reference and through the references and descriptions of others.

I come now to my second question. Since wifehood is only one amongst many components of a woman's life, how far does it go in shaping her 'total social identity'? This question is, to my mind, a very difficult one to answer, partly because it takes us into the complicated realm of individual psychology. The difficulty lies mainly in the uneasy transition of the argument from some image of a collective identity to individual life-histories, in which dissatisfaction and strain may be due to circumstances that are ultimately impossible to disentangle. Some partial answers, however, may be found by leaving the notion of 'identity' in its limbo of loose definition, and turning again to questions of a more empirical or linguistic nature. Is the phrase 'academic wife' just an empty tag or is it a useful communication device, drawing on a wealth of common experiences and interests? Does its use, for example, help generate solidary community feelings?

In order to gain some understanding of ways in which the women themselves relate to the 'academic wife' category, I took an informal sample of thirty-five women, all married to senior members of Cambridge colleges. I first examined ways in which they themselves use the phrase 'academic wife'. Then I studied some of their commitments to activities other than those involved in their husbands' jobs, and some of the implications of such commitments for their own 'identities'.

In their use of the category in speech, I found that the women fell into three groups: those who designate themselves 'academic wife', those who avoid using the expression altogether, and those who use it mainly to describe others. Two out of the thirty-five women never used the phrase, while thirty-three used it habitually. Their answers, however, frequently indicated that the category was a problematic one: those women who had developed satisfactory careers generally used it to designate others, while some of the women who had had their career plans interfered with because of marriage expressed distaste or ambivalence in respect to their roles as wives of academics.

Two main competing, but not mutually exclusive, criteria for self-identification were professional commitment, and family and social background (especially for the well-connected). Seventeen out of the thirty-five women expressed a very strong, but in some instances ill-defined, desire to work. Twelve of these had precise career ambitions and had had full professional training. Six of these twelve felt that their career or training had been severely interfered with because of their marriage to Cambridge academics, while six had developed satisfactory careers (four university, one medical, one in painting). Only one of them admitted to having benefited from her husband's association with Cambridge.

Thus if we take commitment to a career or desire to work outside the house in a paid capacity as one among several possible 'identity' criteria, our sample of thirty-five falls into two, almost exact halves. Seventeen women expressed a desire to maintain commitments other than those imposed (or 'allowed') them in their role as wives, while eighteen others, although themselves often highly trained and intellectually sophisticated (eight had university degrees), expressed no desire to work other than for their families and husbands.

The women in this second group (tradition would have them described as 'ladies') seemed to have adopted to the full what Hilary Callan has very aptly described as the 'premiss of dedication' (1975: 87ff.). They appeared to represent the 'academic wife' category in a way which comes closest to its ideal model as popularly perceived; yet they frequently expressed ambivalence and impatience about their chosen role. Never having had personal ambitions, they had no grounds for complaint about failure to find professional outlets and rewards in Cambridge. Yet they too showed dissatisfaction about aspects of married life in the academic community.

Academic Entertaining: A Breakdown in Reciprocity?

One of the legacies of the traditional conception of teaching as a pastoral activity in Cambridge and Oxford, still present in the sixties, was the custom for senior members of the University and for college tutors to entertain their students and junior colleagues. Undergraduate students would not, on the whole, be expected to reciprocate; but invitations were not entirely one-directional (that is, 'down'). Newly-appointed members of the University, or hopeful candidates for college or University positions, would usually be expected to show their social competence to possible or actual sponsors by returning invitations. One of my informants recalled, for example, that soon after her marriage to a doctoral candidate she was taken aside by the wife of a senior member of her husband's faculty and told with an air of confidentiality that a young man's chance of gaining a permanent position in the University would be greatly impaired if his wife did not give the 'right sort of dinner-parties'.

Such dinner-parties would often, at that time, include people of different ages and standings – a fact often interpreted by European academics as a sign of 'equality' between professorial and junior members of the University. They were, alas, quite mistaken, since conviviality did not imply either the non-existence or the suppression of hierarchies: although it might allow for their short-lived suspension, it would inevitably be followed by their full re-affirmation at work. Such occasions were often described by wives as very trying. Guests might chance to be their good friends, but many were friends at least once removed. Conversation might revolve on some specialist – and often incomprehensible – topic, or (worse still) when entertaining students, they might be faced with some unknown and painfully shy, or else intolerably arrogant, youngster. Their parties, therefore, even if apparently lively, often left them with a feeling of alienation. Some of my informants' main causes for complaint were isolation, the male orientation of Cambridge's lifestyle, and a dearth of truly 'equal' and congenial companions. Entertaining was often described as a burdensome duty.

What is of great interest here, however, is that no uniform view was found as to how strictly such 'duty' was to be construed and how bad it would have been to abandon it altogether. Men and women seemed to hold markedly different views. Women, paradoxically, despite the feeling that entertaining their husbands' students and professional associates was not personally rewarding, asserted that not to do so would have been a serious relinquishment of their social duty; while most male informants, although they took it for granted that some professional entertaining should be done at home, would at the same time deny that failure to do it was of any consequence.

Could a woman then really help her husband's career? Disagreement between the views of men and women on that sensitive question was such a standard theme that, like one of the topics debated in a medieval Court of Love, it often became a ritual argument. Clearly, no real attempt can be made here to establish which view might be closer to the truth, since a wife's cooperation may be welcome in some circumstances, while in others it may be regarded as an abhorrent form of interference. But the conflict itself reveals interesting differences in men's and women's perceptions of marital roles in relation to the difficult world of intellectual work and professional rewards. Both the women's assertion that they could actually help their husbands' progress, and the men's defensive denial of it, may have been influenced by perception on each side of a potential threat to self-esteem. On the one hand, no serious academic would ever admit that anything other than intellectual distinction would ever play a part in his own, or other men's, appointments. On the other hand, the insistence of senior wives that younger women should take on a share of responsibility for the continuation of valued social rituals was certainly an affirmation of their own sense of worth, and of their belief that they too had an active and positive role. When gratitude to a wife was recorded in print, however, the writer usually acknowledged her help with ancillary jobs or her support in the private marital sphere. Social activities which were seen to take place on the borderline where 'private' and 'public' spheres overlap, were usually construed by men as 'purely recreational'.

Most academic entertaining is, in fact, a pleasurable form of exchange and most friendships are non-instrumental, or become so. Yet such differences in men's and women's perceptions of academic social life as I have tried to describe are very significant in the Cambridge context. Insofar as the women seemed to exaggerate the importance of their own contribution, their need to bolster their confidence in the face of overwhelming contrary evidence that dons *could* in fact conduct a full social life and do their own entertaining at college, was indicative of their desperately weak structural position. Such facts, sometimes discussed at those very same parties they had themselves organized, could not fail to generate a deep sense of futility.

Pressure from senior wives to entertain, particularly at a time when lack of domestic help had gradually forced most women to do the actual work involved, was sometimes felt to be a mechanism for controlling younger women and keeping them away from the job market and from professional competition. For wives, the sixties were indeed fraught with contradictions. At the very moment when, with the full complicity of the media and of glossy consumer magazines, food and wine were increasingly treated as clear and readily available social markers (cf. Goody 1982), and young women were encouraged to feel that they too could 'express themselves' through competitive and sometimes outlandish cuisine, dissatisfaction with traditional domestic roles and the need for greater individual fulfilment were increasingly felt and written about.[8] Checked by constant reminders that being in Cambridge at all, albeit excluded from a large part of their husbands' activities, was itself a great spiritual good fortune, signs of dissatisfaction on the part of wives were very often at that time indirect and restrained. This very suppression might nonetheless have been most damaging - witness the high rate of admission of wives to local psychiatric care (Dr Beresford Davies, personal communication).

Conclusion: the Compensations

Despite some examples of painful maladjustment, about half the women in my sample considered that marrying an accademic had its own kind of glamour; they conceived of the University as a community in which they could find plentiful opportunities for self-expression. Their picture of the University as a 'good society', or (as F.R.Leavis termed it) a great 'centre of civilization', was often based on earlier, pre-war and early post-war models. While the dominating atmosphere was one in which intense concentration on humanistic or scientific research - activities from which most of them were excluded - was valued almost above all else, emphasis on humane reflection on the nature and importance of relationships was also rooted in Cambridge. The considerable overlap between Cambridge and Bloomsbury is probably significant; it was certainly well known to wives through a number of biographies and through a wealth of anecdotes. Tales which might illustrate some eccentricity, reveal some interesting character trait, or recall some memorable remark of those impressive personalities who were the academic community's folk heroes, or else gossip celebrating with laughter the arrival of some *Lucky Jim* to the university, often circulated at tea-parties or around the dinner-table. Such occasions undoubtedly helped to create a larger field of discourse than that based purely on the literary or scientific achievements within which different circles in the University community found their distinct identity.

It was therefore in that area of sociability, of private dinner-parties and of the rare college or departmental occasions to which wives were invited, that women could sometimes take conversational initiatives or even specialize in certain social skills, and so feel they had an active role to play. They might, for instance, drop their own bricks and make their own *faux-pas* - sometimes, as psychoanalysts would say, a gratifying release of aggression! Too many such occasions, as we have seen, would cause women to regard entertaining as a duty or an act of piety, rather than a pleasure. But for the more 'dedicated' wives such annoyances were of no real importance, given that the basis and mainspring of their attachment to their role was the fact that their husbands were themselves dedicated to intellectual values. Most of them, therefore, striving for harmony, and determined (sometimes in austere circumstances) to run 'gracious homes',

managed to keep alive their sense that they too belonged to a 'Brahmin'
society in which scholarship and scientific research were dominant
preoccupations, even at the cost of considerable self-sacrifice.

Some of them may have been saints, but, as most made no hypocritical
attempt to conceal, they did hope to reap their rewards on this earth – and
rewards sometimes did come with their husbands' achievement of senior
positions which granted the women, too, some active involvement in the
inner circles of the 'good society'. Some regarded such striving as a
sacrifice, while others, as my interviews made clear, held it a golden
opportunity. But senior positions such as professorial or 'Head of House'
ones are very few, so that backing a husband's ambition could become
quite as frustrating as pursuing one's own.

Looking back on my notes after over ten years, I was surprised that
over fifty percent of the women I knew should have preferred to take on
the role of 'academic wife' to the exclusion of other interests and
commitments, except amateur or voluntary ones. Talking more recently
to the same women, however, I learned that they like other wives are
increasingly finding their roles unacceptably narrow and marginal, not to
mention uneconomical. Now that more opportunities are theoretically
open to women than was the case twenty years ago, there seems to be a
widespread desire among 'academic wives' either to have a fuller share in
the lives of their husbands *or* to cultivate a degree of personal autonomy.

Notes

1. Q.D.Leavis wrote that 'The women's colleges from the beginning had
evidently two functions. If on the one hand they were to provide heads for the
new girls' schools and women's colleges that began to spring up everywhere, they
had an equally important function in providing distinguished academics with
suitable wives' (1947: 3. My emphasis; see also Kirkwood, this volume). That view,
however, was not shared by all the pioneers of women's education. As some
clearly foresaw, if marriage to well-placed academics was to be its outcome, a
university training would replicate the predicament of English boarding schools
for girls and perpetuate women's economic dependence and professional
inferiority. (cf. Okely 1978: 109).

2. A typical example of such opposition between the idea of a 'good wife or
daughter' and that of a 'woman academic' emerges clearly from the letters and
statements of Alfred Marshall (McWilliams 1975). He thought it was right that a
young man should reside at Cambridge 'to fulfil his family's hopes for him'. For a
girl, on the other hand, keeping residence requirements would involve extreme
selfishness; 'if she decides to go her own way and let her family shift for
themselves, she gets honours, but her true life is impoverished and not enriched by
them' (quoted in McWilliams, op.cit: 112-113). What is most interesting is that
some of Marshall's statements were made on behalf of his wife, then a Fellow of
Newnham, as well as himself: 'My wife and I think it would be a mistake to ask
the Senate to admit women to degrees until ... ' (McWilliams, op.cit: 89-90).

3. Women students were strongly advised by their college tutors always to dress
and behave with utmost modesty for fear that they would be thought 'loose' or
even mistaken for prostitutes. As a former Newnham student writes, 'any
conspicuousness in dress or behaviour was strongly disapproved ... if you wanted
to be a social success, you concealed the fact that you came from Girton or

Newnham.' (Quiggin, 1899: 46). Wives, on the other hand, could allow themselves a great deal of freedom and could enjoy wearing flamboyant clothes: *Art Nouveau* styles and Liberty prints. As appears from Lady Jebb's and Gwenn Raverat's accounts, some followed attentively any changes in fashion; they would take pains over their new ball gowns and they made much of those college occasions to which they were invited: May Balls, boat races, and tea or dinner parties. Differences in dress and behaviour were much less conspicuous in the 1960s than in earlier days, but in dress as in other respects grounds for incomprehension between wives and women scholars had been laid permanently and effectively. The tables, however, had turned by the 1960s and it was most likely to be the successful academic women who by their style could arouse the jealousy of the more housebound and dependent wives.

4. 'The wife of some important Cambridge figure expressed thankfulness ... that 'that place' [Newnham] was not there in her husband's younger days. "Why not?" "because, if it had been, I am sure he would have married one of them instead of me ... "' (Q.D.Leavis 1947: 2). 'It was because of such women', comments Leavis rather acrimoniously, 'that women's education was so slow to take off'. But both the concern expressed by the unknown wife and the complete lack of humour and sympathy with which she was quoted over fifty years later show how antagonistic women academics and wives could be, and how uncomprehending of one another.

5. Echoes of an uneasiness associated with 'confusion of categories' are still present; witness the Commemoration Speech for 1982 by the Master of Trinity, Sir Alan Hodgkin. As he reports, when challenged by a journalist to explain why Trinity had contributed so little to political life, ' ... I countered that we had four Trinity men in the cabinet and that unfortunately Mrs Thatcher was too old to have been a Trinity girl - or should I say Trinity person? I do not know the correct equivalent of Trinity man. Neither Trinity lady nor Trinity woman sounds quite right to me.' (Trinity College, Cambridge *Annual Record* 1982: 4) Here the slight linguistic embarrassment is amusingly expressed, but might not the supposed verbal inadequacy reflect a deep-seated reluctance to acknowledge that the female equivalent of 'Trinity man' does in fact exist? And might it not be best to abandon all nicety and use 'Trinity woman' lest the *stylistic* hurdle on occasion turn into an *academic* stumbling-block?

6. Husbands of women dons are similarly excluded from the social life of their wives' colleges, but, since they are more likely than wives to have their own ties with the world of employment and social life outside the home, their position as 'academic husbands' is not really symmetrical with that of 'academic wives'.

7. In *The Times* ('Stay with the Men, Peterhouse', R.Scruton, March 22nd 1983, p.12) a one-time Fellow expresses his grief at the decision of his college to take women students. The writer makes no distinction between women as scholars and women as wives, since in his view both, and above all the marriage institution itself, are to be kept well away from college. The conservative values of college life, 'intellectual companionship', a 'wholeness' and 'a quotidian inwardness', are extolled and contrasted with the vulgarity of modern ideas, such as 'equality', 'fairness' and 'relevance', which now threaten to make Cambridge colleges means towards an end (i.e. education) rather than ends in themselves. If women are admitted, he writes, colleges, like the rest of society, will be ruled by those modern ideas according to which the 'most wholesome' form of association is 'that between the sexes' and the 'primary institution' is that of the modern *domus* - the temporary, nomadic, two-person family.' (sic). But, leaving aside the writer's distinctly phobic reaction, there seems to be no reason why coeducation should *inevitably* give way to the 'tyranny of sex' or why the 'sexual impulse' (unless painfully repressed) should transform colleges into 'cellular structures' of 'exclusive', 'temporary', 'nomadic', 'two-person families' !

8. Academic wives' dinners were often characterized by an amusing interplay between 'cooking' and 'cuisine'. Awareness that college fare, particularly feasts with their vintage wines and French menus, was unequivocally 'cuisine', would induce some of the wives to attempt similarly complex styles. But it was sometimes thought wiser and perhaps wittier to differentiate domestic from college entertainment by including guests in the simple enjoyment of home cooking as a change. Personal preference, as well as the self-conscious need to make 'correct' choices in terms of the economic and social character of dishes, made the entertainment scene most varied and amusing. For example, beef stews, which before coming to Cambridge I had never encountered except as a strictly workaday family meal, were much in evidence at dinner-parties, while an interesting example of culinary syncretism was a 'chicken and lobster casserole' prepared by the wife of a young lecturer when she entertained the head of her husband's college. Each of these dishes has its sources and its orthodoxy, one assumes, within a 'culinary' tradition. But in the Cambridge context they are 'socially' eloquent as well. The lobster, for example, was no doubt offered in recognition of the high status of the guest of honour, while the chicken was a clear statement of humility, but managed to indicate at the same time that some advancement and financial improvement would have been quite in order.

POLICE WIVES: A REFLECTION OF POLICE CONCEPTS OF ORDER AND CONTROL

Malcolm Young

Introduction

This short ethnography on Police wives was collected in a British Police Force. In some respects it is difficult to describe any one Police unit as a homogeneous society; indeed in taking the wives of policemen as an area of study one can ask, as Hilary Callan has,

> whether what I am studying is a society at all, rather than a collection of individuals randomly drawn together by a common definition, location and life-style ... (1975: 103)[1]

The Police Force which I shall describe is an amalgam of some seven smaller Forces and part of an eighth, each of which existed as a separate entity only a decade or so ago. (These small Forces, now drawn together, have a single hierarchy in place of their eight previous Chief Constables and descending rank structures.) Its three and a half thousand members are spread across some three and a half thousand square miles, which include heavily populated metropolitan areas as well as some of the quietest rural backwaters. Some of the smaller Forces which went into the melting-pot ten or twelve years ago had only a few hundred members, and covered small Borough areas of a few square miles.

For the purpose of analysis, I propose (somewhat arbitrarily) to divide the police wives into three groups. By examining each it should be possible to build a symbolic framework showing the syntagmatic chains which make visible a category of 'police wives', irrespective of which group is considered. We will find a society of women whose roles, status, demeanour, modes of thought and consequent action are structured in accordance with the order and control that is imposed both upon and by their husbands' place within the police system. The wives are in effect reflections of the public image of their husbands' occupation and status; but can also influence the lives of their men in ways that are publicly unacknowledged and go largely unregistered.

Categories of wives

Like many anthropological models and classificatory schemes, the three that I have used to display police wives' social space with reference to the

larger male police society are somewhat idiosyncratic. Firstly there is the
'single-beat' policeman and his wife. They are required to live in a police
authority house in a rural village taking responsibility for an area that is
often some miles from the Divisional or sub-Divisional Station, or from
their adjacent colleague and his wife on the neighbouring rural beat area.
Until recently they held a 24-hour-a-day responsibility for their area and
its social control, although this has been amended - in principle if not in
practice. The extremely wide terms of reference that are attached to the
village policeman, and his constant availability, extend to his wife. In
consequence there has been some acknowledgment of the vital role that
the police wife plays in these situations. This recognition has always been
tacit rather than formally expressed; success in her role has inevitably
bolstered the policeman's career chances rather than earn her any
individual reward. Her suitability for the role of 'rural police wife' reflects,
in effect, onto him. At the same time, the strictures applied to the
policeman - and the police role - effectively turn her inwards towards
other police wives, who are similarly constrained by the overarching
discipline expected of the 'total institution' (Goffman, 1961).

Secondly there are the groups of wives who live with their husbands in
the blocks of police authority owned houses, which either surround the
sub-Divisional Stations from which their husbands operate[2] - especially in
the smaller market towns in the Force - or are situated in groups of 4, 5 or
more in suburban areas. In particular I want to explore the structural
position of the dozen or so wives and their husbands in small town police
communities and in a larger group of over 40 wives in police houses on a
site near to an old Police headquarters building. Within this group there is
an inward-looking self-containment among the wives *vis-à-vis* other
outside women's associations. This reflects the generally defensive posture
of their men, who are in an occupation which seeks to control and order
the activities of others within an imperfect society. Consequently they are
required to maintain both bodily and social distance from the rest of
society to ensure that they are not easily seen to be merely human, and so
similarly imperfect. This structural defensiveness adopted by policemen
and their wives produces an insularity that is well documented in the
many volumes on 'the police life'.[3]

The third group that I want to consider is apparently the least visible.
They live in owner-occupied housing, located according to convenience
with no apparent pattern, around the industrial, metropolitan county. Yet,
by the use of 'thick description' (Geertz's term)[4] it is possible to discern in
this group what I suggest is an exact replication of the deep structural
forms that programme the practices of the wives in the much more visible
police housing estates. The same protocol, controls, duties and recognition
of hierarchy exist for these police wives, many of whom have never lived
in any house but their own, and who might not have another police wife
within half a mile. These wives might deny that the structures that

constrain their *colleagues* (my emphasis only) in the 'police enclaves' exist at all for them, but I suggest that each is similarly subject to the inculcated objective structures such as those of language and economy that reproduce themselves in the form of durable dispositions or *habitus* (Bourdieu 1977: 72–95). In this situation as in the others, non-conformity by a police wife to the norms of protocol or social correctness can and apparently often does call forth negative sanctions which affect her husband's career prospects. Indeed I suggest that a positive acceptance and definite involvement in the preferred social roles for police wives is required before husbands can achieve highest rank. Many wives are only too aware that they are indispensable to their husbands' careers, even though there is hardly any written acknowledgment within the police service that they even exist or have a role to fulfil.[5]

I have, myself, been a resident in this last category for some twenty years, with my police wife, and can claim some knowledge of how the experience of police wives within it mirrors the prescriptions and constraints that operate on wives in the first and second categories. At times they are subject to the same structural defensiveness that I mentioned above in their dealings with other groups or associations of women. And although they are perhaps less easily seen to be denying the outside or to be actively forming insular, defensive groups, the wives in this third category have a semantic understanding of their place within the ideology of power and conflict that is constantly reproducing itself in its struggles with the inherent disorder that exists in society.[6] These wives in their suburban homes are, like their husbands, implicitly aware of what is required of them, and especially of what they must not or cannot do if they are to be acceptable wives to *the job*,[7] as the police service is inevitably referred to by those inside it.

Asymmetric classification has almost totally promoted the male, public, police role and neglected any acknowledgment of the important female, wifely role. Consequently there is no written definition to suggest what a police wife is or what she must do to achieve such recognition. As one wife pointed out:

> the definition of police wife does not appear in the little yellow book whose fearsome legal jargon I and many other wives know by heart, from having repeated them *ad nauseam* during husband's training days ... (Ann Hillyer. *Police Review* 21.3.80: 683)

To reveal the social category of 'police wife' in all three settings requires, then, a 'thick description' of police wives' lives, and an exploration of the meanings that their experiences and practices produce for them.

In the country: the 'single-beat' wife
The conditions affecting the single-beat country police wife, even though they have changed over the last twenty years, point to a structural asymmetry between the public world of the policemen and the domestic

roles that their wives are expected to fulfil. As Rosaldo suggests (1974) the avenues by which women gain prestige and a sense of value are often limited by their association with the domestic world; for the single-beat wife, her place and function as a domestiç adjunct to her husband's public role in the village community is still considered to be essential and is the expected norm of success.

Since the amalgamations of the small police forces mentioned above, a certain stability in the 'single-beat' role has been established and consolidated. It was only a decade or so ago that changes of station and house around the county could be expected by a man and his wife every few years.[8] One wife spoke to me of her 12 moves in 30 years, another of her children's 5 changes of school in 10 years. A third complained of her 8 changes of house in 14 years, when curtains never fitted the next house and carpets were always wrongly sized, and the 'removal allowance' - 'I got £10 in 1963 for one move, when curtains needed replacing and school uniform substituting' (from fieldnotes) - never compensated for the upheaval. In the weekly *Police Review*, there is a regular page called 'Homebeat' which concentrates on police wives and their activities. A recurring theme is that of house moves and the problems that occur when a husband is transferred, or has to move on promotion.

In 'Living with the Job' (*Police Review* No.4545, 7.3.80: 462 and subsequent issues) four wives recall some of their moves. 'Janet' tells how she enjoyed living in police houses (she moved 7 times in 8 years) and although claiming to like the life, finds it necessary to describe the moves and their frequency. Margaret Lindsay describes living with parents, moving to a police flat and then to a modern flat before transfer to a police commune ('A Policeman's home' - *Police Review* No. 4573, 19.9.80: 1948). Anne Kellet entitles her article on her house changes 'A Moving Experience' (*Police Review* No.4577, 17.10.80: 2136), while Ann Hillyer considers her experiences have made her a 'Lovely Little Mover' (*Police Review* No.4584, 21.11.80: 2352).

Until the recent past, a move to a single-beat station was seen as a form of promotion for the male constable, even though his rank was unchanged. It was said to be a definite step towards the rank of Sergeant, although this was not guaranteed and it could take two or three further moves before the promotion in rank occurred, when yet another move would be considered necessary.

Of course there are constables who either do not want promotion or find it hard to conform to all the prescriptions imposed by the overwhelmingly male/public police forms; they have resisted moves that were considered essential to advance their careers. Wives similarly can choose to exercise some negative power by deliberately failing to live up to the social expectations of a 'model police wife' on the police estate or in a single-beat station. By deliberately refusing to conform to what is expected of a wife, she is in effect contributing to her husband's eventual political *stasis* within the police system of favour and promotion. This negative power is, of course, itself represented in terms of the 'public' values and beliefs of the police. She has no structure of public power to change the police ideology. Any rejection by her of the anticipated domestic roles can only mean her saying 'no' to a social form that is posed in advance, and very much determined and controlled, by the 'public' structure of police ideas. It should come as no surprise then that the only 'public' voice for police wives is within the columns of the *Police Review*, where the occasional page for wives is described in terms that reflect the male, official world and is called 'Homebeat'.

If the police wife and her husband are willing to challenge the limitations imposed by their allocated roles, and if they are happy to give up his opportunity to reach the higher ranks, they can then exert some individuality. They can achieve something verging on the *power of the margins*,[9] in that they reject the police ideology of success and accept a version that will not be structured in terms of the dominant modes of thought, but will be their own. Such non-conformity and denial of the clearly-defined roles that are specified for both the public and domestic areas of police life, can be expensive. Not many are willing openly to flout the requirements of the police style. Most of those who stay in the police are of a conservative disposition and conform, although they may grumble at the constraints. The lure of large salaries, pensions, the power of rank and early retirement tends to produce a degree of accommodation to the system, so that many achieve middle-management rank and a few reach the lucrative and powerful higher ranks. Their wives gain commensurate domestic status.

When the wife does exert her individuality she needs the co-operation of her husband, and both must expect that rejection of the demands of *the job* will have its results. One wife told me how

> when he had only 4 years' service in, my husband was offered a single-beat station in a village some 8 to 10 miles out from the small town station we were then at. This offer was put to me when the Inspector was paying his 'welfare visit'. There was a definite suggestion of a potential promotion, although I knew it was still some years off, in say another four years, depending on how we made out. But I had worked for a wage and I wasn't prepared to work as an unpaid village police station supervisor and cleaner, and I refused. You see they sounded me out first. Within 2 or 3 weeks they moved us twenty miles to the coast to another town.[10]

The anomalous wife, lacking legitimate authority, can therefore make felt her power of the margins, but will find that her non-conformity will reverberate against her husband and herself in consequence; and may in the long term be financially costly.

The 'welfare visit' mentioned above was something that wives until recently had to accept, along with many other invasions of their time and privacy. This control of the domestic by the public aspect of the man's world would have seemed comical in many other sections of British society. Another police wife complained to me of how she had not only to accept the monthly inspections by the local senior officer, but had to make tea for him as she was being inspected. Margaret Lindsay (op.cit.), although not then a single-beat wife in a village, describes her 'inspection'. She gives us some idea of the disciplines which *the job* transmitted to the domestic sphere, and which reflect the obsession with order. These disciplines applied to wives would surely not have been acceptable in any other section of British society in the late 1960s and early 1970s. She writes:

> in the early days of marriage, we lived with my parents, the house was formally inspected by a Sergeant from the local Station to establish that it was a fit and proper residence for a police officer. He went through it from attic to cellar in silence, his hawk-like eyes missing nothing. So that my mother found herself apologizing for the pile of ironing on the kitchen table ...

This scrutiny commenced even before the offer of a post was made to the man and his wife. He had to be steady, gregarious and a good gardener, while she had to be assessed as acceptable for the very wide and complex, but largely unschematized role that she would have to fulfil. There was, in fact, an unwritten social morality required of the man and his wife because of their visibility in the narrow social space of village life.[11]

Wives had to accept their examination for suitability, and the regular inspection of the house and attached village police office. This was said to ensure that the allowance that they were paid for cleaning the office was being rightly claimed. Inevitably the amount paid has been negligible; even in 1981 it was only £16.34 per month. For this fee, the wife may additionally be required to clean the local Court or the cell, if there is one at the office. One single-beat wife told me that during the period 1969-74, she had been paid £5 per month allowance for cleaning the 12' x 10' office and adjoining toilet. This toilet was used by members of the public who called at the house for a variety of reasons: motor car breakdowns, queries on lost property, requests for directions or holiday accommodation, treatment for cuts and bruises, and the whole array of minor social problems that are the daily round of the village constable. Such activities are far removed from the police force's somewhat single-minded management formula of effectiveness, which is based primarily on the crime-fighting role, criminal statistics and detection rates,[12] and which therefore both under-recognizes and under-values the essentially social style of police work in the country.

The village constable and his wife are only occasionally involved with crime reports; their role is more that of a pair of social workers operating over a broad canvas. The husband will undertake the uniformed patrols and will control local activities, usually through negotiation with local residents and without need to call into process the procedures of law. He will visit licensed premises, issue shotgun certificates; will deal with road accidents, but will also ensure the order of his domain by visiting farms, shops, other villages; will make calls on rural industries and the like, where daily conversation and discussion will build up into a jigsaw puzzle of the social fabric of the rural society.

His wife, totally unpaid, may type his reports, make tea for visitors who merit it (i.e. who need to leave her house with an enhanced opinion of the police); she will answer telephone calls from the Divisional station or other departments and write out official telephone messages. She might have to feed and house the occasional prisoner, without any of the normal facilities that would be found at the sub-Divisional station. One wife recalled how her coal cellar was used as a cell at one village station. The prisoner was locked in the cellar with a broom-shank placed against the door, while her husband went off to arrest a second man. She then had to sit with her husband and the two prisoners in the office, until transport arrived from the sub-Divisional station.

I recall two instances in the early 1970s when, as a City-based Drug Squad officer, I went to villages to arrest individuals and, for the first time, saw this aspect of the life of a village constable's wife. On the first occasion, while interviewing a giant of a young man and trying, in the time-honoured style of the aggressive detective, to get him to admit a burglary at a pharmacy, we found the atmosphere of tension we had built up shattered by the police wife bringing in tea and chocolate biscuits, served on delicate floral china. There is no way of maintaining a menacing style or implying knowledge of foul deeds, when the suspect is sipping tea from best china in the front parlour of a police house in a country village.

On the second occasion, the kitchen staff at a country hotel were all brought in, suspected of dabbling in Mandrax tablet abuse. Again the confines of the village police house and office and the activities of the police wife meant that we were unable to use traditional police interviewing techniques. How can you split up a group for separate interview, when the police office is just off the woman's living room and is only 10' square, so that the children's T.V. programmes were clearly audible from next door as she served tea and biscuits to the potential prisoners?

Often the police house becomes a casualty clearing station in villages. Road accidents are often much worse in rural areas than in towns, because high speed contributes to grave injuries. Some police houses situated near notorious rural cross-roads receive a steady stream of the injured needing initial treatment before the ambulance arrives. From accounts of these incidents in the past, it seems that no compensation has been paid to the police wife for spoiled sheets, pillows, the time she spent, or the tea and coffee she served out. Her husband dealt with the accident, she with its social effects. At one course I attended, where we were all encouraged to discuss recent cases, a colleague from a Norfolk village told of his most recent case of note. While we were discussing burglars and thieves we had 'captured', he told how he and his wife had taken in the wife and children of a suicide victim and how, later, they had spent a week cleaning up the blood and re-papering the walls of the cottage in which the victim had messily shot himself.

In such a situation, where the wife was seen to be an essential adjunct to her husband, it is not surprising that many Forces (including my own) refused until recently to allow wives to take employment. A wife had to be available to act as an officially unrecognized, unpaid, assistant to her husband. At one village, where a wife worked on the local telephone exchange, the husband was told that she *had* to be available at home for a variety of reasons, such as those outlined above. He declined to stop her working and, in consequence, was moved within a couple of weeks to another posting in a town, where the matter of employment, although frowned upon, was not so crucial for police wives.

By steaming open an envelope, the colleagues of one rural constable were able to tell him that his Superintendent (now retired), who had tried to get him to stop his wife working, had written on his assessment report:

> this man is more concerned that his wife is working than with his own promotion. I recommend that he is not promoted until she stops ...

I did not see this appraisal, which was written some twelve years ago, but the belief that the incident occurred as described is strong. The husband is said still to consider his working wife to have been the reason for his non-promotion. Such strictures, however, have been considerably eroded in the recent past; not surprisingly, the entitlement of the police wife to choose her own place to live and her own employment has been a major contentious point.

For village wives, then, the police system prescribed areas of activity which, if adhered to, would help their husbands' promotion chances. The women had been assessed and quietly vetted to ensure that they were suitable for the role of village police wife, because it was tacitly understood that, just like the former Lady Diana Spencer, they could never be just another woman in the village, but would always stand apart. I was told:

> You could never be one of the crowd ... you had to be the Treasurer or Vice Treasurer of whatever committee came into being ... you had to be involved in running the local charities ... you couldn't just be an ordinary member.
>
> As your husband rose in rank in the bigger towns, so the wife's responsibilities rose ... you could never walk up the main street just as a woman; you were 'the Inspector's wife' and it would have been a scandal if you were badly dressed or owed money.
>
> You were a showpiece at the single beats. At any social 'do' the schoolteacher and his wife, the vicar and his wife and the policeman and his wife ran the village occasions.

The wife presented a mirror image of her husband's controlling role within society. Her ordered place and existence were essential to support the images of tidiness and order that the masculine police society promotes at every turn. This tidiness and order is taken to its limits within police society itself. Accordingly, the antagonisms and conflicts that inevitably occur when one imperfect section of a society tries to control the rest, tend to incorporate the wives as well as the men, and they look inwards for support and mutual aid. The men are classified, ranked, institutionalized; and follow carefully delineated public roles concerned with the expression of power and the exercise of authority. The fallibility of the system and the sometimes random application of the rules, which because they are social constructs will always be imperfect, creates tension for the men; this is resolved partially by public acknowledgment of the difficulties of their task, but also by their joining together in a closely protective group, ranged against the outside. The wives, however, lack any legitimate acknowledgment of their part in the construction of public order or any recognition of the power that they can command. They are expected from the outset to form part of a male and female duality in an isolated community that will have to stand *apart* from that community, yet be close enough to understand it totally, in order that control can be successfully maintained. They have to cope with the demands of arduous shift work, with the constant moves to other towns and villages and other houses, and with the very visible task of being a police wife and therefore being, like their husbands, a 'different' sort of human being.

Many wives, of course, like *the job* and the curious form of prestige it can bring. They express great satisfaction with what they are required to do. Like the Army wife, the diplomat's wife or the doctor's wife, a police wife's social and domestic responsibilities will be extensive in support of her husband's public role; many police wives relish this. The power she exerts, however, in her capacity of wife is still determined by the tenets of the male police structure. Acceptance of those sanctions and determinants is the setting for her enjoyment of the prescribed role. As Ann Hillyer says:

> we are always getting letters to *Police Review* detailing the disadvantages of being a Police wife. Nevertheless (I believe) there are wives who actually thrive on it ... (*Police Review* No.2352, 21.11.80: 4582)

On the estate

Until recently the requirement to move house and station when ordered, along with the denial of the woman's right to work,[13] was tied in with a requirement for the man and wife to live where they were directed. We now have over 800 police-owned houses in my Force, although only just over 600 are occupied. Many are to be disposed of. Men and their wives now refuse to live in them and seek to purchase their own houses at an earlier stage in their careers than would have been imaginable at one time.

The provision of a 'free house' was something of a bonus to many, especially before and just after the Second World War; but there are many

drawbacks in accepting tied housing and not all of the accommodation
was up to the highest standards. A major programme of installation of
heating and kitchen units has just been undertaken in many of our houses.
Margaret Lindsay records (op cit) that when she was first allocated a police
flat:

> it was one of six shared by police families ... the flats were not soundproofed
> and with all the men on shiftwork, it was difficult to keep things quiet.
> During the summer we took the children out as much as possible, but when
> the winter came, noise wasn't our only problem. Doors swelled and refused
> to close, floor boards warped and we discovered we could grow our own
> carpets and wall coverings.

In my own force, E., a police wife, told me:

> we had a police house in the roughest part of B. between 1968 and 1970. All 4
> houses on the estate were for Constables. You had to fill the bath from the
> sink with a long hose; there were no taps on the bath, and you had to bail out
> the kitchen every week, it was soaking wet. I never bought any good floor
> coverings in that house, the carpets were always damp and were hung out
> whenever the sun shone.

On the police estates there was rank-graded allocation of housing. On the
largest estate of some 40 houses, near to a complex of police operational
and administrative buildings which all the householders could see from
their windows, I was told: 'the 4-bedroomed houses at the front were for
the Superintendents and the Chief Inspectors, then the Inspectors came
next and the Sergeants. When my husband was a constable, we had one of
the tents at the back'. Association among the estate wives tended to reflect
their husbands' position in the police hierarchy. Eventually there was a
move to obtain individual police houses on certain desirable general estates
for use by the higher ranks, in order to separate them and their wives from
the lower ranks on the Police estates. Today there are few officers of the
rank of Chief Inspector, Superintendent or above living on police estates
or in police housing.

Fraternization was generally *on* the estate and not out from it. Police
wives on the estates create (and created) a social solidarity that reproduces
their husbands' isolation from the rest of the community and obsession
with *the job*. Even everyday topics of conversation become inwardly
directed. The following quotes, from fieldnotes, indicate some of the
cultural restrictions involved and the continual reference to *the job* that
estate wives can expect to experience:

> I didn't like living on a police estate ... all the talk revolved around
> policework - promotion talk - there was no other conversation than the
> interminable one of who was doing well or who was doing badly ...
> we resurrected the police wives' club on the estate; it had died the death
> because everyone thought it was clannish, you know, with the Inspector's
> wife over the constables. We met once a month, then once a fortnight, while
> the men looked after the kids. We met in the Police club on the estate. The
> men thought one night deprived them of their drinking time and we had to
> fight for our one night ... really only two of those on the estate pulled in

outsiders to the bar in the Police Club ... the rest were in police crowds ... it was as if there was an invisible wall around the estate to keep us all together ... it was like living in a field you couldn't get out of and which everybody could see into ...

Peter Evans, *The Times* Home Affairs correspondent, who has written extensively on the police, has discussed how the police are 'tribal by nature'.[14] The ranked statuses and the careful physical demarcations of the system, which Hebdidge (1979: 12) suggests carry implicit ideological assumptions, occur throughout the police system and incorporate everything from uniform styling to house lay-out. Nothing is left to chance; order is everything, for as Foucault has said (1977: 218), 'one of the primary objects of discipline is to fix; it is an anti-nomadic technique'. The police service is nothing if it is not ordered, continually enhancing this clan feeling where form and place are everything.

On one estate, next to a Divisional Station, with 14 police houses, a police wife gave me a careful gradation of wives. At the lower end she placed the uniformed constables' wives. Next came the Dog Handler's wife and the Detective's wife: although still constables' wives, they were slightly higher grade. Then came the Sergeant's wife, and the top rank was held by the Inspector's wife. This woman told of how she thought that she had been 'frowned upon' for failing to adhere to the rank structure for wives.

In the Police Club at the same station (and at most clubs I have been able to collect information upon) there was a ranked structure of seating, which 'was sharply defined and which everyone was aware of. You didn't sit at this table, because it was more or less reserved for the officers and their wives'. This of course occurs in many social situations where staff come together occasionally (such as at the Annual Dinner Dance where the labourer's wife rarely fraternizes with the Managing Director's wife); but in the police case we are witnessing a daily fact of living that obtruded constantly upon estate life.

The police estates and the wives' clubs that operate from many of them are not to the liking of many wives. In the *Police Review* article 'Living with the Job', 'Jenny', a police wife, told how she didn't like the wives' clubs, believing that they are often 'rank structured'. She described the police community, especially on a police estate, as 'being like a small Coronation Street, because everyone knew what was going on'. In the same article, 'Margaret' described the treatment she received from other police wives at a police dance when she first moved to Nottingham: ' ... they just didn't want to know you'. Jenny recalled how one woman 'would never speak to her', because Jenny's husband was a lower rank in the police service, but, as soon as Jenny's husband was promoted, was friendly.

All those living in the 14 police houses adjacent to the Station mentioned above were expected to attend all the local police dances and social *do's* or occasions. The Divisional dance, which was the highlight of the social calendar, was described graphically by one woman as 'the kneepad ball'. Everyone was said to be conscious of their place and to have used their opportunities for social enhancement; there is no doubt that on these occasions an ambitious man, accompanied by an attractive wife who is willing to play the system, can be a formidable duo. Conversation on the following few days will, I was assured, inevitably include comments on which husband-and-wife team had produced the most effective 'crawling attitude'.

Things have changed, however, since the time (within only the last two decades) when, at one Divisional Ball, the Inspector's wife (as she told me) was expected to serve drinks to the more senior officers and their wives in the side room set apart for the 'hierarchy'. The Inspector's wife saw that the logic of this rule related to her position in the police structure. She was 'not quite hierarchy', but was not 'just' a sergeant's or constable's wife. She was half-way up the tree and could therefore expect that she would similarly be waited upon in the near future, if she acquiesced in her role. She was therefore at the right place within the system for this task to be rightfully hers.

Changes have occurred, but at a merely superstructural level. The woman on the police estate still knows that her domestic situation is determined by her husband's position and by the total police structure of thought. Every domestic activity from the allowance received for wallpaper (which is limited in value) to the prohibition on altering any internal fixture without reference back to the police administration, is an extension of the same order that determines where she may or may not sit when she and her husband visit the police club in the evenings. This control of the domestic by the public pervades the thought processes, so that many would deny that controls, as such, exist, and see them merely as the 'natural' order in society.

The owner/occupier wife

Many wives of police officers have never lived on the police estate, nor operated as a village policeman's wife. Since the amalgamations mentioned before, early house purchase has been increasingly pursued, and officers from constable rank upwards are now taking out mortgages in growing numbers. The location still has to be approved in writing, but thereafter the wife's domain becomes more her own than it would on the 'estate' or in the village.

In the past ten years, the number of senior officers above the rank of Chief Inspector who continue to live in police houses has dropped to almost zero, and an exploration of any of the middle-market, semi-detached suburban private housing estates in my Force area would reveal a sprinkling of policemen and their wives. By using my own 'personal anthropology' (Pocock 1973), I hope, in examining this category, to satisfy Pocock's request that the particular humanity of the people studied be put into connection with that of the insider/anthropologist. The unnecessary separation of subject and analyst can thus be avoided, and (in the present case) the analyst's own 20-year personal history within the category can be allied to an objective assessment in order to produce a 'practical mastery' (Bourdieu 1977; see also note 4 below).

This method reveals that despite the apparently detached and individual form of living available to the police wife in the suburbs, there is still an inculcated knowledge of the practices of being a police wife. A good many of the social contacts of these wives reflect their husbands' rank, financial situation, the length of his service and the age-group of his colleagues. In the suburbs wives seem to relate to, know of, associate with, or avoid many other police wives across these private estates. This occurs beyond their immediate consciousness or deliberation. Yet I suspect that they could not describe accurately the corresponding relationships or the active non-event of avoidance in respect to, say, engineers' wives, civil servants' wives or other occupational groups within their local area.

It is no easy task to plot this implicit knowlege shown in the woman's regular or occasional contacts, or her avoidance of other police wives; nor to determine how this understanding goes beyond her awareness of any other category of wife. Her knowledge of, and relationships with, perhaps a dozen or more women, are unconsciously arrived at and are primarily dictated for her by her husband's association with their husbands on *the job*. Yet, if asked, she would be unlikely to acknowledge that she assessed these contacts as being any different from those she may have with other female neighbours.

I have plotted the groupings of police wives within a five or six minute walk of my house in the suburbs of a large Metropolitan city. My wife, whom I would never claim to be especially gregarious or willing to play the 'rank enhancement game' of fawning for her husband's promotion prospects, nevertheless knows well, recognizes, avoids, acknowledges or has contact with some dozen or more police wives who live in the vicinity of our own house. All of these wives are the partners of men who rank upwards from Inspector to Assistant Chief Constable. Factors of age and rank (we are all in middle or late service) are apparent in these links. The cost of the property tends to pull in those on second or third house purchase, rather than the first-home buyer, into which category the young constable and his wife would be more likely to fall. It is noticeable that the wives of the constables in two blocks of 6 police houses, which are within this area, are not encompassed within this set of contacts.

It is also clear that links between many wives that were forged when their husbands were constables tend to be relinquished when one husband moves up the rank structure. The changes that occur for the man who moves upwards to take on more managerial tasks tend to loosen the links of communal meaning that once held the men together when they were constables with common interests, common criteria for success and common enemies. Similarly the wives tend to drift apart as their husbands' shared association with *the job* ceases.

Liaisons among wives in the suburbs are informal and tenuous, but accidental street meetings or local shopping trips, children at the same schools and other activities may mean chances for conversation, or lead to coffee at one another's houses. Conversations invariably include some reference to the common interest – their husbands' jobs – with a mention, perhaps, of the latest chances for promotion, transfers, or the constraints that living with *the job* produces.

Many of these wives attend a number of the vast range of police social functions. The higher the rank of her husband, the more of these a wife needs to attend if he is to move even higher and be 'in with a chance' in the continual politics that bedevil *the job*. There are Divisional, C.I.D.[15] and specialist squad dances, and police clubs holding functions on 5 or 6 nights per week that range from the disco for the younger constables to retirement *do's* for the 30-year-service men. Every week a Welfare newsletter publishes information on numerous intra-force social and sporting events; these consolidate considerable in-group feeling.

C.I.D. social groups, however, are curiously single-sexed. Although there is an Annual C.I.D. Ball, which is the supposed social pinnacle of the Detectives' year, it is avoided by many of the rank-and-file Detectives and pulls in a proportion of non-C.I.D. personnel and their wives. The rank-and-file detectives would probably claim that their 'stag' nights at Christmas and especially those *do's* when another Detective is promoted are *the* occasions. Two or three wives pointed out to me that when their husbands were Detectives, they (the wives) were kept more distant from others than when their husbands were in uniform posts:

> When he [my husband] was in uniform there were shift *do's* where we all got together. We were often at the Police club or at some dance or out for a meal as a group ... When he went into the C.I.D. they had stag *do's* and then when he went back as a uniform Sergeant, my social life started up again ... (fieldnotes)

One Detective summed this up succinctly with the warning, which every Detective would understand: ' ... wives talk! ... '.

This one phrase sums up to perfection the fact that the system, as it operates, necessarily requires many of its Detectives to flout conventions and to live a somewhat ambiguous and marginal life. At the same time, the system purports to uphold the middle-of-the-road, conventional values which are promoted for public consumption. Detectives' wives who do get together can compare notes, and perhaps identify the anti-structural elements[16] that run in rich veins through much C.I.D. life: this can be a challenge to the maintenance of harmony at home as well as work.

In the owner/occupier situation, the wife can absent herself from police practices more effectively than she could in the village. She can avoid other wives and not be drawn into 'police conversations'. She can work today, without sanctions or the need for approval from *the job*; nevertheless difficulties imposed by small children and the absence of a husband on shift work or on the uncertain C.I.D. hours can limit her autonomy. She can seek out relationships with non-police wives. But the continuing fascination that society has for its polarities of good and evil (which have largely devolved onto the police and the villain, replacing the Church and the devil as the binary module by which Western man seems to set up his ethical classifications)[17] means that her husband's employment will continue to obtrude, and she again becomes an aspect of *his* place in the police world, defined by her marriage to a policeman. These police wives, as in the village situation, are expected to be obsessed with the local thefts and burglaries, and to know the details of accidents and fires. She is assumed to have the 'inside information' about the murder, suicide or rape that the local press has recently reported and which form the staple conversations of many in the local supermarkets and at coffee mornings. But she may still be treated by others as 'the policeman's wife': someone special, who should be avoided because of her apparent contacts with those who are charged with the maintenance of the law. So again she may be forced 'inwards', to those other police wives who understand because they share the burden.

Despite these limited opportunities for owner/occupier wives, the creation of a 'total lifestyle', without contact with other police wives, is rarely possible for the wife of the young or ambitious Inspector, Chief Inspector, Superintendent or Chief Superintendent. Together (as stated earlier) she and her husband will have to attend functions throughout the year, often on a weekly basis. The Chief Constable of a Force and his Assistant Chiefs will have a dozen or so Commanders of Chief Superintendent rank to manage the various geographical divisions and support services, such as traffic and C.I.D. They, in turn, have a force of Superintendents who run the day-to-day operations. My Force has about 60 men at this rank, of whom perhaps half accept that they have reached their zenith, while another half of the remainder will be striving hard both socially and in their working activities to make a further upward move.

The Commander's wife and the ambitious young Superintendent's wife will, of necessity, have supported their husbands' climb to power in the past and can be expected to continue to do so. One Commander, commenting on his own continual presence at police functions, said:

> The old man [the Chief Constable] invites you and your wife to certain *do's*; that in fact means that you have to go. She can't not attend, unless there is a pretty good excuse.
> O's wife has some pretty severe illness, so she's excused, but otherwise if my wife didn't go, the old man would make some pointed remark and ask where she was ...

To paraphrase an Army saying about the field marshal's baton in every private's knapsack, it would seem that within many a police wife's handbag there lies a Chief Constable's truncheon.

How they marry: whom they marry

Even before she marries a policeman, a young woman is learning the constraints that she will meet. She will learn that she can never visit certain pubs with her future husband; for he will be recognized by the enemy – the local thieves. She might ask, as my wife has, about the man who has just spoken in the street, and realize that her husband has been recognized and she can therefore no longer go out and about without being seen by others to be with a policeman. Talk will dry up when she mentions that she is engaged to a policeman and, as Anne Hillyer recalls:

> you will be subjected to a peculiar kind of small-talk. For instance, 'Isn't it a lovely day?' will be replaced by 'What a disgraceful state this pavement's in! How can we report all these stray dogs?' It really is quite touching, this blind faith in one's knowledge of the law. I have been consulted on speed limits, local licensing laws and even what constitutes a defective tyre ... (*Police Review* 21.3.80, 'Homebeat': 683)

Another wife recalled that when she had first met her future husband, she was immediately seen by her close relatives to have taken on his law-enforcement functions. They, who had previously included her in a variety of minor fiddles and deviancies, were now afraid she would report them.

Having survived a courtship, the potential wife had until recently to be *presented for suitability* to the Chief Constable. In many forces less than twenty years ago, she had to be reported on in triplicate, with full particulars of her address, age, parents' full particulars and the like, the whole submitted for checking against local records. Once her background, family history and associations were approved, written consent to marry was given. On marriage, the woman had to give up work and understood that she and her husband would probably be allocated police flats or houses at the discretion of their senior officers, and moved again at their discretion. Permission to take out a mortgage and buy one's own house was more common in the small city and Borough forces where police housing was usually less available, but in other forces the newly-weds understood that it would be fifteen or more years before they would be allowed to buy a house. Constant moves imposed from above, and inability to control where one lived, gave to the top of the hierarchy a tremendous source of power over the ranks, and a means of controlling their physical, domestic and social activities as well as their working lives. The amalgamations of the late 60s and early 70s broke this control to a large extent. Men and their wives suddenly found themselves alongside City colleagues who since joining *the job* had, to an extent, exercised their own choice on where they would live and what form their homes would take. No longer were men with 15 or more years' service willing to be moved every eighteen months at the whim of a senior officer.

Each move towards a lifestyle that most of contemporary society would accept as normal, has had to be won. One colleague, who started his police career in a small Borough force in the mid 50s, recalled how potential wives were summoned to appear at Headquarters for the Chief Constable's personal approval, and how, when one woman flatly refused to attend, the legality of these 'horse-inspections' was shown to be dubious at best. They were quickly terminated.

In such conditions it is hardly surprising that an insularity, and a turning inwards towards other police wives who were similarly regulated, was encouraged by those who ran the system and implemented the regulations. The pressures to look inside the group for support are generic, and the new wife finds that support comes best from those who know the system:

> the worst part of shift work is that you lose a lot of friends. People outside 'the job' get fed up with you not being available in the evenings or at weekends ... 'Margaret' aged 50, Nottingham. *Police Review* No.4545, 7.3.80: 460.

> you can't have a career ... because their job comes first and you can't have a good position because you can't work as often as the employers want you to because of the shift work ... 'Janet', aged 30, Hampshire. Ibid.

Many of the wives I have spoken with reiterate this feeling of isolation caused by the shift work and their husbands' role in society: his identity as a policeman. One major way that this structural isolation is prepared for is reflected in the interviews quoted above. Three of the five wives interviewed were themselves ex-policewomen and were consequently prepared for their peculiar role in society; 43 of our policewomen are also police wives.[18] In a paper on the place of policewomen in the masculine-dominated police cultural system, which I presented at a workshop in 1979(b), I discussed the structural role of policewomen. One group of women who remain 'on the job' for only a short term (on average 3-4 years) have been dismissed as 'cheap labour' both by the Police Federation (which represents the lower ranks) and also by some of the better-known senior policemen. Sir Robert Mark described them as ' ... an expensive investment, because on average they serve under 4 years before leaving, usually on marriage ... '(1978: 219)

A widespread denigration of these women's capabilities and 'stickability' followed the slight increase in the percentage of policewomen who were recruited in the mid 1970s,[19] and was used by the Police Federation, the Superintendents' Association and the rank and file to press for pay rises and demands for more *man*power (my emphasis). The 'cheap labour' tag that they acquired, together with the constantly reiterated belief in their vulnerability to violence,[20] was taken up by the media and became a prevalent part of the 'increasingly-violent-society' image that both government and the press have propagated. There is, however, a totally different way to perceive the value of these women and to reverse this negative perception of them in relation to *the job*. Many of them marry policemen and leave after the birth of children, because of the difficulties that they encounter through their husbands' shift patterns. We can add their considerable numbers to the numerous marriages where police-employed civilian female typists, telephonists, clerks and the like also marry 'into' *the job*. We now have a solid phalanx of negatively perceived women, who because of their experience of *the job* and because of their special knowledge of its difficulties and pecularities, can nevertheless play a largely invisible supportive role that is generally unrecognized and receives little public acclaim. Many of these short-stay policewomen and police civilians who become police wives go on to play a vital role in the internal power struggles that their husbands will experience in their efforts for promotion. They also share, to a degree that many other professionals could not imagine, the social constraints and expectations that their husbands will encounter. Sir Robert's description, then, of these 'short-term' women as 'expensive investments' fails, I suggest, to look beyond the surface to the deeper reality that exists for a large percentage of these women and to their long-term value to the police.

As well as intra-group marriage, there are two other female occupations that seem to produce the qualities that the role of police wife will demand. One of these is teaching and the other nursing. It is a regularly expressed belief that police-nurse marriages are common and, although I have been unable to find any reliable statistical confirmation, a glance at the Nominal Rolls of police and civilian personnel (and personal knowledge of colleagues) suggest that there is some truth in the idea. Both occupations of course have some of the character of Goffman's 'total institutions' (1961). They both accept discipline as a major structuring principle and are both involved in the reclamation of individuals in society - one scouring the body physical and the other the body moral. With their unsocial hours and shift requirements, policemen and nurses are often in contact, especially at the age that boy tends to meet girl. Hospitals are constantly visited, especially on nightshifts in relation to accidents and assaults, sudden deaths and the like. Waiting for an unconscious victim to surface provides time for conversation. Many casualty sisters welcome police callers to assist with violent and drunken clients, who may need stitches in a wound and have to be held down. Many of the police wives writing to 'Homebeat' in the *Police Review* mention their nursing backgrounds; and two of the men in my current department of seven are married to ex-nurses, while two of us are married to police civilians.

Acceptance of the many bizarre - to an outsider - features of police life that I have described would not have been possible had wives not previously known, understood and been prepared to manipulate them to their positive advantage. The structures which constrain the wife cannot be controlled by her; and for her to come to terms with such disciplines it is helpful if she is from a comparable background. From their first induction into the police system the men are trained to accept controls, and it is not surprising that suitable partners should be found among policewomen or occupational groups such as nurses. A letter from a Staff member at a Police Training Centre, in the Federation magazine *Police* (February 1981), indicates how far social controls are still seen to be necessary at the Training Centres, where the young men are sent on their initial courses. The author argues a very narrow case in reply to a challenge issued in an earlier edition about excessive strictures:

> It is totally incorrect to say that students cannot leave the Centre, they have been and still are free to go out on a Wednesday night, providing they return by 11 o'clock - in line with ALL centres ...

As he goes on, I am reminded of how, on some of my earlier Police courses between 1958 and 1966, we had reciprocal invitations between Police Training Centres and nurses' homes, and were bused to each other's social occasions. We are told in relation to dances:

> because of the limited facilities open to us ... it was not feasible to invite every student's wife or girl friend and therefore a coach load of nursing staff was brought in from surrounding areas so that everybody had a dancing partner ...

One wonders however whether this 'Police-Nurse' combination is beginning to falter, perhaps because the modern nurse seems not to be steeped in the ordered ways of yesteryear. The author regrets that

> The obvious problem this presented was that the standard of dress worn by these 'guests' could not be monitored, nor could their behaviour in most part. The unfortunate result of all this was that these girls could no longer be invited and therefore discos were no longer a feasible thing to run ... (A.K. May, *Police*, Feb. 1981, vol. XIII, No.6)

Conclusion

By marrying nurses, policemen are reinforcing the meanings that the masculine model of the police world has created for them. They are taking women who exemplify the caring role to nurture their children and to support them as they struggle for promotion. By marrying policewomen, they resolve a paradox. In the paper I mention above (1979b) I have suggested that policewomen are an ambiguous factor in a male-dominated structure which is based on hard, tough, controlling forms and symbols. Women in this situation are problematic and create something of a dilemma. As Heilbrun suggests (1979), they can succeed only if they become surrogate men.

Even then they are still women, and remain ambivalent persons. A more successful solution to the structural problem is for the men to marry them and restore them to what is perceived to be their natural, caring role, in the position of police wife. Even their sensuality, which has led to their being, as policewomen, restricted in their powers of professional and social manoeuvre, is seen to have been resolved. The policewoman who has been denigrated as being, often, worse than useless on *the job* recovers status as a wife and mother. This resolution explains clearly why policewomen, who are subject to much of the condemnation that the marginal and the ambiguously situated generally attract, are still sought in great numbers as marriage partners by the same men who deride their professional abilities. By reconstituting them as wives, policemen are gaining adjuncts to their own careers, re-inserting these female intruders into the male conceptual space 'correctly', and so restoring order.

Notes

1. Many of the features that Callan describes in relation to diplomats' wives, such as conformity, hierarchical structures and the like are replicated in the police.

2. The Force is split into a number of geographical Divisions, each under the control of a Commander or Chief Superintendent. In turn, each Division is further subdivided geographically into sub-Divisions - usually only 2 or 3 to each Division. These have a Superintendent in charge with descending ranks of Chief Inspector, Inspectors, Sergeants and then Constables.

3. Ben Whitaker, for example, in an appendix to his book *The Police in Society* (1979) has a 'Select Bibliography and Suggestions for Further Reading' (pp.334-343), which contains nearly 200 publications.

4. The 'thick description' that Geertz suggests will sort out 'structures of significance' (1975: 10) within categories of culture are only ever practically experienced through the daily progress of activities. These, to quote Bourdieu, 'pass from practice to practice without going through discourse or consciousness'. (1977: 87)

5. And this in a Service where the written order dominates almost every conceivable activity, and where contravention of these carefully described and defined practices constitutes a disciplinary offence under the Police Regulations which can result in anything from a reprimand to dismissal.

6. In 1979(a) I discussed this defensiveness and introspection at length. I suggested that the police use binary concepts based on a paradigm that works through a range of homologies and analogies - 'us and them', 'good and evil', 'human and animal' - and which is awkwardly imperfect in practice. The failure of the model to fit reality creates a defensiveness by the men on the ground, employed on basic patrol work, who are opposed to the 'criminal enemy' and also to their bosses, the hierarchy, who operate the police discipline system. This turns them inward for social and psychological support. Those wives who are subject to the pressures that the system generates will take on the same defensive postures which are embodied in the practical injunctions of control and social correctness, and are implicitly carried out beyond the grasp of consciousness.

7. All the language not otherwise attributed in this paper is direct quotation of everyday conversations on *the job*. Language cannot be divorced from action, and fundamental structures are expressed in everyday language. Implicit concepts can be best revealed by an exploration of word and deed together. Crick (1976: 122) has suggested that ordinary language contains rich conceptual structures relating to action, and I find this to be so.

8. These arbitrary moves still occur in some police forces. In a letter to the *Police Review* (13.2.81, 305), a police wife writes: ' ... our daughter has already lived in 10 different houses in her fourteen years. She has changed schools at every stage in her education ... although [police wives] are supposed to give unfailing support to

their husbands ... and accept disruptions to life caused by house moves ... some police forces are not prepared to give the family any recognition at all ... '

9. Stephen Luke's concept of significant non-events (1974) is based on Gramsci's of hegemony and 'abnormal times', when, as he suggests, structure is both displayed, commented upon, made manifest and subverted for at least a time by those who are marginal, and who may even experience a flash of revelation that negates the ideology of the system and reveals multiple possibilities rather than the single dimension of power that the system would prefer. This allows us to make links to the concept of 'muted groups' (see e.g. Ardener 1975); and also to Victor Turner's (1974: 234) idea of 'the power of the weak'. I find this an attractive means of discussing how people comment on power even when they are submissive to its structures.

10. There is a myth that one can direct one's career in the police. Applications for specialist departments do occur, but the tendency is for authoritarian directives from the top. I have never applied for any of my moves within the service, and often a transfer to another section is known by all but the individual who is to be moved.

11. Ben Whitaker (1979), writing on the police discipline code, has been critical of the restrictive social morality that this imposes. Whitaker fails to see that this control is part of a symbolic system that creates an overarching structure of beliefs in right and wrong, good and evil, by which the entire system of policing is maintained, and which is inevitably some way behind innovative social thinking.

12. A symbolic assessment of the language of police management reveals how valued concepts originate in a primary belief in *real policemen* being *hard*, *thief-takers* and *collarfeelers*. These concepts are continuously set against 'soft' social options for control and ordered management. *Community policing*, or *community involvement*, is a growth industry in most police forces at the time of writing; yet is in effect little more than a return to foot patrolling rather than panda car use, and a formalization of previously existing police/public social liaisons. These new 'police empires' are often contrasted with their opposites, the traditional thief-catching systems; this has produced a dichotomy in which *community policing* is contrasted negatively with the hard, tough, crime-busting image which is still voiced (but not publicly) as *real police work*. My own research (1980) and other work suggests that these concepts of *real work* are sustained by a mythological male image that is created by the use of crime statistics and rates of crime detection as the true measure of success. Such research (see for example McCabe and Sutcliffe 1978; Steer 1980; Bottomley and Coleman 1980) although increasingly quoted in police journals and magazines, has so far failed to modify the very rigid police structures of meaning and consequent practice.

13. I spent some time talking to Mrs H., who in 1942 wrote to the Home Secretary about how her husband, a Constable, had been disciplined for allowing his wife to teach. He had been reprimanded for being *unable to control his woman*, lost his Police house and was denied the regulation rent allowance.

14. *The Times.* 10.11.77. 'The Facts that Cry out for a wider Police enquiry'.

15. Criminal Investigation Department: the detective arm of a British police force.

16. I have used Victor Turner's (1969 & 1974) concept somewhat loosely here, but find it useful. The liminality of living in and around societies' legal constructs, with a close awareness of what is borderline and what is unlawful in the arbitrary constructs of crime and disorder, produces a marginality for the detective, who is taken to the edges of the 'left hand' of illegal realities while he is supposed to uphold the constructs of the 'right hand' of order and decency.

17. The essays in duality by Hertz (1960), Needham (1973), Levi-Strauss (1968), and others, are central to the semantic and symbolic analysis now increasingly used

in anthropology. The concepts they suggest are extremely useful for the anthropologist working with the structures of practice and beliefs that determine police activities. The policeman coming to anthropology finds in them a basis for an interpretation of the daily events that he has been living. As Evans-Pritchard points out in his introduction to Hertz (op. cit.), the analytic notions of Hertz and others of the French sociological school - 'polarity', 'opposition', 'exchange', 'totality', 'liminality' and so on - are the real theoretical capital of social anthropology. Edwin Ardener (1971a: 466) has suggested that these basic conceptual tools are 'richly paradigmatic and ... express the deep structure of cultural facts without violating their surface form'.

18. Of the 215 policewomen in my force, 130 are single while 14 are widowed, divorced or separated; 43 of the 71 who are married are police wives as well as policewomen. Many of the single women are recent recruits and may well marry into *the job*. The civilian employees who are married to policemen and who are therefore very conversant with *the job* swell the numbers of those with close 'job' experience. There are no statistics available at our Force of those wives who were policewomen or past civilian employees, but personal knowledge and a cursory glance through the Nominal Roll of the Force suggest that a good many wives have had first-hand experience of *the job*.

19. The total number of women police only ever reached about 7% of the male establishment, and our current total of 215 women is just 7% of the total Force establishment.

20. Because newly recruited constables are required to undertake the most problematic area of policework at street level, the injuries that policewomen sustained were continually used to suggest their total unsuitability for 'real', masculine, tough policework. Calls for a return to the restricted role they had before the Sex Discrimination Act 1975 were constant. That much of this macho image of police work is a male myth, rather than the daily reality, is indicated by many researchers (see especially 'Women in the Police', Peter Southgate; H.M.S.O. 1980: 24), but examples were used and distorted to support the male logic that women should remain out of the public sphere. Research has also shown (and been ignored) that as many men as women (pro rata) are injured. As Woman Inspector P.K. Sullivan recounts (1979): ' ... the most important aspect of these figures for assaults [on policewomen] when relating them to the new role of women police since the Sex Discrimination Act ... is that over two-thirds of them have been committed by women prisoners and so would have occurred anyway even if the Police Force had been excluded from the Act ... '

CAMP FOLLOWERS:
A NOTE ON WIVES OF THE ARMED SERVICES

Mona Macmillan

Introduction

I do not set out in this brief paper to give a comprehensive or systematic account of the condition of Armed Service wives. My aim is to show that in some very diverse writings and other sources covering a historical span of some two hundred years of British military history, a few distinct themes and dilemmas reveal themselves consistently; and continue to be detectable in the situation of Service wives today. The most important of these themes are: the issue of recognition of the wife as having a legitimate presence and claim on the military institution (and, ultimately, on the State), the corresponding issue of recognition of the wife's contribution to the institution and its function of defending the State, the tension between wifehood and motherhood, and the ambiguous symbolic potency that attaches to the womanhood of wives in 'a man's world'. I shall allow these themes to emerge in their own way as far as possible in the course of presenting my material.

The material in question is drawn from a variety of sources. It is a product of participant observation and family history, both that of my own childhood and youth, and that of a daughter, two sisters and several nieces married to Army officers. I am myself a fourth-generation member of a 'Service' family: my father was a naval officer who became an admiral, his father an Army officer who became a general, and my great-grandfather also an Army officer who fought in the Peninsular War. I have used data from biographies, written correspondence, oral communications and published research relating to the nineteenth and twentieth centuries, and have supplemented these by drawing on two fictional portraits of Army life in the literature of the nineteenth century (both the work of men who had experienced it as journalists). I cannot here discuss the theoretical considerations arising from the use of all these different kinds of sources. I am conscious that I am working entirely within the context of the British Services; that there are other very different traditions was brought home to me in a paper by Tsehai Selassie on Ethiopian women leaders in war (1981). In the tradition of which she writes, violence seemed to be permitted both by and towards women, but in the tradition with which I am dealing women are not supposed to use violence, except in extreme cases of self-defence, nor are men allowed to use violence toward them. 'Little boys do not hit little girls' was an axiom impressed on generations of British children. How far the code was followed, whether it was extended for instance to 'enemy' women, (see e.g. Brownmiller 1975) are questions beyond the scope of my paper, which deals with Service wives alone. I can only record the principles and ideas into which the Armed Services fitted their 'own' women. My material shows that the symbolism which dissociated women from violence was strong in all ranks, as well as being ideologically central to the 'officer and gentleman' code. Yet this very ideological setting-apart of *women* provided no place for the individual *wife* in the men's scheme of things; and contributed to the relative 'invisibility' of wives and to non-recognition of their practical needs.

Armed Service wives show some interesting parallels and contrasts with other kinds of 'incorporated' wives, such as settler wives (Kirkwood, this volume) and diplomats' wives (Callan 1975). Settlers are by definition seeking and establishing a territory; military wives are as clearly defined by being *without* territory. They are camp followers, never settling, never accumulating possessions, not belonging to any social group but their own, although paradoxically they may be looked upon as 'representing' the parent society. If I may be autobiographical, it used to irritate me when people frequently asked me 'where did I come from'. It had not occurred to me that people *had* to come from somewhere, and I would answer impatiently that I came from nowhere; which with my antecedents is true enough. But although I 'come from nowhere' I and my like can very easily 'be at home anywhere'.

Service wives are also close in some respects to diplomats' wives, at least in the British context.[1] This is not surprising when one considers the shared detachment from the parent society, and all the factors making for a common culture and outlook between the two institutions. The 'premiss of dedication' (Callan 1975) is certainly common to both groups of wives. But there are significant differences between them as well. There are of course far more wives attached to the Armed Services than to diplomacy. The classification scheme distinguishing wives of officers, of non-commissioned officers and of other ranks has no practical equivalent in diplomacy, although linear hierarchies among wives exist and are put to use by both institutions. Most importantly, diplomacy has always recognized wives as having a function, if only a secondary one, consonant with their husbands' responsibilities. They may be adjuncts of their husbands, but they are 'incorporated' to some degree into the profession, and share the protection of diplomatic immunity. Service wives, by reason I believe of a *premiss of non-aggression*, have never been integrated into their husbands' profession. Marked by their womanhood as symbolically 'set apart' from the domain of armed force, their exclusion from the central purposes of their husbands' work has a more polar, intended quality than that of diplomats' wives. This, of course, applies only to actual military activities; in matters of welfare work, entertainment and the like, Service wives probably have as many 'duties' as those of diplomats. It remains true, however, that they follow their men entirely at their own discretion, and originally they were not even offered any protection. The trade of arms is seen as a man's trade *par excellence*, and the soldier or the fighting sailor lives in a very close man's world, into which women are not expected to enter. It is because he is called on to give his first allegiance to his mates that a young man must ask his Colonel's or his ship's Captain's permission to marry; in earlier days this would not have been granted before the age of thirty in the case of officers, twenty-seven for other ranks. A Service wife marries on the understanding that her husband's profession must take first place, and that its commands override any wishes of hers. Fiancées are asked to sign an acceptance of their intended husband's terms of service.

The Long Road to Recognition

There is no simple measure by which we can decide whether or not wives, at any particular historical moment, were given formal recognition by the Armed Services. In a sense they are not fully 'recognized' to this day since, as we have seen, the Armed Services in common with other 'incorporating' institutions steadfastly insist that wives' claims on their husbands remain subordinate to those of the Services themselves. But we can take as a partial index of recognition the provision for the physical needs of wives and children, in particular the need for living space or 'quarters'.

Until well into the nineteenth century the Army actively discouraged wives from accompanying their men: the Navy did not need even to acknowledge their existence until much later. The Army began to recognize them officially after the Crimean War, the Navy only after the Second World War. An argument used against the provision of married quarters was that it would encourage marriage (Bamfield 1974: 23). During the period leading up to the Crimean War, from four to six wives were allowed per company as washerwomen. When a regiment was ordered abroad these were drawn by lot,[2] and those left behind had to fend as best they could (Bamfield 1974: 45-47). Those who were allowed, and those who managed to follow illegally, reached even the battlefields, sleeping in curtained-off cubicles in the common tent or dormitory, giving birth on the march (op.cit: 51). Not surprisingly they were often as drunken as the men; Wolfe in Canada and Wellington in Spain heartily wished themselves rid of them (op.cit: 49). Those who went as washerwomen were allowed half a man's food ration, and were paid a halfpenny a day for each man they washed for (op.cit: 23), sometimes as much as sixpence for special articles by their customers. In the 1840s a sergeant in India wrote that women were more trouble than they were worth:

When they are on the march they are very humble and are glad to get some of the men to help their hackeries over the *nullahs* or ravines, but once they are settled in quarters, they turn up their noses to you and get quite saucy and full of dirty pride. If I could do anything in it I would make them wash clothes for the men, as they do at home. (Barr 1976: 96–97).

This was a man's view of the independence of the women, but a civilian woman wrote at about the same time:

A poor soldier's wife is indeed to be pitied ... she is often a young and inexperienced country girl; her health is likely to give way ... she is treated more like an animal than a woman ... she is sent hither and thither at all seasons, and she may truly say 'no man careth for my soul'. (ibid: 97).

But this too was a condescending outsider's view, and the women themselves did not apparently complain. Although the first quotation above seems to indicate that provision of quarters started earlier in India than elsewhere, it was not until 1854 that there was a general agitation for married quarters, led by a Captain Scott, who was censured for this by the Duke of Wellington (Bamfield 1974: 23).

Among the scandals exposed by *The Times* during the Crimean War was the plight of the wives and children living in the basement[3] of the Turkish barracks at Varna (op.cit: 148); it was after this war that quarters began to be built - primitive wooden huts to begin with. Sergeants were allowed married quarters, as were men 'on the strength' - that is over twenty-seven years old, with seven years' service, two good conduct badges and savings of £5 (op.cit: 25).

Before they were accorded even the limited recognition represented by living quarters, women were thus loosely attached to an entirely masculine world without benefit of any support or protection from that world. It might be expected that they would respond by developing relations of dependence on particular men, but the opposite seems to have been the case. From necessity, they built a female world of support and aid which they were able to offer in turn to their men. We find an early representation of this in literature, where Mrs O'Dowd in Thackeray's *Vanity Fair* initiates Amelia into the close-knit life of an Army regiment in 1815:

She proceeded to pour out such a quantity of information as no poor little woman's head could ever tax itself to bear; she told Amelia a thousand particulars relative to the very numerous family of which the amazed young lady found herself a member. (Thackeray 1847: Ch.27)

Mrs O'Dowd and Amelia illustrate the unattached status of the Army wife when, later in the story, they follow the Army to Brussels unofficially and at their own expense. In the world of Thackeray's novel, if any soldier's wife had been asked what she was there for she would undoubtedly have answered: to provide comfort for her husband. This Mrs O'Dowd does; she also demonstrates the confidentiality wives must observe when she is made the recipient of a state secret by her husband - that there will be a battle the next day. While he sleeps soundly she spends the night preparing his equipment and 'portable refreshments', including a flask of 'a remarkably sound Cognac brandy'. Then she wakes her husband and

> had as comfortable a cup of coffee prepared for him as any made that morning in Brussels ... The consequence was that the Major appeared on parade quite trim and fresh, and alert, his well-shaved rosy countenance as he sat on horseback giving cheerfulness and confidence to the whole corps. All the officers saluted her when the regiment marched by the balcony on which this brave woman stood and waved them a cheer as they passed; and I daresay it was not for want of courage, but from a sense of female delicacy and propriety, that she refrained from leading the gallant nth personally into action. (Thackeray, op.cit: Ch.30)

Female propriety did not allow combat. Mrs O'Dowd standing on her balcony is a Mother Goddess from the men's point of view: a mascot, a representative of a different world, a female myth - which is a constant theme in accounts of women attached to the Armed Forces. In practice, however, she and Amelia had immediately to turn their attention to looking after themselves, in an hysterical, threatened city in which they were quite alone: again a theme in the lives of real Service wives.

It is more difficult to find examples in history of ordinary soldiers' or sailors' wives than of those of officers. This is partly because the former were not so literate, but also because the Services were - and are - composed of very young, single, and generally temporary recruits at the level of the ranks. Only officers and non-commissioned officers generally lasted long enough to acquire wives. Even in fiction, there are few examples of the women who followed the ordinary soldier, but it is clear that they had to be tough and self-reliant. Kipling in the 1890s gives this advice to a young soldier:

> And if you must marry be sure she is old
> A troop-sergeant's widow is nicest I'm told
> For beauty won't help if your rations is cold
> And love's not enough for a soldier. (Kipling 1892: 206)

His Private Mulvaney laments 'that the Army has so few rale, good, honest, swearin, strapagin, tender-hearted, heavy-footed wives as it used to have' (Kipling 1891: 205). But he gives the example of one who has the same Mother Goddess attributes as Mrs O'Dowd. She had a figure like the big drum, and her nickname was 'Pummeloe' after a very large type of grapefruit. Cholera breaks out on a troop train. (The ratio of women Kipling gives is twelve, and thirteen children, to eight hundred men.) The women are ordered to go and sit in the shade, but Old Pummeloe organizes them into a chain to carry water to the sick and dying men from a distant well. When she herself dies from sunstroke her little six-year-old girl, who has been trotting to and fro with a bucket after her mother, is adopted as *The Daughter of the Regiment*, the title of the story. When she is old enough, a promising young corporal is ordered by his mates to marry her (Kipling 1891: 206). Orphans were often adopted in this way, and widows re-married almost instantly as they were only allowed six months of their dead husband's pay. There is a long-surviving Army story of the wife who on returning from her husband's funeral was proposed to by the Sergeant Major. She burst into tears and the man was contrite for having been so premature, until she explained that the tears were due to her having already accepted the proposal of the Lance-Corporal on the way back from the cemetery.

Fanny Duberly, the real-life wife of the paymaster of the 8th Hussars in 1854, could perhaps not be taken as a typical wife for her time; she rebelled against exclusion from the men's world, and, as wives had done only a little earlier, followed on to the battlefield. Nevertheless she is looked on by wives of today as their pioneer and champion because, by writing and publishing her experiences, she secured much-needed publicity for the plight of the unrecognized women and children. Though a rebel she maintained the expected feminine stance, dressing attractively and using her femininity to pull strings. This she did effectively to get herself and her two horses onto a transport with her husband's regiment on the way to the Crimean War. A few soldiers' wives were still allowed as washerwomen: all married and respectable, unlike the French *Vivandières*, whom Fanny quotes the men as calling, in an unkind pun, the *hors de combat* (Duberly quoted in Tisdall 1963: 125). The Sergeant Major's wife, who was too superior to be a washerwoman, was only allowed on board as Fanny's maid. But Fanny's own position was very insecure; her strength lay in obtaining the connivance of the men who surrounded her. She was ordered off the troopship by Lord Lucan, but he was overridden by his superior Lord Cardigan. However she often had to hide, and was lucky to get away from the terrible barracks at Varna where the rest of the women and children were trapped.

The Duberlys had a marquee tent at the end of the lines, and here Fanny held court sitting on her bed, with the men on the floor at her feet. After the winter at Sevastopol she had a hut built by some friendly sailors, and even engaged a cook. She took every advantage of her position as the only woman; when another woman appeared she criticized her for her mannish behaviour, her unkempt appearance, dirt and roughness. When the dreadful Crimean winter came she took to trousers and thick boots, but before long she was having a *Zouave* tailor make her a habit on the lines of the *Chasseurs d'Afrique* uniform, sky blue with black braid (Tisdall op.cit: 133). One of the soldiers' wives, a Mrs Evans, also prided herself on her neat appearance, and was one of only three wives chosen by Florence Nightingale to join her nurses.

Fanny's writings show her as rejecting the 'feminine' world on the one hand, but on the other as accepted by the men solely because she contributed something which their lives lacked. She says she will be remembered only as 'the never omitted guest where a dinner wanted to be amusing and brilliant' (op.cit: 148). But she adds 'If you could not cleave your way with a hatchet you would be trampled underfoot' (ibid).

> You must have as much pluck as the men, it is no place for women. Men are
> so eager for their own health and lives, their sports and amusements, that if
> you cloy them they leave you behind. If you go with them it is all very well.
> (op.cit: 54).

She had to make her own timetable and occupations; writing to her sister
she says:

> You ask me how I really endure what I go through. By never thinking of it
> for a moment. I never if I can help it have one idle moment. Work, wash,
> write, all morning, ride from four till seven every day [she was asked to ride
> and train the most difficult horses] then dinner and rum and water till
> bedtime, or the very strongest Turkish coffee. (ibid) ... I wonder [she says
> again] first that I am alive, second that I have kept my good name and my
> mother's memory free from stain, thirdly whether I shall ever know again
> what fear or nervousness mean. (op.cit: 151)

But all this was better than the woman's life she had left behind.

> I am not coming back, I should suffocate. Fancy coming from being the only
> woman back into all the artificial muslin rags, conventionalities and slanders,
> after being out here as free as air ... I love this life, I am living - seeing things
> and feeling them. It is better than morning visits and worsted work. (op.cit:
> 128).

Fanny Duberly finally accompanied the regiment to India, and rode with
the Rajputana column which covered 2,028 miles from Bombay to
Rajputana, of which she rode 1,800. Everyone had terrible saddle sores,
and she had to give up after having an abcess operated on, and riding for a
time on the wound. She had become rather disillusioned with Henry, her
husband, and their relationship is revealed when she writes: 'If only I had a
master under whom I could work, instead of a friend I am obliged to
support' (op.cit: 178). But she earned great admiration from the men, one
of whom wrote: 'I cannot image what it is that carries you through.
When I recall your face and figure I am astounded. You must give an
enormous fillip to the men of your regiment' (op.cit: 179). When she was
most ill and disappointed at having to give up riding she was, she says:

> sitting on a box having a good cry, when a deputation of the
> non-commissioned officers of the regiment came to express their sorrow that
> I was sick. They said that many a man had been saved from giving way to
> sickness because he could not give up so long as I was seen riding at the head
> of the column. (op.cit: 197)

But while the men admired, the women raised their eyebrows. Queen
Victoria refused the dedication of Fanny's book, and when she reviewed
the regiment on its return from the Crimea she would not acknowledge
Fanny who was sitting there in her *Chasseurs d'Afrique* uniform.

Official reluctance throughout most of the nineteenth century to accord
a recognized status to the wives and children of fighting men was
countered, as we have seen, by an ethic of toughness and self-reliance on
the women's part which the men in turn were able to see as a 'shining

example'. It was also countered by efforts to improve the conditions of
Service families within the Victorian tradition of voluntary philanthropy.
Mrs Bowen Thompson, returning to England after the loss of her husband
abroad, set to work without delay:

> Here, at the residence of her sister and brother-in-law, East Coombe Park, she
> immediately commenced various schemes of usefulness. During the Indian
> Mutiny she became a member of the committee formed at the Mansion
> House by the Lady Mayoress, and at once suggested that ready-made articles
> of clothing, mourning, and widows' apparel, should be sent out to India.
> Personal efforts were made on behalf of the soldiers who were sent to the
> scene of action from Woolwich. Prayer-meetings of the men were held,
> addresses delivered, and Bibles and Testaments distributed. Then when the
> soldiers had embarked, the women and children left behind had to be cared
> for. Public meetings were held, and a ladies' visiting committee was formed.
> The women were employed in making underclothing for the Government
> stores; and a small additional allowance was obtained from Government for
> each child. This accomplished, aided by Mrs Angerstein she originated the
> Central Association for soldiers' wives, under the patronage of the Queen.
> (Johnson 1886: 174-5; author gives no dates for the events described).

It is not, I think, carrying conjecture too far to see the historical emphasis
on self-reliance and mutual support among wives as reflected in modes of
thought within the Armed Services to this day. One wife has referred to
the prevailing social pattern of Service life as one of 'instant friendship'
and life is said to be 'never lonely'. But bereavement can be made even
worse for a Service wife than perhaps for others by gradual loss of the
supports on which she has come to count. A Falklands naval widow said
in a Press interview that

> gradually it all stopped and I felt as if I was no longer a member of the family.
> You never find the same camaraderie outside the Forces. (Anthea Hall,
> 'Breaking the Bad News', *Sunday Telegraph* June 6 1982).

The history of official hesitation and reluctance over the recognition of
Service wives, together with a reliance on the volunteer sector to meet
their special needs, also has its echoes in the present - as the recurrent
controversy over the level of financial provision for war widows shows
only too well.

Wifehood and Motherhood

The woman who followed the camp might represent a mother-figure to
the men, but she had to make sacrifices in relation to her own children.
Old Pummeloe in Kipling's story had lost five children and had only the
one little girl left. I have in my possession a long series of letters written
from India between 1842 and 1856 by a mother, Fanny Pratt, to her
young sons left at boarding school in Scotland, which illustrate the strain
on separated families. Fanny's husband, Lt.Col. Thomas Pratt, was on the
staff in Madras. In 1843 she went back with him to India where she had
already spent many years, leaving behind three sons at boarding school in
Edinburgh, and a daughter with her parents in Dublin. It was nine years

before she saw these children again, but in the meantime she bore three more sons, one of whom died at the age of three. She kept in touch with the older children by long letters, some of which seem today to be too emotional for young boys, and it is not surprising that she found their side of the correspondence scanty and inadequate. She begged them not to forget her, and always emphasized that she and their father only remained in India to pay for their education: 'You ask me about our return home, we only remain out here to enable us to afford you all the advantages of education, for your father's public income on retirement is a mere pittance, and while health is spared his duty is to remain where he has a good salary'. (Pratt 11.12.1848, 10.8.1849).

The Services were always badly paid, and social status for the officers was a kind of bonus.[4] Their rank gave them the *entrée* to social events, to institutions like clubs, to credit and, when they retired, to a ready-made place on committees – but very little on which to keep up this standard. This bore hardly on wives, although it also made them very resourceful.[5] Fanny Pratt was pious, and scornful of the gay life led by others. As her husband was not attached to a regiment she was not part of a permanent wives' group. She effectively refused to take part in the life of the Governor's court as she was expected to do:

> The Governor has sent cards for a fancy mask ball, and all the people are in a fuss about it. I settle the question by refusing the invitation as I always do, but your father must probably accompany the Commander-in-Chief and his party. (Pratt 11.12.1848)

As was usual where parents and children were so often separated, he left all the management of the family to her. She did all the writing to the boys, even on money matters and their choice of careers. The Colonel only managed a few lines when she gave birth and was unable to write herself. This type of family was kept together by reliance on grandparents and other kin; 'without your grandmother and Aunt Lucy I know not what we would have done'.[6] (Pratt 12.12.1848).

A good account of a twentieth-century naval officer's wife is given by Joy Packer, a South African, in her biography of her British husband (1975). Her son was born at her parents' home in Capetown, in the absence of his father, who was in the Mediterranean. After a brief time with his mother in Malta, he was sent back to his grandparents for the sake of his health and was brought up for the most part with them. When he was eight his father was appointed for a second spell in China, and his mother joined the boy in South Africa knowing that her husband's life

> would be devoted to his ship for the first six months of the commission. During that period a wife would be frowned upon. (Packer 1975: 24)

She made the journey to Africa, and the second one on to Singapore, as an experimental passenger in a 42 (W) Heracles bi-plane. When she left China again she received a letter from her husband's ship's company, which echoes the men's words to Fanny Duberly:

> The men of the *Kent* wish to thank you for all you have done for them, you have helped to make their lives happy during your stay with us, you have been as it were a foster mother to us all. Your charming presence at our football matches, concerts, dances, etc. has given us the extra will to win. (op.cit: 74).

'Foster mother', 'charming presence': the expected tribute to the woman following the forces. But if she were a foster *mother* to the sailors, the *wife*, again true to type, was separated from her own child, who was now old enough to go to the Dragon School in Oxford. He was able to join his parents in Greece for holidays until the Second World War came, and he had to be packed off to South Africa again for another three years; by the end of which he was seventeen. Separation of parents from children continues to be a major factor in Service life, and the tendency is still to be a wife first and mother second; and for children to spend at least some periods away from their parents.

But even wifehood may have to be improvised to some extent, especially for naval wives. Compared to Army wives, their lives involve more frequent and longer separations from husbands, and more isolation in some ways, since a ship's company is more transient than a regiment, and there is no permanent corps of companions. In the past wives who followed their men were mainly those of officers, since only they could afford to travel. There were no quarters, and they lived in successions of dingy lodgings. My mother went out to Japan to marry my father in 1907, and followed him to China, but once she had more than one child she ceased to travel. Joy Packer writes:

> during thirty-seven years of marriage, constantly interrupted by the Royal Navy's demands, Bertie and I depended on our letters to keep us together: they were a lifeline woven of ideas, confidence, and the sharing of our separate experiences. (Packer 1975, *preface* ix).

This is typical of the part literacy played in Service lives, as with Fanny Pratt: almost all had to be writers, and to live a second, shadow life on paper. Yet in spite of this link, Joy Packer felt on reading her husband's 'log' (diary) that there were things she had not been aware of:

> Every word opened new windows on a life outside a woman's comprehension – the cramped, communal, yet lonely life of a sailor, his involvement with his ship and shipmates, and the need to shake himself free of that 'tin box', and become part of the land again. (ibid.)

As opposed to officers' wives, the wives of ordinary sailors were probably always more locally rooted than those of soldiers. Since the Navy was based on three home ports, sailors' wives were likely to live close to a network of relations, although this may have changed in recent years owing to the provision of married quarters and the establishment of bases in Scotland. Unlike Army wives, naval wives are allowed to remain in a quarter if their husbands are posted elsewhere. In a study of one 'patch' (a name for married quarters common to both Army and Navy) Patricia

Nicholson (1980) found that 20% of a sample of 104 wives lived close to a network of relations, and visited them frequently. At the same time, she suggests, the provision of quarters has in some ways emphasized wives' isolation. Being, for much of the time, an all-female community of very limited age range (mostly 20-30) they feel separate from 'civilians' and strongly thrown in on one another. As noted earlier, this solidarity of the 'patch' comes into its own in a situation like the 1982 Falklands war, which demonstrated how closely the wives on naval estates in Portsmouth and Plymouth supported one another during the long spells of waiting for news of individuals after ships had been reported sunk.[7]

'Womanly' qualities in a 'man's world'

It can be seen from the men's words to Fanny Duberly and Joy Packer, as well as Thackeray's treatment of the fictional Mrs O'Dowd, that women in a military environment could be admired both for *womanly qualities* ('charming presence') and for *male virtues* such as courage, thought especially praiseworthy in a being regarded as physically weaker and more delicate than a man.[8] Fanny was idolized for her gallantry, but her gaiety and vivacity also represented something which the men looked for, a comradeship with the other sex, and a taste of the life which they had left behind. Their fighting lives were tough and ugly, and what they wanted from women, apart from creature comfort, was a distance from the sordid. Fanny with her dinners and her lively talk, her strong Turkish coffee for which she shopped in the bazaars, created a small picture of the other world. If women were there at all they were there to stand for this normal world, for all the civilized graces, and indeed for everything that was the antithesis of war. The idealization of women had begun with the courtly love of the Middle Ages, and it still inspired the attention and support that Fanny received. It had a social purpose also - that of keeping alive a memory of the culture for which the men were ostensibly fighting. But it is not easy to live as a symbol, and in a situation of peace this idealization could create an artificial life for groups of women, separated from their normal communities in Army stations, but trying to reproduce the life of those home communities.

The *memsahibs* of India are conventionally blamed for their artificiality, for taking no interest in Indian culture and for being obsessed with the ritual of tea-parties and dances, protocol and status.[9] But they were there in a sense to recreate their home community, although, being separated from it, they no doubt often represented it in an exaggerated and archaic way. According to one account, military wives were not quite as prim and narrow as the rest: 'they were considered rather fast, free and easy and noisy;' (Barr 1976: 146). The same observer who had pitied the soldiers' wives deplored the habit

> of adopting the strange vocabulary of their husbands and their husbands' friends. It is common to hear ladies speaking not only of their husbands by their surnames (a thing unpardonable except of a peer) but of other guests in

the same manner; talking of 'our kit', 'jolly', 'pluck' or 'cool thing' and other shocking phrases (quoted in Barr, op.cit: 147).

After Fanny Duberly's day the wives of rank-and-file soldiers were not all expected to be washerwomen, although the last of these died only in 1926 (Bamfield 1974: 217). In India there were men prepared to do this chore, and husbands were assigned servants so that wives found they had very little to do. There remained only the social and symbolic role; this, inevitably, tended to become an end in itself.[10]

Conclusion: ways of organizing in the 1980s

Conditions of life for military wives in the 1980s are immeasurably better than they were in the past, but the fundamental structure remains the same. There is still no permanent home, and no opportunity to accumulate one's own possessions. Furniture in Service quarters is identical in every house. Emphasis is still on wifehood rather than motherhood, and there must still be periods of separation either from children or from husbands. My mother, choosing to stay with her children, was separated from my father for two whole years when he was appointed to China a second time. Few wives would put up with that length of separation today. The improvement in Service conditions mirrors the higher expectations of civil life. In order to keep men in a volunteer force, the Services have to minimize as far as possible the disadvantages of Service life. So children's holiday visits to their parents based abroad are subsidised, and air travel for families makes distance no obstacle. But the men still live in a closed world, liable to be called away at any moment for long periods of simulated if not real warfare, and unable to count on fixed periods with their families.[11] So, as in the past, the women have to create a world of their own, and help each other to manage the strains of the position they are all in together.[12] There may not be many circumstances today exactly like the eve of Waterloo, but there are situations of danger. In the early days of the present troubles in Ulster a wife, like my daughter, could give her husband coffee in the morning and not see him again for two days, during which the city of Belfast was torn to pieces. During the last ten years troops have not been allowed to have their wives in Northern Ireland. The men do four months at a time there, while the wives remain in their quarters in Germany. This is often a greater strain on the wives' nerves than actual participation in danger.[13]

It is still the duty of the Colonel's wife to look after all the other regimental wives, and of the Company Commander's wife, herself probably in her twenties, to look after all the wives of that company. They are expected to know individual wives' problems, and to be friend and counsellor. In times of emergency (such as the evacuation from Cyprus in 1974) this social hierarchy, irksome as it can be, will show its usefulness in collecting and marshalling the women and children. In any event the hierarchy is within a very narrow age range; there is no gerontocracy.[14] Conduct is regulated by peer group opinion, which can be severe. Controversial topics are avoided in social intercourse, and argument is frowned on as divisive.[15] Wives are a potential source of discord, since unlike their husbands they have not sworn oaths of loyalty and are not subject to military discipline. (A wife cannot commit a 'military' offence, but in cases of civil offences wives in 'occupied' Germany are subject to the military police and courts.) Wives' theoretical independence of opinion is restrained by loyalty to their husbands, and is not likely to be exercised to the detriment of husbands' careers; but wives known to me have written letters to *The Times* and the *Daily Telegraph* on Service matters.

A Service Wives' Association was founded recently by naval wives at Plymouth. It is as yet small, but in 1978, at a time of great dissatisfaction with the way Service pay had fallen behind that of civilians, this Association organized a protest march from Hyde Park to the House of Commons. (At the time some servicemen could not pay their rents, and wives were being sent home from Germany to their parents.) Four Army wives from a camp at Church Crookham near Camberley decided to join the protest march. They became notorious as 'The Church Crookham Wives', or in the unflattering words of one senior officer, 'the revolting wives of Church Crookham'.

The Army wives felt that their aims were rather different from those of the Service Wives' Association, which has remained largely a naval and Air Force organization. They submitted to the Defence Ministry a paper asking for better communication with Army authorities and suggesting an Association on the lines of the Diplomatic Service Wives' Association, run from a central office in the Ministry of Defence, and communicating through two existing periodicals, *Soldier News* and *Soldier Magazine*. They were disappointed by the reception their suggestions received. The authorities wanted to do things their own way and appointed a committee, with no women on it, which in fact never sat. One of the wives involved writes:

> many of them [the men] have this real bogey-man fear of trade-unions in the Army. I think many people thought that our innocent efforts to improve communication were in fact a disguise for more sinister things. I felt that careful drafting of a charter for an Army Wives' League could have prevented it ever becoming an organization that could undermine discipline. The other problem was a more serious and valid one: that it might have become a way of jumping the chain of command on which the Army runs. This could easily have happened, but again I doubt if it is beyond the wit of man to guard against it. (personal communication).

There is a Wives' Club in every regiment, and a wives' page in most regimental or Brigade magazines, and in the Army paper *Soldier*. The women's page in the latter is perhaps the only real channel of free communication for wives. Wives' Clubs are run hierarchically: the one I had contact with had a committee consisting of the Company Commander's and the Sergeant Major's wives from each company of the regiment, chaired by the Colonel's or the Adjutant's wife. (Now that most Sergeant Majors become Commissioned Officers the protocol between their wives and those of officers is not as strict as it used to be, but they are still not supposed to call each other by Christian names.) The Navy also has Wives' Clubs (once known with hidden sarcasm as 'The Friendly Wives') but these are organized on a port basis, and have never been very successful or well attended. (Nicholson 1980: 36)

A good deal of traditional welfare work is done by the officers' wives. In the Army they are expected to visit and otherwise look after the wives of men under their husbands' command, as we have seen. Modern soldiers and sailors are mostly very young; the average age overall is about eighteen, and thus many of their wives are mere teenagers. They have often married with no idea of what they are going into, and may find themselves in a strange country, with husbands away or unable to give them the domestic support they expect. They may have other problems, financial, psychological or to do with children; nervous breakdowns are not uncommon. They have houses provided, but these are not luxurious. The ordinary soldier will be accommodated in a flat, the NCO in a terraced house, and the officer in one with three bedrooms and an open-plan sitting-room on the model of the average council house. Even the Colonel seldom gets more, and there is extreme difficulty in accommodating Royalty when it descends in the role of Colonel-in-Chief. Rent is charged for all housing, and houses must be handed over in spotless condition on the frequent occasions of what is still called 'marching out'.

Housing is not financed out of the Defence vote, but is paid for in Britain by the Department of Works and in Germany by the Property Services Agency of the Department of the Environment. This is in keeping with a long history of resistance by the Treasury to any direct expenditure on Service families, and with the historical reluctance to give them a recognized status.[16] The new concept of a welfare Army is reinforced by the existence of a welfare State, and is in fact a corollary of the latter. When in Britain, Service families can be provided for by the normal welfare agencies;[17] abroad the Service itself is the agent for the administration of a sum of money voted to cover the needs of families which would normally be provided for by the appropriate Government departments at home such as the Social Services. Since 1970 Service pay has been made inclusive of all expenses; the batmen, latterly batwomen, who were formerly allowed to officers have been withdrawn, and an allowance for service allegedly incorporated in their pay. This is retrograde as far as wives are concerned; few families employ a servant and the extra work falls directly on the wife. Soldiers' kit goes into a communal laundry, but the officer's wife is almost back with the status of washerwoman.

A good deal of welfare work affecting wives is still done on a voluntary basis. SSAFA (Soldiers', Sailors' and Airmens' Families Association) is a voluntary organization which provides, among other things, mother-and-baby clinics in camps managed by a SSAFA Sister. The NAAFI (Navy Army and Air Force Institute) runs the shopping centres, and is an independent co-operative started in the 1920s by a group of high-ranking officers. The Army Benevolent Fund, into which every man contributes a proportion of his pay, provides pensions for widows not entitled to a Service pension. From Marlborough's day onwards officers have paid into a widows' pension fund. In those early days there was a device called a 'widows' man', a fictitious name whose pay went to the upkeep of widows. After the Battle of Blenheim a great many extra widows' men had to be recruited; after Waterloo a group of London businessmen subscribed to a fund for widows. As with other benefits the welfare State now provides the normal widow's pension, while there is an Army pension graded according to rank after a man has served twenty-one years, and the Army contributes a widow's pension for the wife of any man killed or dead as a direct result of his service.[18] The South Atlantic Fund opened for victims of the Falklands war is being distributed through the Army Benevolent and other existing funds. A spontaneous response from the public, it re-emphasizes the continuing dependence on voluntary funds to supplement State compensation.

For all the drawbacks, Service marriages have a good record for stability. To some extent, this is itself a product of Service discipline. Certainly divorce was until very recently an offence against the accepted code, and for officers meant resignation, or at least transfer to another regiment. Adultery within a regiment is still felt to be something like incest. The Officers' Mess was until recently *tabu* to women, and was respected with awe by wives; but most Messes are now open to the girl-friends of the young bachelors who live there, so wives need feel less inhibited. But men still have their close integration, which seems to engender in them a reciprocal respect for the women's world. Soldiers and sailors are thought to make good husbands; they are used to managing the basic chores of living for themselves, and appreciate their wives' work. Their wives enjoy a great deal of financial discretion, as did Fanny Pratt. The Service wife on her side is encouraged by the system to be independent and self-reliant, and to develop relationships easily. Her experience gives her some organizing skill which she, unlike the corporate wife (see Tremayne, this volume) can make use of on return home or to civil life. But she will have an eclectic rather than a deep knowledge of world affairs and will often be ignorant of whole areas of her own society, and of the pressures that drive civilians in matters such as industrial relations and competition for and within work.[19] Both the men and the women value practical experience, and reject or distrust academic study. In this and other qualities the sexes reflect each other, although their lives are parallel and distinct. This distinctness is illustrated by some words of General Montgomery's latest biographer about the General and his wife:

Neither really understood each other's world; and perhaps they respected each other so profoundly because of this, because there was and could be no rivalry, no difference of opinion in spheres so alien to each other ... this attraction of opposites must have represented for each of them the attraction of areas being denied in themselves. (Hamilton 1981: 107-8)

Although this refers to an individual marriage, it has a general application to the complementarity of 'male' and 'female' identity in the Armed Services. Both sexes, however, are generally at one in a deep and tenacious pride in the Service to which in their own eyes they belong, whether by membership or by marriage, however it may treat them.

Notes

1. I am not aware of any tendency on the part of Service wives abroad to see themselves in terms of parallels and contrasts with a reference group such as Embassy wives, as Clark (this volume) describes British Council wives as doing. The difference, presumably, is that in the present case the forces making for an internally generated sense of corporate identity are overwhelmingly strong.

2. I have not been able to find a precise date for the institution of the ballot for wives to accompany their husbands as washerwomen. It seems to have been current up to the Crimean War; and even during it to judge by Fanny Duberly's letters. Most Army reforms date from that war, and were brought about by the response of public opinion to Press coverage of it.

3. Basements would seem to have been thought of as the natural place for families. The composer Sullivan was born in the basement of the RMC Sandhurst, which housed the soldiers' families, his father being the Sergeant of the band.

4. For a few there were eventual rewards. Fanny Pratt became Lady Pratt, and the fictitious Mrs O'Dowd, Lady O'Dowd. The latter, in Thackeray's description, 'was as much at home in Madras as at Brussels, in the cantonments as under the tents. On the march you see her at the head of the regiment, seated on a royal elephant - a noble sight. Lady O'Dowd is one of the greatest ladies in Madras.' (Thackeray 1847: 485)

5. The situation seems comparable to that described by Gartrell (this volume) for colonial life, in which a certain level of consumption was expected and economy was no excuse for social withdrawal.

6. My own grandfather however refused a further commission in India, and his chance of becoming a full General, and retired so as not to be separated any longer from his seven children.

7. During a tense phase of the conflict, handwritten notes appeared on the Portsmouth-Isle of Wight ferries giving times and places for 'open house' tea and chat for wives of those in action. It emerged in television interviews that wives would prefer quicker information on losses even though they appreciated that delays were due to careful checks.

8. Linda Kitson, war-artist in the Falklands, filled much the same role vis-à-vis the men. She had become a mascot, certainly a morale raiser with the troops. She said 'Wherever 5th Brigade went, I went, they were so stunned that I was still with them'. (Jenny Clayton, *The Guardian* 3rd November 1982).

9. See also Gartrell and Brownfoot, this volume.

10. Many of the wives would have been brought up to this role, as there is a high incidence of intermarriage within the Services; inevitable when the young men are outside the normal social network, and most likely to find wives among the daughters or sisters of their fellow-servicemen. My sister's daughter makes the fifth direct link in a Service chain of descent.

11. Field Marshall Lord Montgomery, then a Major-General, was unable to be with his wife during her fatal illness in a seaside hospital. My sister records that he only visited once during a fortnight in which she was with his wife. He was on exercise on Salisbury Plain, and was then taking over a new post as General Commanding at Portsmouth.

12. The President of the Wives' Club of a signals unit in Aldershot was decorated after the Falklands War in recognition of the Club's services. The war itself brought recognition to the Wives' Clubs which have now (1983) been formed into a U.K. Land Forces Federation of Army Wives' Clubs (UKLFAWC) and have begun publication of a quarterly journal *Neighbours*.

13. Note the case (reported in *The Guardian* 18.4.1981) of an Army doctor dismissed for refusing to join a unit in Northern Ireland three weeks after his marriage.

14. The age range is significant. In Army units abroad grandparents are welcomed by more than their immediate families, because their generation is so rarely represented. At the other end of the scale, older children are also absent. Fanny Pratt wrote in 1848: 'It is often a subject of regret to me that there are no young people in this country. Little children there are in plenty, but I miss the gaiety of young girls and youths' (unpublished correspondence).

15. Compare Young's comments (this volume) on the suspect character in police eyes of wives' powers of speech.

16. To be fair, this is not confined to the British case. A recent report quotes a Norwegian official as saying of the Norwegian Army (conscript): 'An added burden on manpower costs is the welfare requirement of allowing troops to visit home and families'. (*The Guardian* 15.1.1981)

17. An article on wives in the 1982 Falklands war says 'support, comfort and help in time of trouble are now firmly built into the Forces, whose social services have developed hand in hand with the growth of the Welfare State since the last war' (Hall, *Sunday Telegraph* June 6th 1982).

18. That the application of these rules is often disputable, is shown in cases like the entitlement to a Service pension of widows of men who die as a possible long-term consequence of early nuclear weapons tests.

19. Conversely one of Nicholson's respondents says, 'I don't try to explain life in the Navy to my civilian [sic] friends' (Nicholson 1980: 26).

THE SUITABLE WIFE:
PREPARATION FOR MARRIAGE
IN LONDON AND RHODESIA/ZIMBABWE

Deborah Kirkwood

Introduction

It might be argued that the optimism of many generations of young middle-class English girls has been sustained by a belief in the myth that behind every successful man is a good woman, intelligent, cultured, sensitive, perhaps witty and beautiful as well; preferably this woman should be his wife. A woman's skills and intelligence could be made to work through her husband to establish for him a position of distinction and authority, not only in the family, but in society. She would thus fully deserve the material benefits and psychological satisfactions which might eventually derive from his success. To achieve a reputation as a brilliant hostess, the *confidante* of politicians and the friend and patroness of writer or artist, has formed the unspoken ambition of many clever girls who perhaps lacked alternative models or a sharp awareness of their own intellectual gifts. Consciously or unconsciously, many young women have secretly hoped to play the role of Mary Anne to a Disraeli, or 'My darling Clemmie' to a Winston Churchill - to be the well-loved and supportive wife to a successful man in public life.[1]

A corollary to this has been a belief that an ambitious man *needed* such a woman at his side to ensure his own success. There are many literary models: Mr Collins proposed to Elizabeth Bennett because of her suitability as a wife for a man enjoying the patronage of Lady Catherine de Bourgh; Darcy, overcome by love, proposed to her reluctantly against his better judgement in view of her *un*suitability as a wife for Lady Catherine's nephew. In declining both proposals Elizabeth spoke for herself and became one of the best-loved heroines in English literature.[2]

Underlying the myth of the good woman behind the great man in Western culture is the teaching of the Old Testament. Woman was created to be 'an helpmeet to Man' (*Genesis* 2, v.18). The *Good Wife* as described in *Proverbs* presents an image of a woman of virtue and authority whose husband 'is known in the gates when he sitteth among the elders of the land'. (*Proverbs* 31, v.23). And inseparable from the image of the *good wife* is the concept of womanly self-sacrifice; this was often implicitly assumed by, or explicitly stated for her. Mrs Beeton, herself a successful writer, business woman and working partner with her husband, wrote in the Introduction to her *Everyday Cookery and Housekeeping Book*, under a sub-heading 'Unselfishness':

> A good woman *should* be a good housekeeper, for the latter must possess one of the greatest of all virtues, namely unselfishness. An utter abnegation of self is almost a necessity with the mistress of a household, for with her rests the question of the health and comfort, if not the happiness, of all its members. (1984 edition: xvii)

While marriage is expected of both sexes it has not necessarily the same meaning for both. In Britain and in most Western societies it has until recently been regarded as a vocation and sufficient destiny for women, but not for men; while non-marriage – celibacy – associated with the religious life has been a clearly-defined vocation for both men and women. Thus in our culture education for marriage has not been *specified* for men; although, in keeping with the present-day emphasis on the personal aspects of marriage, some engaged couples together seek counselling on spiritual, psychological and sexual matters. In this short essay I shall describe two schools – one in London and one in Rhodesia/Zimbabwe[3] – where older girls have received some formal education to prepare them for the role of wife to a man of high status within his own community. I shall also examine briefly some of the myths and realities of a wife's supportive role in marriage and comment on changing contemporary attitudes.

Learning for Marriage

For many generations and classes in European society, the informal teaching of 'wifehood' has taken place at home, within the family, where a mother presents herself as a model to her daughter; the latter observes, too, the role of her father in the dynamic of the marital situation and learns from his (perhaps unconscious) model of husband, as well as his expressed views on suitable wifely behaviour. Parents' example and precept may be reinforced by the advice given in popular women's journals and books on etiquette. As long ago as 1836 Elizabeth Sandford, in her book *Female Improvement*, wrote of the impression made by a wife on the outside world:

> Not only will her husband be gratified by the approbation bestowed upon his choice, but as he is in a manner identified with her, she, by her own conduct and manners either gains or loses suffrages for him ... Her manners should bespeak favour; she should enrich her conversation with whatever information she possesses. (Sandford 1836: 184)

At the same time, there was sufficient substance behind the belief that a woman can help or undermine her husband's advancement by her deportment, conduct and domestic skills (or lack of them) to suggest a need for formal as well as informal education for marriage, particularly for those likely to marry into an elite group. It was assumed that a girl who had acquired certain social skills and graces would be likely to attract an ambitious man, while his own aspirations would be helped by her poise and confidence. During the Victorian era, and through the first half of the twentieth century, there were schools in England which had been founded with the specific if unstated purpose of training girls to be *suitable wives* for men aspiring to high positions in the world.

A 'Finishing' School in London: 1890 - 1950

Judith Okely (1978) has described and analyzed the education which she and countless other middle-class English girls received at a typical girls' private boarding school in the 1950s, which seems to have differed surprisingly little from that which I received in the 1930s. In these schools girls are tacitly encouraged to believe that in marriage they will develop and exercise their 'true' feminine gifts, while boys educated at public (private) schools are intellectually and psychologically prepared for the masculine tasks of career and family breadwinner. 'Finishing' schools provided a one-year course for girls between leaving boarding school and entering 'society'. They formed a bridge between the school-room and the drawing-room. Whereas boarding schools, for boys as well as girls, 'are almost invariably set in rural areas distant from urban concentrations and metropolitan culture' (Okely 1978: 114) the 'finishing' school was normally located in a city or town - London, Paris or Lausanne. The change of *locus* from country to town had, perhaps, symbolic as well as practical meaning; the move to an urban environment was considered essential for girls to gain experience of concerts, opera, theatre, art galleries, museums, more sophisticated shopping and the handling of a bank account; it also signified a first move out of a 'protected' life into the more complex challenges of the 'real' world.

Helen Wisden[4] was the headmistress and owner of a day school in Central London for about 200 girls betwen the ages of 7 and 19. The fact that it was a day school, located in London, distinguishes it at once from the typical girls' boarding school, and indeed it was run on relatively progressive lines: there was no uniform, nor written rules or prefect system. Miss Wisden's period as headmistress lasted from about 1924 to 1958. In her curriculum she included

> A Special Finishing Course for Elder Girls, the design of which is to prepare them, on leaving school, to make a practical use of their previous education whether at home or elsewhere (School *Prospectus*, undated but about 1925, p.6)

About thirty girls were enrolled for the Finishing Course, and unlike other pupils they were all boarders. The following subjects were taught:

> English Literature, Essay-writing, European History, Current Events, History of Art, Diction, History of Music, Practical Arithmetic (to give the girls some knowledge of Banking, Rates and Taxes, Investments and Household Accounts), Housecraft. (*Prospectus*, p.6)

During the thirties 'Interior Decoration' (with special attention to antique furniture) and Flower Arrangement were added and Housecraft dropped. Education in child-care was not included - in due course Nanny would take charge of the Nursery. Never at any stage was there an explicit definition of the course as a preparation for marriage; yet, possibly by a sub-conscious process of elimination - neither a career nor spinsterhood (except as 'failure') seemed to be envisaged - it became increasingly clear to the pupils that it was for this future that they were being trained.

Leisure activities included a daily walk in Kensington Gardens, ice-skating in the winter, swimming and tennis in the summer. Those girls who did not go home or to friends at weekends might go shopping, in groups, on Saturday mornings - usually to Harrods. Expeditions to museums and art galleries were part of the curriculum; visits to theatres, concerts and opera were optional but strongly recommended, although the price of tickets was not included in the fees.[5] Parties of girls were also taken to the main sporting events of the Season: the Boat Race, the Derby, Wimbledon - events whose human protagonists were, of course, predominantly male.

The school was run on the lines of a large upper-middle-class family household of the time. Pupils were attended by a butler and footman-cum-chauffeur, and a troop of housemaids. At breakfast, they were told,

> You may read your letters and the newspaper, girls, but *never* read at any other meals.

Indeed girls were *expected* to read the newspaper at breakfast so that they could make intelligent conversation at dinner in the evening. Lunch was informal and taken with the day girls, but dinner was formal.[6] All were required to change into long dresses every night and to behave as at an adult dinner party. Miss Wisden presided and pupils moved one place clockwise round the table each day, so that each girl might expect to sit next to her at least twice a term - and to be sharply rebuked if her conversational gambits were inept or inappropriate. 'Now that's not a very sensible remark my dear, is it?' was a familiar comment. Long before, Sandford had emphasized the importance of conversational skills for young wives:

> Conversation, for instance, is one great source of a woman's influence and it is her province and her particular talent to give zest to it. She is and ought to be the enlivener of society; if she restrains impropriety, she may promote cheerfulness; and it is not because her conversation is innocent that it may be dull. (1831: 6)

There is a suggestion here that, through the exercise of their talent for conversation, women act as *mediators* in social situations in which the tensions are potentially threatening and dangerous to the man; the critical dinner party at which the husband's employer is guest of honour is a familiar example. Ease in conversation continues to be a major social asset for wives; I heard an Oxford host remark recently of a woman guest that 'she's a first rate talker and can always be counted on to earn her dinner' (see also Ardener and Tremayne, this volume, and Spender 1980).

Posture and language, too, were under the constant scrutiny of Miss Wisden:

> Don't stand like that with your arms folded, you look like a washerwoman.
> Never refer to a friend or anyone you know socially as a 'person'; it sounds very gauche'

Nancy Mitford had not yet identified and documented 'U' and 'Non-U' speech[7] and behaviour (Mitford 1955), but Miss Wisden's pupils were left in no doubt as to which was which. The majority were from English or Scottish upper-middle-class or aristocratic families, but a small number came from the United States and the former Dominions (now known as the Old Commonwealth).[8] Through formal instruction, informal practice and association with one another, they learned 'good manners', social discrimination and a superficial understanding of what must be loosely described as 'culture'.

Romantic love was a recurrent theme in leisure-time talk among the girls. Even those with a brother seemed to regard men as a separate genus. Imaginary, passionate love-affairs with the handsome skating instructor, or with the two young men glimpsed from time to time at the window across the mews (romantically identified as 'students') provided material for fantasy. 'I can just imagine him proposing to me in the moonlight on a Mediterranean beach' confided one girl, thinking of the skating instructor. The subject of sex itself was still veiled in conventional reticence - and ignorance: life after marriage, child bearing and rearing were never talked about.

The 'finishing' process would be rounded off during the next winter at another 'finishing' school in Paris or Switzerland. The following summer girls would move through presentation at Court and the London Season into the adult world and, it was hoped, early marriage. When they tired of discussing their phantom lovers they turned to 'coming out' balls and parties where, it was confidently anticipated, phantom lover and real man would somehow merge in the shape of a *suitable husband*.

The 1939-1945 war accelerated a general process of social change and the emergence of new attitudes. It was generally conceded that, in England, 'finishing was finished'.[9] Thus during the 1950s Miss Wisden's 'finishing Sixth Form' gradually changed into a straight academic class, with perhaps a lingering emphasis on subjects such as History of Art. For over a century feminists had been arguing that young women should strive for economic independence and that, above all, they should avoid being trapped for economic reasons into 'the misery and baseness of a loveless marriage' (Taylor 1865-70: 212).[10] Middle-class parents now recognized that a career and economic independence were the most valuable assets with which they could endow their daughters. Now the emphasis is on examination success and a place at College or University, preferably Oxbridge. A friend, herself a don, spoke to me recently of her daughter's university hopes: 'Of course she'll get in somewhere, but I do hope she manages Oxford. She's so much more likely to meet a suitable man there'. In short, if a girl can get the best of both worlds, so much the better.

A Homecraft School in Rhodesia/Zimbabwe, 1943 - 1981

Christian missionaries working in Third World countries have generally believed that true Christian monogamous marriage provided the foundation for a stable progressive community. Thus the concept of the *good wife* formed an essential component of mission education for girls in African and Asian countries. In 1943 Catherine Langham, an English missionary, opened her Homecraft Village School in a remote country district north of Salisbury (now Harare). During her twenty-eight years' work as a missionary she became increasingly aware of the problems which were beginning to arise when mission-educated men married women who had not experienced any formal education and were unprepared for the tasks of marriage and home-making according to the Western pattern which Christian teaching enjoined and to which many now aspired. Others before her had recognized the problem. Agnes Sloan, in an article in NADA (*Native Affairs Department Annual,* 1923) quotes a comment by 'one of the oldest and most efficient Native Commissioners' to the effect that

> we ought to civilize the black woman ... otherwise we could not expect the men we trained to hold to their training once they went home, to live again in the *kraal* surroundings of native reserves. (p. 61)

In spite of this, Langham received little encouragement and no money for her project from the Bishop and Diocese. A sympathetic European farmer, however, allowed her the use of some land adjoining the 'Native Reserve', and a wealthy Englishwoman, Freda Tulley, provided the necessary funds and helped her to start work on what became known as the Langham Homecraft Village.

News of her plans spread quickly and the first students helped with the building of the wattle-and-daub huts which were to provide the accommodation. From the start the Village was to a great extent self-supporting and much of the food was produced by the students themselves; thus it was possible to keep the fees very low.[11]

By January 1943 a few cottages, a dispensary and sick-room were ready and the term opened with 37 women and girl students. Married women and their young children and expectant mothers as well as young girls were accepted. Tulley was a qualified midwife. A brief history of the Village is included in the National Council of Women of Southern Rhodesia publication *Women in Central Africa* (1953):

> By 1949 our numbers had risen to 103 with 46 children and babies, these latter increasd to 51, as five were born in the little maternity hospital; 980 applications had to be refused. (p. 105)

And in 1953

> Term started on January 27, with 121 women and girls. We have 39 toddlers
> and babies, 6 of whom have been born this term. The village now consists of
> Church, dining-room, four class-rooms, industrial room and kitchen, four
> single cottages, two bathrooms, kitchens, stores and open-air
> nursery ... Though full to capacity we had to refuse 890 applications for this
> year. (Ibid)

Langham pioneered homecraft education; other missions quickly followed
her example. By 1951 there were

> four homecraft schools for women, namely Miss Langham's school near
> M'Sonneddi, and three Beit Homecraft schools at mission centres at
> Morgenster (Dutch Reformed), Masasa (Church of Sweden) and Empandeni.
> These schools are meeting a definite need and exercise an influence for good
> on African homes. The Government will assume responsibility for the three
> Beit Homecraft schools in 1951. (*Official Year Book of Southern Rhodesia*, 1952:
> 329)

Christian precept formed the basis of Langham's teaching, and her
students would certainly have been presented with the model of the *Good
Woman* of *Proverbs*. Instruction was designed to promote

> The Life of the Spirit ... the Life of the Body ... and the Life of the Family.
> (*Women in Central Africa*, 1953: 105)
>
> Miss Langham's vision was quite simply to help to build up homes where
> 'health, love and laughter might prevail' and to this end she trained her pupils
> in things both spiritual and practical. (*Profiles of Rhodesia's Women*, 1975: 146)

There were lessons in reading, writing, simple arithmetic, hygiene and
sanitation, first-aid, home nursing, dietetics, cooking, gardening, sewing
and knitting, toy-making and 'simple crafts to beautify the home'.
European women wrote frequently to ask Langham if she could
recommend a cook or children's nurse, but would receive a polite refusal.
She was emphatic that the aim of her Homecraft Village was to educate
young women to be *suitable wives* for husbands who were entering
professional life, or who held positions of authority within the traditional
structures, or who had simply heard of her work and wished their wives
or daughters to learn the skills she was teaching.

A Zimbabwean woman, daughter of an Anglican priest and of a
woman who was one of the early pupils at M'Sonneddi, recalls that her
mother was well known for the high standards she maintained in her
home and for her emphasis on personal integrity, order, hygiene and a
balanced diet for her family. It is perhaps relevant that, by Western
standards, the children in this particular family each achieved remarkable
professional success, especially considered in the context of white-ruled
Rhodesia of the fifties and sixties, when there were limited educational
opportunities available to blacks.[12]

Anthropologists might argue that Langham was replacing traditional
gender roles with new ones based on Christian morality, without regard

for time-honoured custom and practice, and an observation by Agnes Sloan about pre-colonial society might be quoted to support this view:

> The quality that is common to all the women in their homes is a sense of what is becoming and proper in their relations with their elders, their relatives, their husbands, their husbands' other wives, their children; and in their relations with the world about them and with the opposite sex. (1923: 63)

From the feminist perspective of the 1980s Barbara Rogers writes critically of

> The domestic science movement which promoted 'home making' as a vocation justifying the unemployment of women, in order to serve men. (1980: 23)

Langham might have replied sharply to such criticism because she believed that much of the human suffering which she had observed during her years of work among rural communities could and should be avoided by education in hygiene, diet and domestic skills. But her special concern was that those, mainly men at that time, who were receiving Western-style education should be helped by their wives' domestic skills, rather than hindered by their ignorance.

'Lucy', interviewed recently, described her experiences at the Village during the 1950s. She was a trained nurse and a member of the staff. However, as an African she identified more with the students than with the white missionaries. She seems to have shared the students' experience to a large degree and described it as follows:

> Catherine made a deep impression on me, and I believe on all the students. I often wondered where she came from and what her origins were. Though I was qualified as a nurse, I too learned a lot, especially knitting, sewing and cooking. There was a strong Christian emphasis; Church on Sundays, prayers every day, bible study; Easter was a 'very special' time.
> We made all our own recreation. On Sundays after church we went for long walks in the veld. In the evenings we would have sing-songs and we made up many of our own songs. I remember especially one song we made up about Catherine herself, 'Poor Catherine, She's old and has never known the joys of marriage and motherhood. She will die without having a child'. I got married while I was there and I remember that Catherine was very strict about pre-marital sex. I remember too that she tried to teach us a sense of personal responsibility for our own decisions and to be independent and not rely on others, parents or husbands. (Personal communication)

The emphasis on 'independence' may have been in conflict with the social values of the extended family. Lucy and her husband are both well established in their respective professions; I met her in London where she is doing advanced training.

The Village was forced to close during the later stages of the war which preceded independence, but it re-opened in January 1980, with sixteen second-year and twenty-seven first-year students.

> In the face of uncertainties about the future education policy, the new Ministry of Education has assured the Chairman that it firmly believes there

will still be a need for Homecraft Schools, in spite of the expansion of Form
I's to accommodate all Grade 7 pupils, and Langham is allowed now to take
students with some secondary education. Organizations such as Red Cross
Refugee camps are coming more and more frequently to Langham for
Courses to learn about the Project and to carry the message back to others.
(*Langham Homecraft School Annual Report*, 1980–1, private circulation)

Today the elite in Zimbabwe mainly send their daughters to one of the
Government or private high schools, or to one of the long-established
mission schools (where many of them received their own education) and
hope that they will go on to university and a career.

Contrast and Comparison

At a superficial glance it might seem that the circumstances in London and
Rhodesia were so different as to make any comparison irrelevant, but
there were similarities too. At Langham the emphasis was on practicality
and Christian morality; at Kingsway the stress was on culture and
conformity to an elitist social code. Zimbabwean pupils learnt how to
grow, as well as cook, the food which would provide the daily diet for
their families. The English girls dabbled once a week in a little extravagant
cooking and learnt the 'language' of gourmet food; at lessons in 'interior
decoration' they learnt to recognize and identify styles of antique
furniture, while Zimbabwean girls learnt 'simple crafts' to beautify their
homes; it might be argued that the designation 'interior decoration'
described more accurately the latter than the former. Practical arithmetic
appears in both curricula. London girls learnt how to operate their own
bank accounts and the principles of the stock market and property
ownership; Zimbabwean girls were taught basic numeracy and simple
arithmetic, essential knowledge for successful transition from a subsistence
to a cash economy. Many of Langham's pupils were already married,
pregnant or with children, and most of the unmarried were betrothed; the
birth of children as a sequel to marriage was a self-evident fact and
child-care formed a major part of the training. Among Wisden's girls
motherhood was vaguely envisaged, seldom explicitly discussed and not
'taught' at all.

It was observed by Okely that the mistresses at her boarding school
were not themselves true models for their pupils:

> The majority of our teachers were unmarried and, apart from a few proud
> and self-sufficient ones, they presented themselves as victims of
> misfortune ... perhaps to justify self-confessed failure. They did not teach us
> to emulate themselves. We recognized our teachers as of a lower social class.
> (1978: 121)

Neither Wisden nor Langham were or could be personal models for their
pupils either. They were not married and each regarded her work as
teacher as a vocation; in no way did they see themselves as 'failed' women.
By comparison with Langham, Wisden might appear frivolous, but this
was far from being the case. A graduate of the University of London, she

was a serious educationalist. While at some 'finishing' schools girls received instruction in make-up and dress, the emphasis at Kingsway was on 'culture'. Her general aims as outlined in the early *Prospectus* could have been wholly compatible with those of Langham.

> The Principal and Staff make it their constant aim to train the girls to manage their own lives, but always in relation to the comfort and happiness of others ... In this way the girls are enabled gradually to acquire self-discipline and to form their own standard of good manners, courtesy and consideration towards those with whom they live. (p. 4)

But while the virtues of self-sacrifice might have been emphasized by Langham, the *leit-motif* of Wisden's training was *self-assertion*. For a young woman about to take her place at the 'court circle' level of society, and who would in due course become mistress of a household of domestic servants, this was a useful quality, rooted as it must be in self-confidence.

What, within the *milieu* served by the finishing schools, constituted 'suitability' in a wife? There are many dimensions to this concept; in the present context I would suggest that a wife needed to possess, or acquire, the necessary skills to act as a mediator between her husband and the social tensions and material discomforts which could threaten his advancement in the 'real' world. (Husbands as providers and protectors traditionally shelter their wives against different hazards). If her social origins were different or inferior she should at least have learned to 'talk the same language' as her husband and his associates; where the husband had 'married up' she should be able to instruct him herself in these subtleties. In other words, both, but she especially, had to be able to decipher and transmit the socially encoded messages that are exchanged by speech, gesture or behaviour between members of an elite – or indeed any – group. She had also to know how a complex household should be managed, although actual domestic tasks might have been performed by others.

In Africa the priorities were different. Monogamous marriage, physical and social mobility demanded new attitudes on the part of both husband and wife including perhaps a 'distancing' from the obligations and benefits of the extended family; thus a young woman had to learn self-reliance and independence as new values. Wives of men who now lived in Western-style houses rather than traditional village dwellings had to acquire the skills to maintain and manage their modern homes. The change from a subsistence to a market economy meant the availability of a wider range of material goods, and women had to learn to use money itself, often for the first time. Viewed in one way, this contrasts with the more sophisticated management of personal finance taught to the London girls. From another perspective, however, there is a parallel: in each case what was imparted was seen as a limited competence, sufficient and appropriate for the needs of a wife.

'Good' wife, 'suitable' wife, or 'Superwife'?

In English culture the role of a wife remains relatively undefined as to content; this vagueness is reflected in the varying experiences of the women married to men in different occupations which are described in this collection of papers. Leaving aside the undefinable and subtle benefits which derive from a 'marriage of true minds' and the physical comforts provided by a well-managed household, how can a middle-class wife expect to help her husband to advance and consolidate 'his' position in life? In some occupations such as farming or small-scale business, husbands and wives may have to work together to survive. In others the wife's practical support must remain marginal. A doctor's wife answers the patient's telephone call, but can never diagnose or prescribe:[13] a clergyman's wife is expected to live according to the gospels, but not to expound them or she risks harming rather than helping her husband's work in the parish.[14] A don's wife can sometimes help directly in her husband's work by informed criticism and research assistance. Traditionally, too, she types articles and books, reads proofs and compiles indexes, and is rewarded by dedications and acknowledgments in prefaces.[15] Many perhaps share the fictional Dorothea Casaubon's disappointment and frustration when she discovered that her own idealized view of an intellectual working partnership with her husband was not what he had ever envisaged. Some men too may sympathize with Casaubon himself, who felt at first irritated and ultimately threatened by her over-zealous concern with his work.[16] Doubtless there are similar limitations on the direct help which a wife may supply in most other professions.

A distinction must be made between the 'statutory' and the informal ways in which wives may assist husbands in their work. There would seem to be an at least quasi-statutory obligation on police wives to fulfil certain duties, for example,[17] but the wife of the Oxbridge College steward who recently recalled how she had worked all night at home to make the sausage rolls for a private college party did so as a true volunteer – contributing nonetheless to the high reputation which *her husband* enjoys.

The British Medical Association booklet *Getting Married* (1977) addresses itself to both men and women and the emphasis is on shared responsibility; the self-sacrificial role for women is specifically criticized in a section headed 'Home's No Place for Martyrs' (p. 20). Within marriage the debate turns increasingly on the issue; two careers or one, and if one whose? In many cases two careers are possible and are pursued with satisfaction by both partners. Meanwhile a new model is being presented to women for emulation or rejection. Shirley Conran has defined 'Superwoman' and in her two books *Superwoman* (1975) and *Superwoman in Action* (1979) explains how to be one. Superwife is an extension of Superwoman; she reaches eminence in her own profession, marries and presides over a well-organized family and household, entertains and in

general fulfils the role of the *good wife*. This new myth is projected by the
media generally and especially on Women's Pages, and in women's
magazines. The writer Hunter Davies paid generous tribute to his wife,
novelist Margaret Forster, in an interview with *Good Housekeeping*
magazine on the occasion of the publication of her novel *The Bride of
Lowther Fell*:

> She hated Oxford and was very glad to leave and become a Housewife
> Superstar ... She's always done her own housework - as well as having two
> other careers. There's her books - and she's produced almost one a year for
> the last 14 years. Then there's being a critic. She's chief non-fiction reviewer
> for the *London Evening Standard*. People are always asking her how she does it.
> A big house. Three kids and all that shifting words and no help whatever. No
> wonder she's a legend in NW5. Not a popular legend. You don't get liked
> for being that clever. (*Good Housekeeping*, October 1980).

While those who lack the energy and drive to succeed as Superwives, or
who fear the stresses and strains which this entails, continue to accept the
rationalization of their position which is provided by the concept of the
good wife, they are likely to be realistic about the limitations of the role.
The desire to have 'something of my own' - an identity as well as an
income - which derives from neither husband nor children, is now clearly
articulated. For many the sense of loss which is the consequence of the
forfeiture of an independent career on marriage is mitigated by
opportunities to engage in part-time professional work. A new model is
being presented to men too - *husband of* - satirized by *Private Eye* in the
regular feature 'Dear Bill'. The majority of married women probably
continue to accept the definition of themselves as *wife of*, but few today
would accept the implications of *suitable wife for* - one famous
contemporary example notwithstanding.

Conclusion

Wherein lies the interest in 'schools for wives' now, in the 1980s, when the
notion seems outmoded and inappropriate? I am not convinced that the
concept of education for marriage has been completely discarded.
Finishing schools, of a sort, still exist; Winkfield Place,[18] near Windsor, is
one and there are others. The emphasis is generally on practical skills that
are also conventionally 'feminine': cooking, flower arrangement, interior
design and secretarial training. Girls who attended finishing schools in the
30s are the mothers of young women today and are thus, inevitably,
models (or counter-models) for their daughters. For many men of this
milieu the perception of a wife's role remains conservative: I spoke to a
friend very recently about his 22-year-old daughter. 'Oh well,' he said,
'she's done a *cordon bleu* course, she studied French and Italian and history
of art, and now she's doing interior decoration - she'll make a first-rate
wife for someone'. Women themselves, of all ages, still both suffer and
benefit from the non-specificity of their role as wives. This lack of
definition is perhaps a principle in itself and, it might be argued, one to be

preserved, since it allows many women a choice which few men enjoy. A few women are able to have the 'best of both worlds', combining familial with 'public' status and achievement. But the pressure on them to become *superwives* should be seen for what it is - an opportunity for the energetic and exceptionally gifted: a new[19] form of servitude for many others.[20]

Notes

1. Rosemary Brown, the journalist, in an article headed 'The Real Kitchen Cabinet', based on interviews with the wives of three Ministers in the present government, wrote of the reality of being married to a man 'at the top': 'Some people say they have the toughest job in politics ... the Ministers' wives who play a variety of roles and provide a service known as AWW - *available when wanted*. Their life is usually a seesaw between public glamour and private loneliness. On the plus side there is the de-luxe entertaining, the occasional trip overseas and the spice of being close to the nerve centre of power'. Men, of course, frequently honour half-ironically the image of the wife as 'the power behind the power'. On the same day in the *Evening Standard* the following appeared under *Sayings of the Week*: 'Only one person in the world alters the vote of an MP - his wife (Joe Ashton, MP).'

2. Jane Austen, *Pride and Prejudice*, 1813. In the end, of course, Elizabeth accepted Darcy, but only when the question of her *suitability* had been ridiculed and finally dismissed.

3. I was a pupil at the London school in 1935-36 and I have maintained fairly continuous contact with the Zimbabwe School since it started in 1943.

4. I am using fictitious names for the school and headmistress in London, but will use the real names for that in Zimbabwe.

5. In 1935 basic fees were about £100 per term; in 1981 they were £1,180 a term.

6. On a return visit to the school recently I was delighted to find the dining-room almost unchanged. According to the current prospectus, 'Everyone is expected to change for dinner, but for this only a very simple dress is necessary'. However, conversation is not what it was and the Headmistress remarked on the resistance of girls to the idea of 'making' conversation.

7. Professor Alan Ross of the University of Birmingham published an article in an academic Finnish journal on 'Polite English Usage' in 1954, and first used the letter *U* to denote *Upper Class*. Nancy Mitford developed and expanded his definitions in relation to *U* and *Non-U* speech and behaviour in her satirical essay, 'The English Aristocracy' in *Encounter* (September 1955).

8. I was a 'colonial' and was thus able to observe the school and its pupils with some detachment. Coming from another country I felt myself less of an outsider than I would if I had come from another class. Perhaps I can claim to have done my first anthropological fieldwork in London, at the age of 16.

9. I quote here the present Headmistress.

10. Mary Taylor was a lifelong friend of the Brontë family and of Charlotte in particular, and a committed feminist. Her article 'On Marriage' in the *Victorian Magazine* was one of a series on *The First Duty of a Woman*.

11. When the school opened in 1943 the fees were £8 *per annum*, everything included. In 1979, by which time teachers' salaries were paid by Government, they were about £75 *per annum*. This was roughly the level of boarding fees at the big mission schools providing straight academic education.

12. The two sons are doctors, and the two daughters trained nurses, each with specialist qualifications. This is a truly creditable family achievement, notwithstanding the evident sex-typing of the children's occupations along European lines.

13. A friend, married to a general practitioner, whom I questioned recently about her role in his professional life, replied; 'When David was practising on his own I used to enjoy answering calls from patients and it made me feel involved, but now he's part of a group practice they no longer ring us at home. I missed this and felt that I no longer had a role, so I've taken a part-time job'.

14. Rosalind Runcie, wife of the present Archbishop of Canterbury, in an article in *The Times*, 'Clergy wives are people too' (August 7 1982), describes the increasing number of clergy wives, including herself, who have full- or part-time jobs.

15. See also Ardener and Sciama, this volume.

16. George Eliot, *Middlemarch* 1872.

17. See Young, this volume.

18. Winkfield Place was founded by Constance Spry and Rosemary Hume in 1946, as a residential extension of the Cordon Bleu Cookery School in London. According to the current *Prospectus*, 'Although sometimes described as a finishing school or a school of domestic science neither description quite fits Winkfield Place ... The training at Winkfield is designed for those who wish to bridge the gap between leaving school and taking up a profession or making a home of their own ... The training is also suitable for a girl who may plan to enter a University after a year's break'.

19. It is of course 'new' only to middle-class women. Many working-class women have had perforce to be 'superwives' to ensure the survival of themselves and their families, certainly since the industrialization of Britain and perhaps long before.

20. For a discussion which is comparable in some respects see Friedan 1981.

SHELL WIVES IN LIMBO

Soraya Tremayne

Introduction

The aim of this paper is to examine the process by which some women married to Shell company employees become *Shell wives*. Its scope is restricted to the wives of men of managerial rank within Shell. A separate study would be needed to understand the impact of corporate culture on the wives of blue-collar employees; common factors as well as interesting contrasts might emerge. The phrase 'Shell wife' is an umbrella expression for a number of women who, as wives of Shell men, develop certain common characteristics in order to adjust to the requirements that their husbands' profession makes of them. These characteristics will be referred to in this paper as the *Shell wife identity*: it is by acquiring these attributes that wives gain entry into the world of Shell and become accepted and adjusted members of Shell communities overseas.

My own experience as a Shell wife has been gained in the Middle East, West Africa, Eastern Europe and Great Britain.[1] In addition I have carried out a number of formal and informal interviews with Shell men and their wives. I was first tempted to write about women married to Shell employees when we were on a posting in a politically highly sensitive country, in which my husband was the only Shell man. We were closely supervised by the local authorities, who interpreted every gesture we made as made *by* the Company. We also received Shell Company visitors, who would come on business trips from Monday to Friday and often stay over the weekends as well. No line was drawn between our private and public life: our entire existence was laid open not only to the microphones and cameras of the local authorities but also to the magnifying-glass of our regular Shell visitors.

The compensation for living under conditions of such pressure was, for my husband, the sympathy and maximum collaboration of other Shell men. To my surprise, I did not get the same reaction. Although courteous and kind, they uniformly treated me not with respect for my ability to cope, but in a way which I found patronizing. Visitors of all levels of seniority in the Company felt entitled to give advice about my conduct, even after three years in the post; so too did women working for Shell in the head office, who had never even visited the country concerned.

At first I thought that this treatment was the result of our special conditions of life. But as I talked to other wives on similar postings and analyzed, in retrospect, other Shell communities in which I have lived, I began to pose general questions about the Shell wife. Such a woman cannot conceivably remain indifferent to, or untouched by, the character of her husband's profession; but through what processes does she become marked by the culture of his occupation and so turn into a *Shell wife*? In this way I was led to look at Shell wives in the context of the deeply rooted corporate culture from which emerges the *Shell man* as a recognizable product.

Shell Company and the 'Shell Man'

The term *Shell empire* is much frowned upon by senior management; nevertheless it describes something real. Over one hundred thousand people all over the world are employed by about fifty operating Shell companies. These companies, although fundamentally similar in organization, vary in size and function and exhibit different facets according to the historical, political and social conditions of each host country. In some countries Shell appears as a predominantly commercial enterprise, in others the representational character dominates the profit-making side of the business, and in some there is an equal emphasis. In most countries in the past, Shell men have been thought of as equivalent to diplomats and have enjoyed a similar social prestige. This is still the case in many States, and senior Shell men, particularly in large Shell companies overseas, have an almost ambassadorial status.

Despite the diversity of culture and nationality of people working for Shell, the 'corporate culture' seems well anchored among the Company's employees. In an article entitled 'The outdoor trail of management training', the organizer of a course, an outsider to Shell, writes:

> The Shell course was the first time the Leadership Trust had catered to such an international mix and it provided some interesting comparisons and insights into the 'Shell corporate culture'. One thing that particularly impressed me was the fact that Shell culture seemed to be stronger than the national differences between the participants, and there was a high degree of teamwork. (Taylor 1981: 24)

Even among the most powerful and efficient multinationals, Shell has earned a high reputation for the amount of effort and expense the Company puts into the training of its managers. The result of this effort is a type of man who is moulded in specific ways to satisfy the needs of this giant and demanding Company. Throughout their careers Shell men try consciously to distinguish themselves from men belonging to other corporate cultures. They take a pride in being 'branded' with the Shell label, they use anecdotes to convey their differences from others, they seem to have definite ideas as to where the differences lie between their own and their competitors' styles of operation. They will refer to Esso men[2] as 'too aggressive' and 'too direct'; they consider British Petroleum men to be 'not quite international enough'. Corresponding judgments are made of Shell men by men belonging to other corporate cultures. One retired senior British Petroleum man told me 'Shell men like to think they are as nice as us and we like to think we are as efficient as them'. Hundreds of examples of this kind could be cited to reveal the strong tie that exists generally between men and their various corporate cultures (see McCall and Simmeons 1966).

My twelve years of participant observation, together with the many interviews which I carried out, show that on the whole Shell men do not regard themselves as mere regular attendants at the Shell offices. In an overseas post especially, these men do not leave Shell and its world behind at the end of the day; their private lives become an extension of their office existence. They share not only a managerial culture, but also a deep sense of loyalty and commitment which crosses the boundaries of business and becomes a total way of life. The professional identity of the *Shell man* becomes the dominant aspect of his personality as long as his career with the Company lasts.

One of the professional qualities required of a Shell man is an ability to work with people of many different nationalities. In other words, learning to be, himself, 'multinational' is an imperative. In this paper I do not intend to explain in detail how a man is affected and transformed by this aspect of his profession. There is an abundant literature on managers and their cultures in various occupations (see e.g. Pahl and Pahl 1971, Kanter 1977).[3] But a picture, briefly as I have sketched it, of some of the forces that go into the making of the *Shell man* is essential background to a study of women who at marriage are subjected without any special pre-exposure or training to the culture of 'multinationals' and 'internationals', and who are expected to adjust and perform in a manner that is harmonious with that of their husbands, in order to meet the requirements of the latters' profession.

Shell wives

Women married to Shell men may, for convenience, be divided into three groups. First, there are women married to men who work in the head offices of Shell in Great Britain and Holland. These women do not travel or appear publicly in any formal capacity as *Shell wives*, because they are considered to belong to their husbands' private life which can itself be kept separate from work. Some of these women may pass their entire married life without once meeting their husbands' colleagues. It is therefore hard to discern any common characteristics among these wives.[4] Accordingly, I shall be mainly concerned in this paper with wives falling into the second and third groups: namely those who live overseas in Shell communities as *Shell wives* and those who have lived overseas but who have returned home and so ceased to be *Shell wives*. What distinguishes this third group of wives is the way in which, with the overseas posting at an end, the attributes and skills which they have cultivated in order to cope with the special demands of Shell community life become suddenly redundant.

Later in this paper I shall be concerned with some of the responses to this sudden loss of the *Shell wife identity* and of Company-generated structures of simultaneous control and support.

Going overseas

When a Shell man is posted overseas, his wife is treated by the Company with a curious mixture of care and concern for her needs, and refusal to recognize her as a separate social person. This non-recognition comes about partly through her being seen, like the rest of his belongings, as a *management problem*; and partly through the collapsing (in the Company's eyes) of her needs and claims into those of the *family*.[5] She benefits from all the measures to ensure safety and comfort that the Company is anxious to provide for its employees when they are sent abroad. The biological family of each employee is considered part of the larger *family* of Shell, and in times of need, emergency, sickness or disaster (such as earthquakes and revolutions) very prompt and efficient help is provided by the Company. The family of the employee is met at unknown places by other Shell people and taken care of by Shell 'cousins'. At other times extra effort is made to include the family of the employee in all kinds of activities outside the business but within the Shell world. The family is entitled to use sports and social facilities such as clubs, and to take part in competitions at home as well as overseas. But no special provision is made for wives as such. Not one of Shell's various magazines mentions wives, whereas children are often given attention. When I made enquiries about any material on wives at the Shell library, my request was received with great amusement and the answer was negative.[6]

Wives are not distinguished from the family because the Company does not recognize that they have any separate needs *as* wives. Only when a wife overseas acts in a way that puts the Company's interest and reputation at risk is her presence and negative effect acknowledged, and the assumed but unspoken role that a woman should play in her husband's professional life articulated.[7] Otherwise she is structurally invisible. During one of the visits of a senior Shell man to a foreign country, the Shell representative there was ill and had to be away. In his letter of thanks, the senior man stated: 'I was so delighted to see how well the office was run during your absence. We also had a very enjoyable meal in your house. It is a sign of good management that in your absence both your home and office were run so smoothly'. Although I cannot reveal other particulars of this letter, the sense is clear that it was not the wife who was credited with the 'good management'.

Before a Shell man is sent abroad he receives weeks of training and briefings. Wives, however, must resort to informal means of preparing themselves. They may get help from the Company if they seek it,[8] but in many cases, particularly when going abroad for the first time, wives do not realize that they need to find out more about the place to which they are going, nor that if they asked they might get help. By the time they realize this, it is often too late and they have to use their own inner resources and initiative to cope with unforeseen situations.

Typically, then, a first-time Shell wife enters a Shell community unprepared. She comes from 'home' where she has mixed with neighbours and friends whom she has chosen, has behaved as she wished and has generally directed her life as it has suited her. Overseas, in sharp contrast, she enters a far more rigidly organized community where a single interest dominates the social aspect of her life to a great extent, and the private aspect of it to some extent. The interest of Company business now dictates almost every social activity of the wife. It is almost entirely through her husband and his Company position that space, both physical and social, is made available to her and its boundaries specified.[9] I have often heard Shell men refer to some colleague in words such as: 'He is a lousy manager, he cannot even control his wife ... '

Shell communities are usually welcoming to newcomers, and help them adjust both to their new environment and - even more - to their rank within the community. Each woman has a rank, determined by her husband's place within the office hierarchy. The newcomer soon begins to feel the weight of the expectations laid on her; but although she is conscious of the atmosphere of pressure (this is truest, naturally, of the more resistant and independent personalities) it takes her some time to detect exactly what *is* expected of her, and make an adjustment.

The recognized contribution of wives

Wives overseas are expected to accede without question to a view of themselves as fully defined by virtue of marriage. Their presence in the community, although not considered integral to the success of business, is valued as helping to cement social life, and making life more pleasant for husbands. The wife is a part of her husband's 'private' life; but in this character she acquires, paradoxically, an indirect 'public' role: for the 'private' lives and character of its employees are an important resource for the Company in disseminating a favourable 'public' image of itself overseas.

Wives may also have some direct involvement in public duties, depending on their husbands' seniority. The more senior the man, the more conspicuous the representational role that may be accorded to his wife.[10] This role, however, seems to be less specified in content than in the only other comparable case so far investigated: that of diplomats' wives abroad. Hochschild (1969) notes the part which can be played by an Ambassador's wife in conveying indirect political messages, and continues:

> While the ambassador communicates both political and social messages directly and indirectly, the ambassador's wife, lacking formal authority, avoids direct and specializes in indirect communication through the use of ... 'covert message systems'. Therefore the ambassador's wife specializes in a more purely symbolic aspect of diplomatic life.

In similar vein Kitahara (1982) notes that:

> Sometimes a diplomatic wife can say things to foreign contacts of her husband which the husband would find difficult to say ... Sometimes it is possible for a wife to say things, seemingly by being carried away in the conversation, which her more restrained husband might find difficult to say ...

The Shell case provides a contrast in that the senior wife's representational role is manifested in her mere presence at high-level functions and in her ability to signal her husband's importance through charm and good dressing. Wives of very senior men nonetheless have some additional duties and are truly initiated into the *Shell wife identity*, even at home; they are expected to accompany their husbands on short trips abroad. I have on several occasions heard Shell men make such comments as 'She has to go with her husband to reduce the social pressure on him. At least he will not have to be *charming* to wives, as well as doing business ... '; 'Besides, his wife can find out about many aspects of the community life that he could not. She can listen to complaints from other wives ... ' As I in my turn listened to those senior wives, I gained the impression that not all of this reporting is respectfully received. The wives would claim that although they pass on their findings to their husbands, only the points which are of direct interest to Company business are taken into account; the rest are brushed aside by Shell men as 'female nagging'.

Conformity and tolerance

In their relations with Shell society, wives must strike some sort of balance between preservation of a sense of self and accommodation to the norms of management and of the community. Not only that, but 'accommodation' itself presents problems special to a multinational company overseas, as I shall show shortly. An important part of the task of becoming a *Shell wife* is the development of qualities of initiative and independence. The paternalism of the community does not guarantee protection of its members against every possible difficulty. Not all of the practical problems which wives are likely to encounter are resolved for them. But while initiative is essential for a wife if she is to deal with such problems, the excessive use of it is discouraged by the community. Non-conformist individuals are admired, but are also seen as a threat to the stability of the group. Resistance to any show of independence in wives comes mainly from men, who consider it undesirable and potentially trouble-making for Shell: a wife might, unknowingly, risk Shell's reputation and cause an *unnecessary headache*.

Thus a wife's failure to conform to expectation can result in a tense atmosphere for her husband to work in. Her refusal to accommodate can even force the husband to ask for a transfer. A wife should be

1. highly adaptable, 2. highly gregarious, 3. realize her husband belongs to the corporation. A good wife is good by not doing things, by not complaining,

by not being fussy, by not engaging in controversial activities. (Whyte 1951)

Although this was written some thirty years ago, Whyte's words are highly relevant to Shell attitudes today. Wives should also be 'stabilizers', 'good listeners' and 'sounding boards' for their husbands. They 'should not be outstanding in personal ways' (ibid).

Most wives justify their submission to the rules of the community as a sacrifice they make for their husbands and therefore for the life of the couple. Many remember their life abroad with great pleasure, delight and nostalgia; but others attribute a sense of alienation to this 'to-ing and fro-ing' in and out of Shell communities, living in 'limbo lands' and 'no man's lands'. Having to 'borrow' a personality each time they are posted, having repeatedly to give up the job (if not the career) they have built up at home in order to go abroad again, has made them feel marginal in every society and has stopped their personal progress.

The point of compromise between expected conformity and tolerated independence in wives must, of course, shift over time. Non-conformity is a fact for management, more now than even a decade or so ago. My experience of Shell communities indicates that both age and level of education have a direct bearing on wives' tolerance of the community's discipline. The younger generation of Shell wives, particularly the relatively career-minded and highly educated, are - as one might expect - the least tolerant. They see total integration into the group as a threat to their own identity. While they thought they had chosen a man as an equal and partner for life, they now find themselves in a segregated and very unequal position in which any control that *is* possible is exercised by him. They resent being vetted by the company, if and when the case arises, before going on a posting. They are unwilling to give up a career for which they may have spent many years training, in favour of their husbands'. If they do so, however, they expect to retain some personal autonomy rather become totally absorbed within their husbands' professional identity. I believe that, in general, less educated wives are more shy and diffident *vis-à-vis* the Company's expectations; although I cannot at the moment produce firm evidence to substantiate this impression.

The community in its turn uses tolerance as a mechanism to reconcile its members to their position. Tolerance thus becomes a device for the protection of the group's solidarity. It eases the integration of new members at an initial stage, and it provides a safety valve for those wives for whom adjustment is especially difficult. The degree to which deviance in wives is tolerated varies from one community to another: groups formed by the exploration/production side of Shell are less tolerant than those on the commercial side. Whether broad or narrow, the tolerance shown by the community is itself an effective means of control: it often shapes the dissident wife into the Shell mould, even at the cost of according her some degree of special treatment and licence.

Given that some measure of accommodation remains necessary for wives overseas, this accommodation itself carries complications which can be brought out once more by comparing the situation of Shell wives with that of diplomats' wives abroad. Two major functions of a diplomatic mission are to assure continuity of contact between its own country and the host State, and to recreate a consistent image of its own country abroad. These goals generate stable expectations, both within posts as individual personnel change, and for personnel themselves as they move from post to post. Diplomats' wives in turn are able to benefit from these stable expectations in negotiating their relations within the mission and with individuals and institutions of the host State. Shell wives, on the other hand, are expected to 'represent' the *multinationality* of Shell; here, by definition almost, there are no stable expectations to go by. The image that the wives are supposed to cultivate for Shell varies from place to place, and the rules must be learned afresh each time. To be a successful *Shell wife*, then, a woman needs more than a satisfactory balance between independence and conformity. Accommodation itself calls for imagination, initiative, versatility and resourcefulness: the very qualities, ironically, which management views with suspicion.

The 'Shell wife identity'

Shell wives to whom I spoke did not seem to have a separate, conscious image of themselves as *Shell wives*. In many cases women seem to adopt some version of their husbands' professional self-image while living abroad. Some kind of working relationship develops between the couple, and wife and husband see themselves as one towards the world outside Shell. When asked by non-Shell people 'What are you?' they reply 'We are Shell'. This unity, as we shall see, is disrupted at the end of the posting.

It is however possible to speak of a *Shell wife identity*.[11] The collective representation of the group's identity among wives is manifested in their loyalty, resilience and sociability. Wives either already possess these attributes in a visible way, in which case they immediately become popular with the group, or they will have to try and acquire some of them in order to be accepted as members.

The material as well as the moral aspects of group identity are remarkably uniform. Common values acquired through living a Shell way of life are displayed in matters such as dress, education of children, type of housing considered desirable, ways of spending leisure and holidays.[12] Some women, when interviewed, insisted that for them going overseas had meant giving up advantages and life-styles superior to the ones abroad, rather than bettering them. But in most cases the financial situation had improved through the postings abroad and values had altered accordingly. Many wives stated that from choice they would never have sent their children to boarding schools and that both children and mothers had suffered initially from the separation. Nevertheless, when they returned home they had chosen to keep the children as boarders in spite of the opportunity they now had to bring them back home. This was partly justified by mothers as 'for the child's sake they did not want to disrupt the continuity of the children's education'. The same transformation of values and appropriate reasoning applied to other aspects of the corporate life-style among the cases in question.

A last example of the refractions of collective thinking is to be found in the attitude wives develop towards the outside world, and their judgment of it. Wives seem to assess the world outside the Shell communities through their husbands' eyes (a judgment which is often itself a reflection of the way the business operates). Living in a socialist country, for example, is considered to be a 'pressurized posting'. Going out into the 'free world' at frequent intervals to reduce the pressure has taken the form of a ritual for Shell people posted in those countries. When we were on a posting in a socialist country, I was sometimes asked by other wives how often did I 'get out of the place?' When I replied that I did not have the urge to get out and was perfectly happy, my reply aroused astonishment and my non-conformist thinking was interpreted in a variety of ways; other wives tried hard to find reasons why I was 'not thinking like them'.

Loyalty, resilience and sociability

Life in a Shell community places special and sometimes dramatic demands on these three qualities in wives. In this sense they can be considered 'pillars' of the *Shell wife identity*; they are, as we shall see, closely interconnected. For a new Shell wife who has not lived in a Shell community before, loyalty to the Company is a new concept. At home, wives have no special commitment towards Shell and its world. As Pahl and Pahl put it:

> the two worlds of wife-at-home/husband-at-work rarely meet, but rather are mediated to each other through the person of the husband.(1976: 176)

Abroad, the integration of private life into the more public life of the community helps reduce the tension of the 'two worlds' - for the husband. Wives are expected to share their husbands' loyalty towards the Company: a loyalty which, in women, is developed under the pressure of group opinion. Critical remarks by wives about Shell receive an obvious and unfavourable reaction, particularly from men. In a small community, being seen to buy one's petrol from a station other than Shell is noticed and causes comments to be made and eyebrows to rise. In a positive sense, the loyalty of wives is a valuable practical resource for management. This has been well explained by Eric Miller in a paper on Foreign and Commonwealth Office wives, who are in this respect a parallel case:

> Loyalty of wife to husband and the expectation that she will do what is necessary to service him in return for dependence on him as a breadwinner have been taken-for-granted behaviour in our culture. Questioning of it is very recent and the wife who departs from the traditional norm - allowing him to cut his own sandwich for lunch or to wash his own shirt - is in most

British sub-cultures still frowned upon as a deviant. The Diplomatic Service has used this loyalty and dependence and incorporated it into the organization of the missions. (1977).

The exercise of loyalty demands resilience, of which adapting to cultural differences is the mere beginning. A wife may easily find herself preparing meals for sixteen visitors who turn up for two days, or having to receive them three hours later than expected. Resilience at its extreme is called upon when a Shell wife has to live in one hotel room with three children for months or years under conditions of stress.[13] In a case like this the financial compensations are high but so are the expectations laid on wives, where the Company's interest is involved.[14] In matters of daily conduct, wives are expected to follow their husbands' lead almost blindly; since any independent action on their part in a sensitive post is thought to carry a risk of harm to the Company.

It is, finally, a salient fact of Shell community life that the key qualities of loyalty and resilience are simultaneously displayed in, and demanded by, structures of sociability both within the community and outside it. Pahl and Pahl among others have emphasized the importance of analyzing social gatherings in order to reach the more subtle realities of social relations:

> If it is in their informal life, in the interstices between institutions, that people are most free, while yet social pressures are still felt at these times, then it is in informal life that certain sorts of social realities are most clearly revealed. (1971: 143)

Structures of sociability are encountered in two major contexts: that of female gatherings and patterns of association among wives; and that of mixed gatherings. Although both kinds of gathering obviously may or may not include outsiders to the Company, I shall concentrate here on what happens 'internally'.

Female Gatherings

M.Helfrich in the 'Social Role of the Executive's Wife' writes:

> In the business world of today, which transcends the office and enters the home ... the wife of an executive entertains and is entertained by her husband's associates, clients, potential clients and superiors. Each may require a different pattern of behaviour. (1965: 44)

Shell wives are very conscious of the structured character of all their relationships, both with the outside world and among themselves. A junior wife who tries to make friends with the general manager's wife will be singled out and criticized. Eric Miller points out in reference to diplomats' wives – again comparable in this respect –

> The loyalty to the husband therefore has the effect of distancing her from other wives, and maintaining status distinctions among them, even though many may feel a similar predicament. (op.cit).

Likewise, their place in the formal sphere of the Company prevents all but a few spontaneous relationships from developing among women in Shell communities. *Friendly* but *distant* relations dominate the socialising scene of these women. While at home there is very little contact between wives and perforce no formality at all, there is a rigid code of conduct among them when abroad.

According to the older generation of Shell wives the Shell community in the 'old days' was an extension of the English way of life, and was similar to the Colonial and Foreign Service communities abroad. Joining clubs or forming them, organizing bazaars, parties and the like were the main ways of socializing for wives even fifteen years ago. My experience as one of the younger generation of Shell wives indicates a change of approach in recent years and a more 'cosmopolitan' way of thinking. The fact that Shell does not provide its employees with the same kinds of facilities as do the Foreign Office or the Armed Services,[15] and the fact that Shell wives often move around more freely than (for example) diplomats' wives, makes it easier for them to contact local people as and when they desire, and gives Shell wives wider opportunities for socializing outside the Shell group.

Ways of socializing within the group vary from community to community, since (as already stated) wives have to develop different skills in each post to ensure their place as a wanted member of the group. For example, in countries where food ingredients are scarce, cooking and the art of displaying food becomes a main and constant occupation and gives an incentive to friendships and the formation of sub-groups. The sight of picnic baskets full of appetizing food beside the swimming-pool in Nigeria at a time when many ingredients were not easy to find, is still vivid in my memory after many years. The same crowd of women gathered by the pool every day, played cards, did not set foot in the water, and spent most of their time displaying the elaborate food they had spent hours preparing specially for the occasion. In another country where it was difficult to establish contact with local people, competition among Shell wives was to see who could make the most friends among the locals.

Mixed Gatherings

Purely male gatherings overseas are rare outside office hours. At mixed gatherings, however, the underlying interest remains the business which, in a subtle manner, dictates the rules of social interaction. The office hierarchy is visibly at work: I have often been told and heard others say 'I am trying to think what I can say to my colleague's wife', or 'She is the boss's wife', or 'Her husband is only a junior man'.

It is usually easier for men than for wives to know what to say to whom. Their common interest and knowledge of business and of other Shell men gives them a secure area in which they can relax their guard, and which the wives on the whole do not have. Lack of knowledge of office politics and of the relationships between men makes it prudent for women to adopt a more passive, defensive posture. This passive behaviour can be partly explained as the only possible response to 'shop-talk' on the men's part. (At mixed gatherings, shop-talk typically is apologized for, then continues unabated.) But the wives are never sure to what extent what they are saying or doing can be damaging or helpful to their husband and his career. Casual conversations with wives are an effective means whereby Shell men 'check up' on their colleagues. One of my husband's superiors once told me 'It is amazing how much I have learnt about the unknown aspects of my subordinates' personalities through their wives' careless remarks'. Men regularly try to withhold business information from their wives lest they should unwittingly give it away.

Senior men enjoy considerable freedom in their manner towards subordinates' wives at mixed gatherings. They are licenced to treat the latter in ways that would elsewhere be considered patronizing; and to flirt. Gallantry towards 'junior' wives is not of course sexually motivated on the whole, but is a way of signalling seniority within a well-understood code. Needless to say, the licence is not symmetrical. For a junior man to adopt the same manner towards the wife of his superior would be seen as a violation. Likewise a senior man's wife cannot patronize or flirt with her husband's juniors. She has no 'messages' to convey to the males present; any such behaviour would be not a tool of communication but a matter of moral concern.

Social gatherings reveal very clearly the degree to which the life of the community penetrates and prevails over the life of the individual and the 'private' sphere. Traditional and personal festivities which at 'home' are culturally marked as private - Christmas, anniversaries and the like - become important collective ceremonies. In addition, competence in personal life becomes a matter of public concern and this concern is publicly exhibited. Men are very conscious, for example, that their wives must be capable of entertaining; and may even refuse a posting where a great deal of this is required if they think their wives could not cope. One of our visitors once told me: 'But ... cannot possibly go abroad however much he would like to, his wife cannot cook.' Once they are in a post, a man may deal with his wife's failures in matters thought to concern the community's interest by a form of 'public confession' at social gatherings. The wife may be present or absent, but if the husband feels that the community is critical of her or that she falls short of its expectations, he volunteers criticism. This, ironically, is seen as *self-criticism*. In this way, mixed gatherings can function as a forum for public correction and control of wives.

The end of the posting: home or Limbo Land?
Coming home at the end of a posting frees women from their duties as Company wives. Returning to where they were born and brought up, however, proves to be more than just crossing physical boundaries and falling into an already-known culture: home, for most Shell wives,

becomes a 'limbo land' where they face yet another culture shock, and a new learning of a different way of life.[16] In the majority of cases the family on its return moves into a bigger house in a different area from the previous home. The wife, no longer a *Shell wife*, often finds herself in surroundings as foreign to her as when she first went overseas. Her old friends, even when within reach, are not particularly interested in her experience of life abroad, her relatives are not necessarily nearby, and the effort of contacting them or visiting them can be more a burden than a help. There is no such thing now as a Shell community. The husband, who from the very first day of his return has resumed his work at the head office, leaves to his wife the management of the house-moving, taking the children to and from school, finding new friends, and generally coping with everyday life. Contrary to her expectation, the qualities which she has developed to deal with the pressure of life overseas, and which she has considered a universal recipe for survival in a new environment, do not work at home and are largely redundant. The special context for which those attributes were developed – the Shell community – has vanished and so have its demands. The gap is too unexpected and deep for women to avoid falling into it. From having lived in the *limelight* of the community's life[17] and under the magnifying-glass of its members, the woman suddenly finds herself in the *dimlight* of private life where she has no incentive and no place for displaying her most hard-won qualities. Worse still is the abrupt interruption in the relationship she has developed overseas with her husband, where they both aimed at the same target and developed in the same direction. While the husband *continues*, she *starts again* in search of a new identity.

So the learning begins again, and by the time the woman has managed to master her environment, to overcome the feeling of marginality in her society, and, at best, to start a career or job, it is time for another posting overseas. Margaret Sullivan writes of the diplomat's wife: 'She, more than any member of the family unit, is called upon to provide continuity and stability for her husband and children ... ' (1977) The same is true of the Shell wife and yet her life, of all the members of the family, is the most lacking in both.

Appendix. Learning to be a Shell wife: extracts from fieldnotes

Case 1: Jean. 'I got married to my husband in the late 1950s. I was already a graduate with a prospect of good jobs, but instead I joined my husband in an African country and later in the Far East. At the beginning I did not want to mix with all those wives who did nothing but play bridge and run bazaars and go out to cocktail parties. I felt excluded from the community because of my reluctance to join in the female activities and yet did not want to join them. In the evenings when my husband came home I used to complain to him, to which he replied, 'if you want to be like them, give parties and take part in the community life; then you will be one of them, but is this what you want?' The gap caused by the conflict over whether to join the community or remain oneself narrowed as Jean's husband grew more and more senior. She learnt how to behave as a *Shell wife*, and how to compromise between being that and being 'herself'. She now found on walking into new and grand houses that even the servants expected her to behave like other Shell wives before her. Although Jean has managed to keep her personal interests going by doing various jobs abroad, she has also had to perform to the full the duties of a *Shell wife*. Between postings, at home, she has found jobs but as soon as she has established herself her husband has been posted overseas again. She said she felt that 'every time she rolls herself up, and when she reaches the top - in terms of personal achievement - the reel unwinds itself and she finds herself at the bottom again'. One of Jean's last comments at our interview was, 'I don't know why we women who already have an interest of our own give it up and follow men around, but we always do.' Jean's husband is now very senior. Her message to more junior wives is, 'I do admire you for having learnt to play bridge, but I admire you even more for not playing it.'

Case 2: Caroline. Caroline was a trained nurse and had her own job when her husband was posted. His job was not a senior one but he was the general manager and the only non-local Shell man in the post. Caroline said, 'It was lucky that I learnt the job on a junior posting because when we got posted to our next posting which was fairly senior I knew exactly what to do and was not half as nervous.' In other words Caroline, unlike Jean, had learnt quickly and easily how to be a *Shell wife*.

Acknowledgments

I would like to thank Shirley Ardener and Pat Holden for their help and advice, and all the Shell wives who agreed to be interviewed. I would also like to express my very special thanks to Hilary Callan for the help she has given me in the editing of this paper.

Notes

1. No *Shell communities* are however formed in Great Britain because the business is too large and its interests too diverse. The conditions that give rise to the formation of a community do not apply to the head office.

2. Esso is Shell's most powerful competitor.

3. For more general reading see Bridger (1980), Cohen (1974), Goldberg *et al* (1965) and Sampson (1975).

4. For comparable cases, see Callan (1975) and Clark (this volume).

5. See Callan (1975) for a comparison with the treatment of diplomats' wives.

6. Since this paper was first given, in 1979, I have heard that Shell has funded the Social Science Research Council to study the wives of North Sea divers and their special problems.

7. Young (this volume) provides a more extended discussion of non-conformity, deviance and the 'power of the margins'; much of this would apply well to the Shell case.

8. In reply to a letter I sent to Shell's Personnel Department, I received the following comment: ' ... it is normal practice now for couples jointly to attend

courses both about the specific country they are going to, and about awareness of
other cultures in general. These events are rightly supplemented by personal
contacts which staff in Personnel Services are happy to arrange if required.'

9. For a further discussion of special features of wives' access to space, see
Kirkwood and Young (this volume). See also Ardener (ed.) 1981.

10. Kanter (1977), in her chapter on 'Wives', has made an excellent study of the
corporate wife in the U.S. She analyzes the course of the wife's relationship with
the corporation as it moves from a concern with the boundaries of inclusion and
exclusion at 'junior' levels to the representational responsibility of the 'senior'
years. I do not, in this paper, emphasize this 'life-trajectory' aspect of the moral
career of Shell wives.

11. See also Malcolm Young's discussion (this volume) of the use of 'thick
description' to arrive at an understanding of a given group's implicit knowledge
and 'practical mastery'.

12. For a comparison with homebased managerial lifestyles, see Pahl & Pahl
(1971). See also Ifeka-Moller (1975).

13. In this particular case the wife attempted suicide.

14. Shell visitors who come on short visits to a post expect to be entertained and
looked after by the Shell representative, and reckon that the Shell man's house is
the *Shell house*. In the larger communities the visitors are received by different
people according to their grade; but in a small post the one Shell man has to look
after all the visitors regardless of their seniority. In one such small post the wife of
the representative (a fairly senior man) was harassed by two of the regular visitors,
who were always drunk and persistently misbehaved. Finally she stopped being
pleasant and told them to leave. The two Shell men were surprised, and protested
strongly that when they were away from their home and family they should have
a home to relax in; naturally the *Shell home* was it. Whether those men were in any
way disciplined by their superiors was not known to the community, but the
general feeling was that the blame lay with the 'intolerant' wife.

15. These would include for example the special shopping facilities such as
NAAFI stores and commissaries to which diplomatic and Armed Service families
may have access. See also Macmillan (this volume).

16. By 'home' I mean Great Britain. I have not had the opportunity of looking
at other 'homes' such as Holland.

17. 'Limelight' and 'dimlight' are here used metaphorically without any
prejudice or other implication.

THE NEGATION OF STRUCTURE:
A NOTE ON BRITISH COUNCIL WIVES

Isobel Clark

Introduction: the British Council as an institution

The British Council was created as a voluntary association in November
1934, and received its Royal Charter in 1940. Its founding was a result of
the realization by the then Foreign Office that Britain was suffering in her
overseas trade and relations from the lack of an efficient information
agency comparable to that of France, Germany and Italy. A Joint
Committee was set up in 1933 by the Board of Trade, and the Board of
Education pointed out to the Government the problem of ignorance
overseas of Britain's achievement in the fields of education, culture,
science and technology. The pressure of these two Departments of State,
together with that of the Foreign Office (which had been urging the
creation of British 'centres' in certain capitals since 1920) resulted in a
'British Committee for Relations with Other Countries' being established
in 1934 under the auspices of the Foreign Office. It was to be financed by
the Treasury and a combination of private companies, the Federation of
British Industries and the Association of British Chambers of Commerce.
The name was changed to the simpler 'British Council' on its official
inauguration by the then Prince of Wales on 2 July 1935. In the first years,
the Council was concerned mainly with Europe and South America
(owing to their importance in overseas trade), with the Near East (for
strategic and political reasons), and with the task of counteracting the
concentration of German and Italian influence building up in the latter
area. In 1939 a move to incorporate the British Council into the Ministry
of Information was resisted, and in 1940 a Royal Charter guaranteed its
permanence and independence (White 1965).

It is important to stress that the British Council has never been an
explicitly political organization at any time: although financed through
the Treasury it began as, and still is, an independent institution along the
lines of the BBC. This point is crucial in understanding the sense of special
identity which Council staff and wives experience in overseas postings,
since it provides the basis for a radical distinction between themselves and
corresponding British Embassy personnel. This distinctiveness in turn is
the more sharply felt and insisted upon because of the overall
comparability between the Council and the British Diplomatic Service in

areas such as pay scales, overseas allowances and living conditions, and career structure.[1]

Internal Structure

The Council is a loosely-structured organization, especially in its overseas posts, and this spirit characterizes the wives as much as the male staff. There is a *deliberate* lack of hierarchy, and this is seen as contrasting sharply with the diplomatic community. The wife of the head of post (the Representative) is regarded as 'senior' in the sense that other wives are expected to help in her official entertaining at large parties. Beyond this it is left to the individual Representative's wife to relate to the group in her own way. During my time in Jordan the 'senior wife' tried to structure the group fairly firmly, with 'obligatory' weekly meetings. This however soon broke down: the wives reverted to informal friendly relations and showed a certain amount of resentment towards her. In the Sudan, the wives of two of the three Representatives who served in the six years I was there laid no claim to authority in any form. The third Representative had no wife, and the lack of a 'senior wife' made very little difference to the pattern of life among the women. I have, on the other hand, heard a wife observe that this lack of hierarchy could result in inefficiency when things had to be done, such as joint entertaining, since people then acted as individuals and were not co-ordinated behind a leader.

The relationships of wives among themselves were informal, predominantly friendly and non-hierarchical. No wife that I knew during my second tour abroad took a position towards any other by reference to their husbands' relative seniority in the Council, and everyone mixed on apparently equal terms. This was made simpler by the fact that Council-employed staff are, in general, more homogeneous socially and culturally than those of a British diplomatic mission abroad. All are graduates, and there is no equivalent of the *administrative/executive* division which exists in the British Diplomatic Service.

Sources of group identity

As we have seen, internal relations within a British Council mission abroad are typically relaxed, and this quality is emphasized and valued in the life of the post. Other sources of the community's strong feeling of common identity are its small average size (there were five wives in Jordan when I was there and six in the Sudan) and, especially, a shared attitude to outside groups.

The most significant reference group for both staff and wives is the local British Embassy. The self-perceived role of the Council as *non-political* affords an important contrast in felt identity between the two local organizations. The work of the Council is more closely aligned with the institutions of the country of residence than is a diplomatic mission (which, of course, while being *accredited* to the host Government, looks to its own for political direction.) This difference creates corresponding attitudes on the part of wives. Council wives tend to see their social lives as directed towards local people rather than the British community, and to choose their friends through a much wider range of contacts than is typically available to diplomatic staff and wives, especially in 'sensitive' posts (see also Tremayne, this volume). They are invited, even expected, to take part in Embassy wives' social activities such as sewing-circles and coffee-mornings, but they tend to resist this. In doing so they reflect the overall Council feeling that there should be a definite *distance* and *separateness* between Council and Embassy.

Council wives lay stress on their own lack of formal hierarchy, as against what they see to be a much stricter internal structuring within the Embassy. They feel they have greater personal freedom than their diplomatic equivalents, and they resent any apparent attempt to infringe this. They also, in general, feel that they are much closer than diplomats and their families to the country in which they are serving. Fewer obligations are placed on them by the Council than is typically the case in an Embassy, and they see themselves as able to be altogether more individualistic in personal style than the diplomatic wives in the same post. All these points combine to build up a sense of independence and apartness from the Embassy among Council wives. Since a good proportion of Council wives have higher education in some form, their personal friends are predominantly found among the intelligentsia and academics, both local and expatriate, of all nationalities. As a Council wife I felt no constraint from the Council on my own choice of friends, although positive emphasis, as in all aspects of Council work, tended to be placed on local people.

Employment

There is no formal bar to wives' taking paid employment at post: the Council has, in fact, no overall policy on the subject. Indeed, the British Council's official efforts to work closely with local agencies and people provide a basis on which wives are encouraged to work. Such work tends to be within the Council's sphere of influence, partly because ready-made contacts ease wives' entry into paid work in these areas. A good example is the sphere of education; many wives work in the administration of University departments, and a few taught in local schools in Khartoum while I was there. The Council saw this activity as enhancing its own reputation, since it had the effect of involving the wives in local concerns and so of widening even further the Council's range of contacts.

For these reasons, most Representatives in my experience encouraged wives to have jobs. In this way wives were able to have at least some earned income, but were also genuinely drawn into the wider aspects of Council work; this in turn strengthened their own sense of 'belonging' to the Council. At the same time it drew them deeply into local society and gave them a status of their own in the eyes of local people. In the Sudan in particular, during my time there, the Council wives had very easy access to, and informal relations with, local people as a result of working in local paid jobs; this was regarded by them and their husbands as a valuable contribution *to the Council's* work and general objectives.

Wives are thus seen – and see themselves – as aiding and extending the Council's interests by having paid jobs. At the same time this approval itself is often expressed as a recognition of the wife's 'freedom' to work. The right to work is, however, real in the sense that it can be honoured even when the interests of the Council are not necessarily served by a wife's employment. One Council wife in Khartoum, working with the Sudanese Ministry of Education, ran a volunteer teacher recruiting agency on behalf of the Sudanese Government which drew staff from the same sources as the Voluntary Service Overseas programme administered within the Sudan by the Council itself. This put her, to some extent, into unforeseen but direct competition with the Council. The Representative considered the case, but allowed it. It would have been within his brief, in fact, to refuse her permission to work; but to do so would have been to go against the overwhelming feeling within the Council as a whole that the wife must be considered as a 'person in her own right', rather than an adjunct of the employed husband. A case once arose in India of a Council wife, who was Swedish, working in the Swedish Embassy there. The Representative, while once again allowing this, was unhappy about it since he felt that it took her away from the Council community into the Swedish wives' group.

Thus while, as in the British diplomatic case (Callan 1975), the question of 'permission' for a wife to work does technically arise, the restriction on individual freedom that this implies is effectively countered by the community's own consensus of values. It is far more common, in fact, for wives to be prevented from working by local restrictions or language problems than by the Council itself. In Jordan when I was there the employment of wives was virtually ruled out by the civil war taking place at the time. In the Sudan by contrast there was an open market and all the wives had jobs, although not all worked full-time.

Attitude of wives to the Council

Wives in general do not feel 'threatened' by the Council. The relative freedom they enjoy makes for an easy relationship between wives and Council. This is greatly helped by the Council not putting pressure on wives through their husbands, or the reverse: wives are never interviewed in connection with their husbands' appointments, nor do they figure in the annual reports filed on all employed staff. Most wives are in practice willing to help Council work overseas alongside their husbands, precisely because very little pressure is put on them to do so.

The majority of the wives whom I knew overseas between 1968 and 1977 were contented with their place *vis-à-vis* the Council, although the loose structure of command and communication could at times cause frustration in situations of difficulty, when what began as a respect for the individual ended as a failure of support. Wives sometimes felt that it was not so easy to 'know where you were' as in the tighter structure of an Embassy; and that a more visible distribution of responsibilities would be on occasion welcome.

The attitudes of wives have changed, not surprisingly, over the last five years, and new expectations have come to the fore. Mrs Valerie Coombs, Chairman of the Wives' Association, whom I interviewed on 27 February 1981, felt that younger wives put more emphasis on their own jobs and careers today, and frequently resent the necessity of abandoning or interrupting their own pursuits to travel overseas with their Council husbands. This appears to be a general tendency, not confined to those professionally trained. There is thus a growing discontent among younger wives at the inevitable partial taking-over of their lives by the Council. A rising incidence of marital breakdown among overseas personnel may be one symptom of this change. While the Council itself 'allows' the wife considerable freedom of choice in working overseas, her career must of necessity depend on what is possible in the local country rather than on her own personal wishes. As stated before, much depends on local limitations and conditions. As a result, many younger wives are involved in tensions of personal identity.

Such tensions can be exacerbated in cases where the *wife* is a former *colleague*. Among the wives as a whole, female Council officers who marry overseas serving colleagues are not popular as a rule. They lose their official status on marrying, but, knowing the system from inside, they sometimes continue to operate as if they were 'staff'. Consequently, they may be seen by other wives as 'pushing' or even 'self-seeking'. Such cases afford an interesting comparison with those described by Young (this volume) of policewomen who become police wives.

The Home Posting

Council staff spend most of their careers overseas, but all return to Britain for home postings from time to time. Thus wives alternate between small bounded groups overseas, and the very different conditions at home. Tremayne (this volume) describes the dissolution of the net, of Company-based relationships and obligations surrounding a *Shell wife* when the overseas posting comes to an end and she returns to a 'home' environment which may itself have altered beyond her recognition. The Council wife enters a comparable organizational 'limbo' (to borrow Tremayne's expression) when her husband retires or is posted home. In Britain there is far less group cohesion than abroad, one reason being that families are scattered geographically. Council centres in the United Kingdom cater for overseas students in the main, and do not function as meeting-points for home-based staff or wives. After leaving the Sudan posting in May 1977, I was very little involved with the Council at all. In London itself, some group feeling is kept up among those who can attend

Wives' Association meetings; the Association also attempts to keep wives in touch with one another and with Council affairs by means of a journal. However, because of the built-in looseness of structure described above - but also because in this country there is no felt need to operate *as* a group - wives when in the U.K. tend to 'go their own way' and not to have any form of common life.

The British Council Wives' Association

All wives belong by definition to the BCWA: there is no condition of membership other than marriage to a serving Council officer.[2] It is operated by home-based wives with a Committee of six members, including the Director General's wife *ex-officio*. Despite this formal connection, the BCWA (like the corresponding Diplomatic Service Wives' Association) is constitutionally independent of the Administration. This independence enables it to do a certain amount of lobbying in the Council for changes in regulations and improved 'conditions of service' such as more frequent fare-paid visits of children at boarding school to parents at post, and extension of entitlement to these visits for children of University age. There is a tendency among members who are ex-Council officers to urge that the Association adopt a trade-union model in its negotiations with the Council; but this is not a popular idea among the membership at large. The dominant opinion (reflecting no doubt the complex and mixed loyalties of wives themselves) is that the Association is most effective as 'an informal lobby'.

The most general function of the BCWA is to bridge the communication gap between the home and overseas Council. It acts as a common focus for wives, and is in fact very helpful in solving all manner of individual problems. Much concern and real aid is offered to wives overseas in emotional difficulties, confronted with problems of settling-in and adapting to often uncongenial conditions, and experiencing every kind of personal worry. Letters are received and answered in confidence, without anything going on file. In this way it is a confidential welfare service, whose declared aim is to help wives to find an acceptable role and identity within their differing situations. It also provides more practical services: an escort service for unaccompanied children going to and from parents at post, including putting them up if necessary; looking after elderly relatives as needed, and passing information to those overseas; shopping for goods not available at post and sending them out. These services are paid for by the people concerned, as the BCWA is self-financing. A quarterly publication is distributed to all wives; this is open to all topics for discussion, to correspondence and news of general inside interest.

Within the BCWA is a group for 'retired' wives. Members automatically become part of this on the husband's retirement, and a representative sits on the main Committee. The Association also continues to extend services to divorced and separated wives, especially in helping with children to and from overseas posts. They are no longer invited to meetings, although their letters are welcomed.

It can therefore be argued that the BCWA constitutes a 'support group' for wives, albeit one that is inevitably tied in with the Council's own objectives and attitudes. (The help given to the divorced and separated might, for example, be interpreted in more than one way). But the influence of a more radical feminism is also being felt, if only in small ways. A member from Hull wrote to the Committee to object to the word 'wives' in the Association's title (see *Appendix*). The BCWA response to this initiative is that one day they may become the 'Spouses'' Assocation, that it is willing to move with the times, but that at present the existing title 'fits best'. There are currently (1982) three male spouses of Council serving officers, and these are regarded as full members of the BCWA. So far they have not been active in the Association.

When interviewed by me, the Chairman stressed the *non-hierarchical* character of the BCWA; reflecting once again that of the Council as a whole. As a contrasting example (echoing yet again the importance of diplomacy as model and counter-model) she described the Annual General Meeting of the Diplomatic Service Wives' Assocation, which she had attended. At this meeting, unlike the AGM of the BCWA, representatives of the Foreign and Commonwealth Office Administration were present and answered each question from the wives in an official capacity. Each woman identified herself by her husband's name and grade before asking her question. The report of the meeting, requested by the BCWA Chairman, was checked throughout the hierarchy before reaching her five months later. The comparable BCWA report is prepared by the Committee present and is not shown to any other Council body.

Conclusion

In this brief paper, I have indicated that in many ways the lives of British Council wives abroad reflect, as one would expect, the values and organizaton of the Council itself. The wives look on themselves as an *egalitarian community* with shared intellectual and cultural interests. The character of their husbands' work encourages them to seek friendships outside the organization within the local community, and especially the local intelligentsia, rather than within British expatriate society. In most respects they consider themselves privileged compared with other wives; but they do experience tensions, notably that between the theoretical independence accorded them by the Council and the limitations of opportunity imposed by mobility and local circumstances. There are thus clear contrasts, as well as some similarities, to be seen between their situation and that of the other groups of 'incorporated' wives living abroad who are described in this volume. The most revealing comparisons however are with the position of Embassy wives abroad, since the latter constitute the main reference group against which the Council wives themselves see and define their own identity.

The BCWA also reflects, in the final analysis, the strengths and weaknesses of the Council itself. It is loosely structured and relaxed in style, relies on individual initiative and aims to be a 'free association of equals'. It has almost no printed literature: a deliberate policy to avoid having to *define itself too closely*. The gain is in flexibility, and in the capacity to respond imaginatively to most situations. It is a genuinely caring body giving both practical help and moral support to wives over a wide range of problems; even though, naturally, in so doing it also eases the Council's own management task. But there is a loss. Its lack of formal structure and hierarchy means that the BCWA finds it difficult to make known its services in an efficient way to all who may need them. Consequently many wives do not know quite what to expect from it, and may miss the benefits it has to offer. Briefly as I have described it, the situation of wives in the British Council affords a useful limiting case when set against other instances of 'incorporation' discussed in this book. It suggests that where an organization has values which promote the studied *avoidance* of formalized roles and statuses among wives, there can be a price to pay as well as a gain for the individuals concerned.

Appendix

Letter in *Compass*, January 1981:

What has happened to equal opportunities for men ? Let us start at once a Council Husbands' Association ... [which] could debate such topics as the role of the Council husband in the 1980s. Should ... [he be] involved in all Council activities, or should he be allowed the option of non-participation if he is content to immerse himself solely in his own career ? (Gillian Crossley, Hull)

Reply in *Compass*, February 1981:

Gillian Crossley of Hull ... seemed to find the idea of a "Council Husbands' Association" wildly funny. Why should she assume that a man married to a globally transferable British Council officer has no problems of status, work availability, and involvement in the work of the Council etc. ? At several of our recent meetings this very problem has been aired. The situation many of us find ourselves in ... stems primarily from the fact that we are married to British Council officers and only secondly from the fact that we are women. When more women Council Officers are both married and globally transferable we might well consider changing the name of the Association to the BCSA (S for Spouses of course). (Valerie Coombs, Chairman, B.C.W.A.).

Notes

1. The material put forward and discussed in this paper is based on my own experience in Jordan (1968-70) and the Sudan (1971-77), supplemented by information gained from interviews and internal Council publications.

2. For much of the following information, I am indebted to Mrs Valerie Coombs, Chairman of the Association at the time of writing, whom I interviewed in February 1981. The Assocation will be referred to as the BCWA.

SETTLER WIVES IN SOUTHERN RHODESIA: A CASE STUDY

Deborah Kirkwood

Women are the necessary guarantors of permanent settlement through a second generation. (Dillard 1976: 71)

'Your people may come in and take away this stone [gold quartz] as they take away ivory in their wagons. They may load up as much as they please of it, but on no account are they to bring with them a woman, a cow, a ewe or a she goat, because the permission is to carry away stones, not to build houses and towns in my country.' Words spoken by Moselikatse to gold concession hunters in Matabeleland in 1867, quoted by John Mackenzie (1871: 353).

Introduction

The premiss that the continuing presence of wives is intrinsic to the *settlement*, as distinct from the *exploitation* form of colonization would seem beyond doubt. It is a truism that where men go, women follow, sooner rather than later; settler women follow with the implicit understanding that they will sever effectively their ties with the mother country and will remain and make their homes in an overseas colony. I have chosen to describe the experiences of a particular group of such women who, simply by their presence, confirmed their husbands' status as *settlers* in a 'new' country, then Rhodesia. In this instance the country was 'new' only to the white immigrants; it had been the familiar homeland of the half million indigenous black population for centuries. Here I shall confine myself to a description of white society there, and to the whites' perception of themselves and their universe. For a short period the whites of Rhodesia experienced a notoriety disproportionate to their numbers and their personal qualities, though not their political significance. The European woman interviewed for television against the background of an affluent home, domestic servants and the inevitable swimming pool in the garden, became a familiar symbol of white intransigence in black Africa. Nevertheless, the experiences and role of the European wives during the ninety-year span of settler rule were more complex than the image might suggest. The ways in which they reacted to and acted upon an environment which was unusual, if not unique, may be of interest to those concerned with the study of women in society.

Preparatory reading for this essay involved a study of many of the early,

mainly autobiographical books written by travellers, traders, hunters and
the *pioneers* themselves. Predictably these were almost all written by men,
although there were a few women travellers and observers, notably Miss
Alice Balfour and Mrs Theodore Bent. Alice Balfour described her
journey in her book *Twelve Hundred Miles in an Ox Wagon* (1895); she was
a gifted artist and her watercolour paintings of the country are of
exceptional quality. Observations and illustrations by Mrs Bent, who
accompanied and assisted her husband in his research into archaeological
sites in Mashonaland, are included in his book *Ruined Cities of Mashonaland*
(1892).

As I read these old books I noted all references to women; these were
scant and were in themselves revealing:

> Mrs Hepburn gave us some delightful home-made bread and real, fresh
> butter, the first I have eaten for six months. (Leonard 1896: 118)
> Mrs Kirsten asked us to wait a little and have lunch. (de Waal 1896: 102)
> There were some lemon trees and his wife [Countess de la Panouse] was
> making a lemon drink. (de Waal op. cit: 242)

Such observations were typical. Hugh Marshall Hole, an eminent early
Rhodesian, in his book *Early Rhodesian Days* (1928: 22) commented:
'There was said to be a white woman somehwere in the camp, but she
must have remained in *purdah* for we never saw her'. In this book (facing
page 80) there is a photograph of a Salisbury group of four men and a
woman; the names of the men appear at the bottom, but there is no
reference to the woman.[1]

I shall try to convey something of the reality of life for settler women in
the new growing towns and in the country. More detailed attention will
be given to the wives of European farmers, miners and administrators.
Regrettably, limitation of space has precluded any close consideration of
the wives of missionaries; they were the earliest white women to settle in
Rhodesia, arriving during the 1850s, and their lives and experiences merit
detailed study.[2]

The Environment
It was a pre-condition for settlement that a new colony should be
geographically and climatically suitable. To early European explorers
Southern Rhodesia, situated on a high plateau just north of the Tropic of
Capricorn and south of the Equator, seemed eminently so in both respects.
The climate seemed excellent, the land appeared fertile, but more than this
there was a confident belief that the gold fields of Rhodesia would rival
those of the Transvaal, which had just been discovered. An early settler
wife, Mrs Mary Lewis, writing home to her mother in 1897 described 'An
enchanting view. We looked down the valley where Umtali is
situated ... and beyond towards the lovely mountainous country just
crying out for people and homes.' (1960: 20). Of course she meant white
people. Earlier she had met Cecil Rhodes himself, and noted that 'He was

pleased to see a woman coming out to settle and make a home in his country.' (op.cit: 19). This observation contrasts significantly with the official attitude towards Colonial Service wives, who were *permitted* to join their husbands after a prescribed period, but even then sometimes felt themselves to be admitted on sufferance.[3]

An Historical Framework

The ninety-year span of settler dominance can be divided roughly into three periods. The first, from 1890 to 1923 (following the grant of a Royal Charter to the British South Africa Company) was that of occupation, conquest, pacification and settlement; it was marked by the Matabele War (1893), the Mashona and Matabele rebellions (1896), the Anglo-Boer War (1899-1902) and the Great War (1914-18); it culminated in the attainment by the settlers of *responsible government* in 1923. The 1896 rebellions, a foretaste of the 'bush' war of the 1970s, were bloody and frightening but were speedily quelled by the invaders. Of the 450 whites killed 9 were women and 23 were children. In 1898 the Southern Rhodesia Order in Council regularized British South Africa Company rule, and the territory was brought under stricter metropolitan control.

In 1922 a referendum was held in which the alternatives of *responsible government* or union with South Africa were put to a white Rhodesian electorate which included women by virtue of the Women's Franchise Ordinance (1919). A substantial majority voted for the former option and in 1923 Southern Rhodesia became a self-governing colony; its status was unique in the then Empire. It was no longer administered by the Company and the British government retained only the most tenuous control over the locally-based government.[4]

During the middle period, between 1923 and 1945, a local white *mentalité* became more apparent than formerly; there was consolidation of national feeling and a growing sense of Rhodesian-ness. From the early days, however, whites had had a keen awareness of their identity as Rhodesians. The heroine of Cynthia Stockley's novel *Virginia of the Rhodesians* declares:

> Though Ireland was the land of my birth I am chiefly and above all things a Rhodesian. Mr Rhodes is mine own familiar friend, his quarrels my quarrels and his country my country. In fact, I belong. Everyone who has been through the Matabele War and the rebellions of '96 feels like that. (1903: 235)

She was expressing here a sentiment which became more and more manifest throughout the history of settler rule and culminated in the tenacity with which the 'bush war' (1972-79) was conducted right up to the end. Rhodesians also felt themselves to be distinct from, and superior to, white South Africans. It was said of them in the Union (of South Africa):

> They are not only intensely British, but quite intolerably Rhodesian ... and they are inclined to vaunt themselves and to be puffed up by the mere fact

that they *are* Rhodesians. (Tawse Jollie 1924: 7)[5]

The third period lasted from 1945 to 1979. After the end of the Second World War in 1945 the whites made determined efforts to attract immigrants from Europe to swell their numbers. In an attempt to consolidate their position and extend their influence in Central Africa they pressed the British government to create a Federation to include Southern Rhodesia, Northern Rhodesia (Zambia) and Nyasaland (Malawi). This Central African Federation was constituted in 1953 and led to a further rapid increase in white immigration. The demise of the Federation in 1963, due to African opposition to it in all three territories, led to a sharp swing to the right in white political attitudes which resulted in the declaration of unilateral independence (UDI) in 1965. Despite their wish to increase their numbers in Southern Rhodesia, old settlers came to feel themselves 'swamped' by the new white invaders and for many years there was a conscious cleavage between the old and the new Rhodesians; nevertheless they closed ranks after UDI, during the period of international sanctions and war.

Population

In 1891 there had been an estimated white population of 1,500, but no details of the ratio of the sexes is available; Africans were estimated to number about 500,000. By 1911, however, the number of whites had increased to 23,606 (male: female ratio was 100: 51), while the Africans then numbered 752,000. In 1941 there were 69,370 whites (male: female ratio - 100: 88) and 1,425,000 Africans. At the last official census in 1969 there were 228,296 whites (male: female ratio - 100: 97) and 4,846,930 Africans. It was impossible to conduct a census during the emergency and war; but it was estimated that the African population increased to nearly 7,000,000. While there was a steady exodus of whites there were white immigrants too, and the Europeans probably numbered over 200,000 at the time of independence and majority rule.

Pioneering

The Pioneer Column of 1890 was followed by a more-or-less continuous stream of men seeking land, gold or simply opportunity and adventure in a 'new' country. Women were first officially allowed to join, or seek husbands, in 1891;[6] according to W.D. Gale, in his 'Introduction' to the reprint edition of *Old Rhodesian Days* (Hole 1928):

> The embargo on women entering Mashonaland was lifted in 1891, and several of the married men ... sent for their wives ... The appearance of the women had a noticeable effect on the menfolk; beards were trimmed, hair was cut and the standard of dress improved. (pp. i,ii)

The women quickly took their places as wives of farmers, miners, administrators, policemen. A few single women arrived during those early years to make their own way in the new community: as early as 1898 there was reference to a milliner and an office assistant. Nursing and teaching were the two professions which provided openings for single women in the colonies (see also Brownfoot, this volume). The marriage rate was high; Tawse Jollie wrote of teachers: 'Without being unduly exacting one could wish that the Rhodesian Education Department had less success as a matrimonial agency' (op. cit: 237) and of nurses: 'The hospital was an even shorter cut to matrimony than the school. Together they have provided two thirds of Rhodesian wives' (ibid).

Some came as children's nannies and mothers' helps; amongst these too the marriage rate was high. From the employer's point of view plainness was a stronger recommendation than character; a young woman wrote to her mother in England about the new nanny: 'Everything about her was perfect, elderly, ugly, squints, has false teeth, partially bald, lean, sallow and a heart of gold, oh paragon of nurses !' (Macdonald 1927: 182). This extract comes from *Sally in Rhodesia*, a collection of letters written by Sheila Macdonald to her mother in England during the early years of the century and happily preserved by the latter. Today 'Sally' sounds naive, even coy, but given the period her style was perhaps natural:

> Life amongst men is apt to be trying at times ... When I first came here I was amazed to see so many men at dances and practically no unmarried girls at all. Consequently all love their life here. They are almost all young, many very attractive and lively and one and all have plenty of men friends. We discuss quite openly many subjects that would make your hair stand on end ... Life is very simple in many ways. Tiny houses help of course, and then living so much on your verandahs and having neighbours drop in at all times, staying for a chat if one is not busy, and going off in a hurry without offence if one is. We all love our 11 o'clock teas and it's as much a solemn rite as the Man's sundowner. (op.cit: 89)

In some families wives remained at home in Britain until husbands had established themselves in the new colony; in other cases, especially among the lower-paid artisans and clerks, husbands sent their wives and families back to England because of the excessively high cost of living in Rhodesia. The Cost of Living Committee of Enquiry (1913) heard, in evidence, artisans argue 'that they can better afford to keep their families out of the country than in it'. A Civil Service witness said, 'It pays to keep the families out of the country'. The Committee's conclusion was that 'The effect on the men is bad in every way. Prostitution is an abnormal evil owing to men sending their wives away' (Report: 68–69). The moral laxity resulting from the imbalance of the sexes prompted 'one stout, elderly and worthy matron to institute a 'Purity League' (Macdonald op.cit: 179).[7]

If the early days were adventurous and gay they were also very rough and uncomfortable. In generous acknowledgment of the hardships which women living in Salisbury experienced during the early 1900s G. H. Tanser dedicated his book *A Sequence of Time: The Story of Salisbury, 1900–14* (1974) to: 'The Unsung Heroines, the Housewives of Early

Salisbury'. Mary Lewis described her house on arrival:

> In the daylight it looked less promising. No shelves and plaster so sandy that
> no nails can be put in; no sink but a small kitchen table where I shall have to
> make all my dishes. So far everything stands on the floor ... I have a staff of
> two natives who call themselves cook and houseboy. The cook *can* boil water
> and the houseboy has never been in a house before and does not know a plate
> from a saucer, or the use of knives and forks. (op.cit: 23)

Life in the Towns

As the population increased Salisbury and Bulawayo expanded, and the
early untidy sprawl of shacks and cottages gave way to neat geometrically
planned towns. They were laid out in rectangular blocks. In Salisbury the
avenues ran from east to west and it was a case of 'the norther the posher'.
North Avenue was in fact the avenue of the elite and included
Government House and large one-acre plots on which senior officials and
the more prosperous citizens built comfortable colonial-style houses. A
character in Doris Lessing's *Martha Quest* uses the descriptive phrase 'ever
so North Avenue' (p. 149, paperback edition). Between the back gardens
of the avenue houses ran the *sanitary lanes* which were necessary for the
collection of sewage. All lavatories backed on to these lanes, and buckets
were replaced during the night by the municipal night-soil carts. Indoor
lavatories with water-borne sewerage were only introduced in the 1930s.
The servants' quarters also invariably backed on to these so-called
'sanitary' lanes, which frequently served as the highways of African social
intercourse.

As early as 1897, and long before the avenues were laid, it had seemed
to *matter* where one lived. Mary Lewis wrote:

> Round the foot of the kopje [hill] the town has sprung up, at least the
> commercial part of the town. The government offices are about half a mile
> away ... and this half of the town is connected by a road or causeway. I hear
> the Causeway people look down on the Kopje people. Why I cannot tell, but
> time will show. (op.cit: 25)

Sheila Macdonald too gives more than a hint of social hierarchy:

> Now I must hasten off to pay some belated calls. None of the tracks called
> avenues have names to them, and finding out where people live is a
> nightmare. Added to which no boy knows the name of his mistress, but just
> grins cheerfully and says, Ja, Missus! when you ask for Mrs Brown and you
> go in and find yourself in the bower of Mrs Smith, who hasn't called on you,
> or perhaps is not of the callable-on species, to put it nicely. (op.cit: 103)

Servants were more sensitive to such finer social distinctions than their
employers sometimes realized. Much later, in the 1950s, a socially
ambitious lady reproved her male house servant for calling her *Missus* and
tried to insist on *Madam*. She was firmly corrected: *Madam* was reserved
for ladies living in North or Montagu Avenues; those further south had to
be content with *Missus*.

From the earliest days *calling* - that is paying courtesy visits - was an important part of the daily life of a married woman (see also Brownfoot and Gartrell, this volume). It gave a certain formality to an otherwise casual, easy-going social pattern. The lady of the household would set out equipped with printed calling cards; narrow ones engraved with her husband's name, broader ones with her own. The elite *called* periodically on the Governor and his wife; they wrote their names in the Visitors' Book kept in the Guardhouse and left cards. Until the 1939-45 war *calling* was, of course, a regular feature of middle-class provincial life in England; in the colonies it served the important function of introducing newcomers to the community and of reinforcing solidarity in a small and isolated society. Women and men accepted with little questioning the social rituals which derived from the metropolitan culture and which emphasized important institutions in the social structure which they wished to reproduce.

Southern Rhodesia, like Kenya but in contrast to Northern Rhodesia and Uganda, was frequently described as a 'white man's country'. However, it was acknowledged that white women found the climate 'trying' and thus it was believed that an afternoon rest for them and for children was essential. 'Home before lunch and after that the lovely long afternoon rest all the women and children enjoy and which their men have to forego' (Macdonald, op.cit: 87). The siesta habit was never adopted by men; the working day was, and still is for Government officers, from 8 am to 4 pm. In neighbouring Mozambique the Portuguese never contemplated working in the heat of the day and in Beira everything closed between noon and 3 pm. However, the working pattern of the day in Rhodesia was largely dictated by the Englishman's passion for games. Night falls quickly and the precious two hours between four and six were devoted to sport by the men and by some of the younger women. This was also the most popular calling time. Later, in the 30s, afternoon bridge became a widespread fashion. The Governor's wife of that period was a dedicated bridge player, and an *entrée* to Government House was assured to any keen, competent player, provided always that she had reasonable claim to be regarded as a *lady*.

Life was a curious blend of living in the provinces, being at the centre of affairs, and pioneering on the frontiers of civilization. The total white population was probably less than that of an English country town, so a certain provincialism of outlook was unavoidable. Officials were responsible for important territory-wide administrative duties; those who were on friendly, often Christian name terms with Government ministers, charged with national policy decisions, basked in reflected glory. During Royal visits to Rhodesia, at international conferences or when received at Court in Britain, white Rhodesians operated at a level of privilege unlikely to have been theirs in larger social communities. Tawse Jollie, in the 1920s, described white Rhodesians as 'third class people travelling first' (op.cit: 5, and cf. Brownfoot, this volume). Meanwhile farmers struggled

to cultivate so-called 'virgin' land which had never before been subjected
to European methods of agriculture.

Women married to Farmers

Farm life in Rhodesia has been described fictionally by many writers,
several of them women. Judged by contemporary popularity and sales,
Gertrude Page in the 1900s and Doris Lessing in the post-war period have
been the most successful writers.[9] Page, who was married to a farmer,
claimed to have done as much to promote Rhodesia as Cecil Rhodes
himself. Lessing, a farmer's daughter, might well claim the opposite. Her
brilliant first novel, *The Grass is Singing* (1950), presents a dreary,
dispirited view of farm life. It is the story of an unsuccessful farmer and his
wife who suffer increasingly from isolation, poverty and depression, and it
culminates in the murder of the wife by the black house servant. White
Rhodesians found it hard to forgive Lessing for daring to suggest a sexual
tension/attraction between a black man and a white woman, and for
depicting in such stark fashion the decline and failure of a white farmer.
Page, on the other hand, romanticizes farm life in the spirit of a woman's
magazine serial. *The Edge o' Beyond* (1908) ran to the 380,000th impression
and was dedicated to 'All the women in the colonies who are roughing it
for the sake of husbands, fathers, brothers and their country'. Badly
written and unashamedly racist, it was dramatized and ran for six months
in the West End of London. Occasionally, amid the romantic, crude and
often offensive sentiments, an authentic note is struck, in the words of her
homesick heroine:

> I've never been able to take to this new land, I can see that it's beautiful, but
> after the sea it all seems so dead ... I can't explain it but there's a deadness
> about *kopjes* that almost hurts. (p.53)

The quality of farm life varied, depending on comfortable success or near
failure, and on the type of farming operation: maize, tobacco, ranching. It
was a lonely life; nearest white neighbours were usually several miles
away. Entertaining provided the highlights in an otherwise monotonous
life. Children had perforce to go to boarding school very young, although
during the middle period the Government established a correspondence
school for country children. Mothers had then to supervise their children's
study programme in co-operation with town-based teachers to ensure
sound basic education, but only, as a rule, to the age of eight. (Mothers in
outback Australia act as teachers under a similar scheme.) A readiness to
improvise was essential; in common with pioneers throughout history,
settlers had to devise novel ways of building houses and furniture, baking
bread, storing food so as to keep it safe from pests, and the like. Some
knowledge of that hybrid *patois* or pidgin, offensively labelled *kitchen
kaffir*, had to be mastered to organize domestic and farm workers.
Elementary home nursing and first-aid skills had to be acquired by women
to look after their own children and to run the informal 'clinic' which

farmers' wives held almost daily for workers and their families.

Because of the isolation, because farming was such a precarious occupation and failure and bankruptcy seemed often so close, the farmer and his wife were partners in the enterprise in a very real sense. Frequently ruin was avoided only by the wife's work with poultry, dairy and vegetable garden and the immediate cash which this produced (see also Brownfoot, this volume). Farmers were not ruined only by natural disasters - droughts, floods, locusts, epidemics of animal disease - or their own incompetence. Lack of labour could cause the collapse of a farm; workers would boycott a farmer for reasons difficult to discern. From observation it is clear that a wife's attitude to workers and their families could be crucial. If she handled morning 'clinics' and other encounters with patience, sympathy and interest a genuine *rapport* developed between the two worlds of white and black; a readiness to interest herself seriously in the health and education problems of workers' families was undoubtedly appreciated.

There were two other activities in which wives sometimes played a direct role. To serve and attract farm labourers, a farmer sometimes opened a small trading store on the farm and started a school for the children of workers. The store was an additional source of income and in some cases wives helped with the purchase of stock and the accounts; occasionally the wife might serve in the store herself. A school would be run with the support of the Government education authorities who would appoint and pay the teacher, the farmer providing the land and school building. In many instances the wife would negotiate with the education department and visit the school regularly, maintaining a friendly contact with the teacher.

Although farming families paid less attention to the social distinctions which were evident in the towns, there was an awareness of who should be included, and who not, at social events such as tennis parties and dances. In more recent years country clubs became the centres of social activity in many districts, and there was more social mixing than in earlier days when country families had to entertain each other in their own homes. Like attracted like, and each district acquired a certain social character.[10] Tredgold remarked on this in his autobiographical book:

> It has puzzled and interested me that so many districts in Rhodesia have so distinct a character. This district may be tougher, that more aristocratic, the next more Afrikaans, and so forth. I am sure that the explanation lies in the fact that the first people to settle tend to gather round them their friends and other like-minded people. The same trend, operating on a wider basis, may well have influenced profoundly the whole of the first settlement of Rhodesia. (1968: 51)

Hylda Richards, in her autobiography *Next Year Will Be Better* (1952), conveys accurately the tragi-comedy of farm life in which the farmer, his wife, the African farm manager and the cook play the lead roles. The Richards' were typical of many settler farmers. Their farm in Kent had

failed and a warm climate was prescribed for a delicate son, so their
relatives clubbed together and lent them just enough money to get them
to Rhodesia and a farm managership. They arrived with practically
nothing, but in due course scraped together enough money to get a farm
of their own. The next ten years were a period of acute poverty,
punctuated by a series of farming disasters; locusts, army worm, drought,
veld fire and flood. Hylda Richards wrote topical and funny verse for the
local newspaper, and the money she earned helped to save the family from
total financial collapse. Describing the start of life on their own farm she
wrote:

> We could only afford a minimum of furniture; four iron beds, six
> secondhand bentwood chairs, and a plain round table which was reduced
> because it had a crack in it. I also bought a chest of drawers for NKosi's
> [nickname for her husband derived from the Shona word *chief*] clothes.
> Looking back I can see no reason other than that of sheer stupidity for giving
> him the luxury of smoothly sliding drawers while my clothes lived in a petrol
> box cupboard. (op.cit: 22)

Of her loneliness she wrote:

> There were very few neighbours and I found them difficult to get on with.
> Looking back I think it must have been my own fault because I did not like
> Rhodesia. My heart was in England, but instead of trying to understand the
> people I was angry because they were not like those I had left behind. (op.cit:
> 29)

Ethel Tawse Jollie and her husband were more prosperous and secure, and
in her book *The Real Rhodesia* (1924) she wrote this of farm life:

> Of one thing there is no doubt, this is essentially a man's world ... but for the
> right woman - with the right man - it offers much that she would never find
> elsewhere, and notably a chance to prove herself a helpmate indeed. The
> woman in the back veld is, therefore required to be mistress of several trades,
> and by the time she has organised her household, ordered her flower and
> vegetable garden (on which she must rely for a great part of her supplies)
> looked after her dairy and her fowls, and done all the sewing for the family,
> she will not have many idle moments. She is, in fact, more like the virtuous
> woman of Proverbs than most of her sisters, for she is the loaf giver, the
> provider, not in name only, but in fact, and if she does not set her hand to the
> tasks her family will neither be fed nor clothed. (pp. 196 - 203)

A description of farmers' wives would be incomplete without some
reference to widows. When a farmer died, all too often he left nothing but
the farm as a going concern for his family. In the early days there were no
government pensions and no form of social security. A widow frequently
had no alternative but to run the farm herself, sometimes with a young
white farm assistant, otherwise a black foreman.[12] Mrs Jeannie Boggie
was an example. After her husband's death she engaged a European
manager who proved untrustworthy; so she took over the running of the
farm, describing herself as a *farmeress* in her autobiographical book *A
Husband and a Farm in Rhodesia* (1957: 197). With children away at
boarding school it could be an extremely lonely existence, with many

responsibilities. While the physical work was carried out by black labourers, the farm owner normally had to plan and supervise, arrange for the marketing of the crop and negotiate the complicated financing of the farming operation. The average white Rhodesian farmer was in debt for eleven months of the year; he or she borrowed from the Land Bank to finance the planting and growing of the crop and paid off the loan when the tobacco or maize cheque arrived at the end of the season; a month or so later the whole cycle was repeated. (Compare the situation of widows in Malaya: Brownfoot, this volume.)

Wives of Miners

Early explorers believed that they had found evidence of very extensive gold deposits in the rocks in Rhodesia. In the event these deposits proved disappointing; there were few major reefs, and none to compare with the Witwatersrand. Most of the gold lay near the surface and a great deal had already been extracted by the original black inhabitants and sold to Arab and Portuguese traders. Apart from a few comparatively large mines the *small working* became the characteristic mining enterprise. A *small worker* would develop a reef or deposit and when it was exhausted he moved on, ever hopeful that the next find would make his fortune. Many, indeed most, had no professional engineering or geological expertise; if they were unsuccessful at mining they might try trading or farming. When a miner moved on his wife, of course, moved too. The life was precarious; many of the small mines were located in the more remote and less healthy districts, often near low-lying streams; illness, malaria in particular, took a heavy toll especially of the very young and the old. Compared with the farmer's wife, the miner's wife had little scope to become an active working partner with her husband, and the outlets for her creative energies were more limited. It is difficult to find documentation of the lives of this group of women. But in a collection of personal reminiscences edited by Madeline Heald (1979) there are contributions by miners' wives and children which tell of their lives and experiences. Mrs Heald's mother, Mrs Coe, for example:

> was a beautiful, gentle woman who had never been accustomed to such hard living conditions. The African women were primitive, the nearest white woman was many miles away, and her husband was busy all day at the mine or prospecting. (p.72)

Later he gave up mining and they went to live near Bulawayo, but:

> after living nine years in the bush, with, at times, only her children for company and without any form of social life and feminine companionship, she became a very shy and retiring person and never really enjoyed the conventional social activities which were prevalent at that time. Attending sedate At Home tea parties, paying formal calls on specified days and leaving the customary visiting cards (one for herself and two for her husband), bridge parties, working committees and such like were not for her pleasure ... The memory and effect of those nine years of loneliness in her youth never left her. (pp. 77, 79)

As suggested above, many, probably most of the settlers were relatively uneducated 'generalists', lacking any systematic training or qualification in agriculture, geological survey or mining. In this they were probably little different from other settler populations like those who moved to the Americas or Australia although only a rigorous analysis of the social and educational characteristics of each group can establish this. As pioneers in a new environment they had to produce to survive and to improvise whenever necessary.

In addition to the women who endured the hardships of pioneering life because they had accepted the supportive role of wife to a farmer or miner, there were some who chose a life in the colonies for themselves. Mrs Frances Kennedy had come out as a single woman to visit an old school friend. She quickly married her friend's brother-in-law, a mining prospector, entered her new life with zest and enthusiasm and became a working partner with her husband in his various enterprises.[13] She recalls:

> For one whole year I never went into Bulawayo. I was miner, housekeeper, wife and mother and they were strenuous years ... My husband gave me £20 for my birthday and I bought a little mine with it and called it the B.P. and tributed[14] the sands. I made about £100, but every little helped. (Heald 1979: 190)

She describes being lowered down a mine in a bucket:

> I was terrified of a bucket and in fact of looking down a shaft. I was persuaded to go down between 75 and 100 feet - will I ever forget it! When I got to the bottom I was so impressed with the size of the reef that I forgot to go up again. (ibid)

Wives of Administrators

The administration of the African population was the responsibility of the Native Affairs Department.[15] Mrs Joy Maclean, wife of a Native Affairs Department Officer, has written an unofficial history of the Department and she describes the day-to-day life of officers and their wives (1975). These women lived under conditions which are closest to those experienced by Colonial Service wives. Their lives were broadly similar; they moved from station to station and from one government house to another, making their gardens and striving towards some sense of continuity despite frequent moves.

Social precedence in small outstations was respected. The District Commissioner's wife was always the *first lady*, and wives in general took their status from their husbands' position in the administrative service (see also Clark, Gartrell and Tremayne, this volume). Instead of sending their children to school in England they sent them to local schools in the larger towns. This fact underlines the most significant difference between Rhodesian administrators and Colonial Service officers; the former, though they may have been recruited in Britain, became in effect settler Rhodesians. Their working lives were spent in Rhodesia and there was never any question of a transfer to another colonial territory; in most cases they stayed on when they retired. The supportive role of their wives is described by Mrs Maclean:

> By entertaining and opening their homes to the local people, to visitors from Head Office ... to missionaries, hunters, traders and VIPs the wives and daughters of Native Department officials in the 1900s established the traditions which most Native Department wives carried on. Their cheerful ingenuity in making attractive homes and gardens ... must have greatly helped their husbands. (Maclean 1975: 137)

She goes further and suggests that Native Department wives contributed significantly to the genesis of a Rhodesian *ethos* and tradition which extended throughout the whole European population:

> It is impossible to lay too great a stress on the women of this era, for it was they who formed the traditions that are still held dear in Rhodesia, who brought up their children to respect and live for God and their country ... These women also very largely helped to lay the tradition of the old Native Department which grew into an extended family with deep bonds of loyalty and affection between the members. (op.cit: 198)

She also remarks that African messengers' wives were included in the family feeling of the Native Affairs Department (p. 263),[16] and she describes the setting up of *homecraft clubs* through the joint efforts of European and African wives.

Space: Physical and Social

Women and Space, the theme of a recent volume in the Oxford Women's Studies Series (Ardener (ed) 1981), suggests an illuminating perspective in this study of the experience of settler wives. The physical space in Rhodesia is wide and relatively unconfined; for women, the social space proved very limited. For many women the 'wide open spaces' seemed a void rather than enlargement of freedom. In Page's novel *Love in the Wilderness* (1907) the heroine, while still in England, imagined 'the glorious morning gallops across the windswept veld ... the sense of a wide breathing space all round unfettered by the pettinesses of town life' (p. 6) but found that the reality of farm life reminded her of 'one of those terrible prisons of the Inquisition that closed in a little more each day ... and seemed to mock her with vain longings and vain dreams' (p.81).

The most immediate reason for the limitation on their freedom which women experienced was the lack of public transport.[17] There still is very little public transport, apart from the railway, which whites would consider using. The towns spread over very large areas, and to cycle from home to the centre could be a matter of several miles; it was always regarded as unsafe for a woman to cycle alone at night.[18] Women were, and still are, cut off from a wide range of activities unless they have an escort or a car. Settler society, even more than English provincial society, very quickly became a community of married pairs. With the high marriage rate among girls it was difficult for those who remained unmarried to find a satisfying role-identity which did not bear the stigma of social misfit. For those young women who did not fit the pretty, non-intellectual, sport-loving stereotype so popular among young settler men, life could seem limited and depressing with the threatening prospect of lonely spinsterhood; this appeared more daunting there than in a country such as Britain with its richer cultural and recreational resources. In the early days, of course, and right through the middle period, there was a significant surplus of young men and the opportunity to marry was not lacking for girls; nevertheless some found themselves in the new trap of an unpropitious marriage. Mary Turner, the heroine of *The Grass is Singing* (Lessing, 1950) is a fictional example of a not infrequent reality.

Tawse Jollie wrote of this 'shadow' side of a woman's life in the colonies:

> When one is still young the world appears as an environment which can be shaped to suit one's own tastes, and unless it can be so shaped one feels that life is going to be a failure and not worth while - but it is not till youth is going that the failure will be admitted. Young women ... in Rhodesia or other new raw countries ... will have their pre-conceived ideas of the amount of amusement, sport, admiration or other distractions that are necessary for the filling of their days, and when they find themselves hemmed in by the inexorable conditions from which there seems to be no escape, and in which there is little variety, they have the feeling of caged birds. (1924: 193)

During the middle period, work opportunities for girls were limited more in scope than in number; there were plenty of jobs in offices, schools and hospitals, but few other openings. With the rapid increase in the white population after the 1939-45 war the social space for women widened in the sphere of recreation as well as work. Indeed towards the end of the settler period Rhodesia was remarkable for the range of cultural activities in which whites engaged; standards reached in drama, music and the visual arts were high considering the size of the white community.[19]

Domestic Servants

It would scarcely be an exaggeration to say that every white household, no matter how poor, employed at least one servant.[20] Every white women was an employer - somebody's mistress. The *Report of the Cost of Living Committee* (1913) includes a section which is headed *Extravagance*; among various manifestations of 'high living' the question of domestic servants is examined. Witnesses agreed that 'women always required a servant here' and a 'working man's wife' claimed that 'everything is so different, water has to be drawn, wood has to be cut ... it would be very difficult for a woman to run a house, however small, without help.' (p. 26)

The subject of domestic servants merits fuller treatment than can be given here. Are they liberators or tyrants? There can be no doubt about the tyranny that servants exercised unconsciously and sometimes consciously, as discussed also by Brownfoot (this volume). In most households the cook and house-servant jointly ruled the establishment. Members of the family were expected to get up early, be punctual for meals and be generally circumspect in their behaviour if good relations with the domestic staff were to be maintained. 'Difficult' employers were those who interfered too much in the cooking and housework rather than those who were merely strict. In another, more indirect, way servants act as agents of discipline over housewives; unless a woman knew and could explain household tasks and routine, chaos quickly resulted. Mary Lewis summed it up in one of her letters home:

> Other young women who have been reared in homes refined or luxurious shoulder their responsibilities nobly. They learn the domestic routine in order to teach the raw native; cooking and laundry and gardening have to be learnt before one can instil these sciences into the brain of the Mashona. The natives are quick to learn ... but ... in teaching them a duty such as turning out a room, no detail must be overlooked the first time, or the same omission will be repeated *ad infinitum*. (1960: 36)

As in other colonial territories in Africa (Nigeria, Ghana, Kenya and in Malaya, for example) house servants were almost invariably men.[21] In Rhodesia, African women began to enter domestic service as nurse-maids during the 1930s and in recent years have been more widely employed as cooks and general maids. The relationship between mistress and servant was one of the primary and often the only point of interracial contact for women. For the great majority of white women their servants were the only Africans whose names they knew; indeed they generally knew only the first name of an employee – which was often a 'name' (such as 'Sixpence') which had been conferred on him by a previous employer – and had to consult his *situpa* (pass or registration certification) to remind themselves of his family name. Anecdotes about servants are endless; usually, though not always, they are at the expense of the servant. We have heard much about white employers' views of their black servants, but little as yet has been recorded of the servants' opinions of their white employers.[22]

In the domestic context the concept of space, shared and separate, is again illuminating. Families occupied the identical overall space of their houses and gardens with their servants, but there were separate 'islands' within that space. In formal social relations they interacted only in the sphere of housework and service. The servants' quarters were always situated some distance from the main house; as noted, in the older parts of the towns they backed onto the *sanitary lanes*. The mistress of the house seldom ventured into these quarters, even for the inspection of hygiene and cleanliness. Servants on the other hand, here as in Malaya (see Brownfoot), knew intimately every corner of space occupied by the family. White children were adjured to keep a proper distance: 'Don't drink from the servants' cups.' (This was a serious offence; it was feared that some nameless disease might be transmitted). And to the girls, 'Keep your skirts down, don't let the natives see your knickers'. In most cases these same knickers would be washed, ironed and put away by the male servant. In the days before water-borne sewerage a visit to the lavatory was a public excursion for whites; they usually had to walk past the servants' quarters, often in dressing-gown and night attire, and would be observed by servants and their friends. Given white assumptions, it may seem surprising that there were so few 'Black Peril' incidents; this was the local euphemism for sexual assaults by black men on white women. Tawse Jollie wrote:

> compared with other countries with similar conditions Rhodesia has a good record as to *Black Peril* cases ... a good many cases which are sometimes called by another name are undoubtledly attempts at stealing in which the culprit, being disturbed, hides and is subsequently unable to get away, but when one considers the number of women who are obliged to live without a male protector it must be owned that the natives of Rhodesia have a good record in their relations with white women with whom they are brought into far too intimate relations. There is only one remedy for the evil as it exists and that is the employment of women as house servants. (1924: 276)

She claimed she was the only woman, outside a mission, who had a whole staff of girls in her house (p. 275).

What of *White Peril* cases? Did black fathers and husbands fear the seduction of their daughters and wives by the white men of the household? This diagonal in the square of black/white/man/woman relationships is seldom referred to explicitly by whites. Reliable evidence is difficult to obtain, but there were undoubtedly many extra-marital liaisons in the early days when the sex ratio in the white population was so predominantly male; and African women informants also suggest that sexual relations between white men and black maids were more frequent than is commonly supposed. Stereotypes as to the respective sexual attractiveness of blacks and whites, males and females for one another may have played some significant part in encouraging or discouraging sexual adventures.[24]

Women and Work

If domestic servants are to be regarded as 'liberators' some attention must be directed to the ways in which women used the time which was made available to them through this relative freedom from household work, although it must be remembered that 'managing' a staff of servants required time and effort. During the early and middle periods few married women engaged in paid work; in 1946 women formed less than 10 per cent of Europeans in employment. (*Southern Rhodesia Yearbook* 1952: 192) The impression gained from personal observation during visits at intervals in the 1950s and '70s is that younger married women have tended increasingly to work outside their homes as soon as their children were at school, and that former patterns of morning tea parties and afternoon bridge have been largely abandoned.[25] This process of change was greatly accelerated during the years of war and national emergency, when more and more men were called up for increasingly long periods of active service, so that women were required to fill their places in offices and on farms. *Profiles of Rhodesia's Women* (1976), published by the National Federation of Business and Professional Women of Rhodesia to mark International Women's Year, describes a wide range of white and black women engaged in a variety of professional, para-professional and commercial activities. These included administration, education at all levels including university, medicine, veterinary science, pharmacy, nursing, commerce (at managerial level), journalism and television; it contains, however, no detailed analysis of occupations nor any statistics which would indicate the numbers involved.

Settler women took with them the Anglo-Saxon tradition of voluntary service and 'do-gooding' so characteristic of British and American middle-class society (cf. Ardener and Brownfoot, this volume). Within the first ten years of settlement several charitable societies were founded; these were nearly always connected with church or synagogue. As early as 1897 the Jewish women of Bulawayo started a welfare committee. The Loyal Women's Guild originated in South Africa during the Anglo-Boer war, and a branch was started in Rhodesia in 1907. Its aims were: 'To draw together the various races, sections and classes in a common community and to band women together for their mutual benefit.' (*Profiles of Rhodesia's Women*: 154).

Whom were they loyal to? The Loyal Women's Guild was typical of nearly all the charitable activities in the early days; they started at the 'white' end of the racial spectrum and it was only later that the good work was extended to benefit first 'coloured' families and much later 'blacks'. From the earliest times the decline into *poor whitism* was regarded as the ultimate failure for whites, and voluntary bodies directed their efforts towards the relief of these casualties of the process of colonization.

Another, and perhaps more significant, voluntary movement began during the 1940s. Individual women, black and white, began to perceive the educational needs of African women in remote country districts:

> These women were usually those who, by the circumstances of their lives, were in close contact with the majority race in Rhodesia. Missionaries, African teachers' wives, demonstrators' wives, farmers' wives, nurses or doctors, were all made aware of the crying need of the African women to be taught the simple basic rules of hygiene and health in order to combat the dreadful child mortality and to prevent such diseases as malaria, dysentery, trachoma and malnutrition. Accordingly these individuals, in towns and in the country, set up classes and taught simple rules of health and such domestic arts as simple cookery, knitting, sewing and some knowledge of nutrition. (*Profiles of Rhodesia's Women*: 146)

The white Women's Institutes joined in the club movement and in 1947 the first Women's Institute Homecraft Club was established. A Federation of Women's Clubs was constituted in 1953 to co-ordinate the work of individuals all over the country. By 1975 there were about 1,000 clubs with a membership of over 20,000 women. This type of educational club for women was not exclusive to Rhodesia; Women's Institutes in both Kenya and Malaya (now Malaysia) organized similar activities for the local women in these countries. The wife of a Government forester living in a remote part of Matabeleland describes the beginning of a club in her district:

> One day I received a well-typed letter asking me if I would help the women in the *Insuza* (compound) start a club where they could learn to sew and cook. As my Sindebele is limited to understanding rather than talking, and neither sewing nor cooking are my strong points, I doubted that I could be of much use but having met the teacher's wife who could interpret for me I decided to have a try. To begin with the meetings were a little strained and the women shy and reluctant to give their opinions. If given some mending or sewing to do that was beyond them they expected me to be angry and stayed away from meetings ... It is mostly the younger women who come to these meetings. They enjoyed cooking and child care discussions most of all and I enjoyed them too ... In getting to know them and the way they spend their lives I have come to admire them for their fortitude, stamina, dignity and humour. In helping them with their club I have learned far more important things than cooking and sewing. (Farquhar 1974: 95-97)

A black woman interviewed in 1980 paid unreserved tribute to the work of the clubs; but she suggested that there was an element of 'maternalism' among some of the white organizers which gave offence, though not to the point of disruption. African Nationalist leaders, advocating the boycott of all such white initiatives, forced the closure of many clubs, especially during the war period. MacLean describes how, as early as 1962, she and the wives of messengers in the Native Affairs Department were obliged to close a club in the face of such pressures (1975: 263).

Related, but separate, was the Adult Literacy Organization. Here again an initiative was taken by a settler wife in 1960. The activities of the Organization covered the whole country. Modern educational techniques were used. Subsidised by Government, the staff is now (1980) entirely black, but the work is under the overall direction of an American literacy specialist.

The late Tom Mboya is said to have remarked, *à propos* Kenya, that the white women were the most dangerous enemies of African nationalism, not only because their sympathy and co-operation with African women blunted the cutting edge of resentment against white domination, but because of their tenacious attachment to the homes they had created. Certainly there is abundant evidence that whites held on to power so long and so stubbornly in the face of overwhelming odds because they believed their families' living standards and security were at stake. *Rhodesia Front* propaganda in the critical election and referendum of 1964, which led up to UDI in 1965, was directly aimed at the women voters. One of the most widely displayed election posters showed a picture of a white Kenyan woman leaving the family home in the Highlands with the caption: 'Do

You Want This To Happen to *You?*'. In a more direct way, women helped to prolong the conflict in Zimbabwe. Outnumbered as they were, the whites could not have fought the guerilla war so long and so effectively if the white women had not rallied to help guard and manage the farms, and to work in offices and industry to release men for longer and longer call-up periods.

Conclusion

The period of settler rule must be regarded as an interlude in the long history of the people of Zimbabwe. Throughout, the European community remained largely self-contained and inward-looking; however, no social encounters are without consequences, and it will be a task for future analysts to assess any enduring changes which might conceivably be attributed to the presence and activities of white women. Here I have presented a broad impressionistic view of the experiences of women married to settler men in Rhodesia. This has been documented by historical writings, official publications, written and oral reminiscences, fictional works and by my own personal observations and memories.[26] A more detailed analysis, with supporting statistical data, would be required to assess properly the complex role of women during the 90-year period of settler rule. Certain generalizations appear valid; the particularity of the experience and role of women in Rhodesia was dictated by (a) the geographical and climatic environment and natural resources, (b) the minority position of the whites *vis-à-vis* the indigenous black population, and (c) the unique constitutional position of Rhodesia in its relationship with the metropolitan government.

Town life has been compared and contrasted with life in the country on farm, mine and administrative outpost. In the towns the women were the bearers and conservers of what they took to be British middle-class social values and mores. In remote country areas women were obliged to assume the role of pioneer frontierswoman, to improvise, to endure loneliness and often material poverty. The sense of *Rhodesian-ness*, remarked upon by so many visitors to the country, was strongly reinforced by the women in both town and country. Women experienced a continuous, though socially distant, day-to-day relationship with the indigenous population through the universal employment of domestic servants, who were usually male; these latter became the unwitting mediators between the two cultures. The popular view that life in the colonies provided an escape from the constraints of English middle-class convention proved to be only partly true. English conventions were quickly replaced by Rhodesian ones, made all the more restrictive by the smallness of the white community and the largeness of the country.

The women's club movement provided new areas of contact between white and black women where specifically female interests were pursued. While it remained rare for true friendships based on acknowledged equality to develop between black and white women, the atmosphere in such encounters was generally less politically charged than in those between groups of men. The effectiveness of the movement as an agent of informal mutual education should be examined more closely. Once again, a significant comparison can be made with the distinctive situation described for Malaya by Brownfoot and for Uganda by Gartrell (this volume).

Politically, women were more directly active in local than in central government. Individual white women served as town councillors in most municipal areas. However, during the whole period of self-government from 1923 to 1979 only three women were elected to Parliament. During the latter days of republican government (1969-79) three women were nominated to the newly constituted Senate. Many were active workers and supporters in each political party and in this way they will have exerted some influence on policy decisions. At this distance in time one can only speculate on the direct influence of women voters in the 1922 referendum and in the critical elections of 1933, 1958 and 1962, each of which resulted in a change of direction in Rhodesian politics.

Accepting the original premiss that without the presence of wives and children on a continuous and permanent basis there would have been no true settled community, I have suggested some of the ways in which white women may have influenced and contributed to the structure of Rhodesian society and to the 'settler dilemma'. The intriguing question of how they have responded to Zimbabwe's independence and will adapt through the various phases in the future will be data for historians to come.

Notes

1. Mrs Marshall Hole arrived in Salisbury in 1892 with her small daughter after a journey which was 'a veritable nightmare of discomfort and exhaustion'. Before she died many years later (in England), she requested that the epitaph on her gravestone should read simply 'Pioneer of Rhodesia' (Boggie 1938: 63, 65).

2. Emily Moffat, daughter-in-law of Robert, arrived with her father-in-law and husband in 1859; and they established the London Missionary station at Inyati about 40 miles north-east of Bulawayo. She was one of several wives who came with their husbands to work jointly as missionaries before 1890.

3. Officers in the Colonial Service were not generally permitted to have their wives with them until they had completed at least one, and more generally two tours of overseas service; in the latter case this would amount to a period of about five years.

4. Foreign relations remained the responsibility of the United Kingdom but internal policy, save for certain specified matters, notably African administration, was entrusted to the locally elected representatives and their executive. Measures affecting Africans had to be reserved for metropolitan approval.

5. Mrs Ethel Tawse Jollie was the first woman to sit in an Empire parliament (not including the British Parliament). She was elected to the first Rhodesian Parliament in 1924.

6. I have so far been unable to find documentary evidence regarding the prohibition against women entering Mashonaland during the earliest months of the Occupation, but this quotation from such a reliable source as W.D.Gale

suggests that there was some explicit ruling on this matter. A young English woman, Fanny Pearson, subsequently married to the Count de la Panouse, disguised herself as a boy and came up with the Count at the end of 1890. Her story is told in *Countess Billie* (1973) by Robert Cary.

7. MacDonald makes a very brief reference to this initiative and suggests that the organiser was equally concerned with the morals of her native servants. To date I have found no other references to it.

8. Very soon the focal centre of Salisbury moved towards Causeway, and the kopje area became increasingly 'marginal'. Pioneer Street, which ran due north of the kopje, was notorious for a time as a 'red-light' district. Until a special suburb was constructed for them south of the railway line, the *coloured* (mixed-descent) community lived in the kopje neighbourhood occupying houses which had been built for people such as Mrs Lewis in the early days. The area was located on the margin separating white Salisbury from the *native location* where African migrant workers were housed.

9. Doris Lessing needs no introduction to the contemporary reader. Gertrude Page (Mrs Alec Dobbin) wrote nearly twenty novels of which twelve are set in Rhodesia. She propounds imperialist ideology and displays an almost mystical reverence towards the men and even more the women who settled in Rhodesia. *Jill's Rhodesian Philosophy* (1919), written in the form of letters from a farmer's wife to friends in England, is thinly veiled propaganda to attract settlers.

10. For a more analytical treatment of this aspect of white settlement in Rhodesia see Hodder-Williams 1978.

11. Groups of Afrikaans-speaking South Africans trekked to Rhodesia in the 1890s. Their history has been described and documented by Professor S.P. Olivier in *Many Treks made Rhodesia* (1957). They tended to concentrate in the eastern Melseter district and more centrally around Fort Victoria and Enkeldoorn.

12. African foremen and managers frequently played a very significant role in European farming and other sectors of production. Widows no doubt benefited from their knowledge and services, but would have had to accept ultimate responsibility for the management of the farm.

13. The hypothesis that suggests itself here - that those women who came out on their own initiative made a more positive adjustment to the challenges of colonial life - requires closer examination before it can be accepted.

14. In the context of mining operations a *tribute* is the proportion of ore or its equivalent paid to a miner for his work, or to the owner of the mine (OED).

15. The Native Affairs Department was established in the years following the Southern Rhodesia Order in Council, 1898, and was responsible for the administration of the African people. In the early 1960s the work of this department was taken over by the newly established Department of Internal Affairs.

16. *Messengers* had a more important function than the name would suggest. They were responsible for communicating Government administrative and policy decisions to the tribal authorities.

17. The advent of apparently safe, cheap and readily available public transport has made a significant contribution to the liberation of single women from protective male control in all advanced industrial societies; a fact which is sometimes overlooked. Brownfoot (this volume) draws a comparable picture for rural wives in colonial Malaya. However, urban wives seem to have been differently situated as regards mobility in the two territories.

18. Defying convention, the real Doris Lessing and the fictional Martha Quest appear to have cycled alone at night from one political meeting to another throughout the length and breadth of Salisbury.

19. According to a report to the national Arts Foundation on the state of the arts

in Rhodesia by George Maxwell Jackson under the title *The Land is Bright* (1973) there were '22 organisations for Arts in General, 13 for Art, 2 for Ballet, 8 for Literature, 16 for Music and 38 for the Theatre' (quoted in *Profiles of Rhodesia's Women*, p.137).

20. During the last decade there has been an increase in the number of households without servants. Modern flats and houses are often built without accommodation for resident servants.

21. In 1932 a Committee was appointed to prepare a *Report on Employment of Native Female Domestic Labour in European Households in Southern Rhodesia*. The committee was unanimous on the general desirability of the wider employment of women as domestic servants. Aware of the problems and dangers to which young African girls might be exposed in towns, it listed various possible measures to ensure their maximum protection and to reassure the families of such workers.

22. No doubt this perspective on the servant-mistress relationship will have been illuminated in some of the many novels recently written by Zimbabweans. These are not easily available in Britain and I have not yet had an opportunity to refer to them.

23. A.K.H.Weinreich in a paper delivered in the First Congress of the Association for Sociologists in Southern Africa (1973) comments on the link between domestic service and prostitution, 'which is not confined to Nucheke. Simone de Beauvoir recounts the same phenomenon in France.'

24. That white women were *attractive* to black men was, of course, a widespread assumption of racist myth. Current Zimbabwean writings will also no doubt shed light on this important question. See also Brownfoot's comments (this volume) on the corresponding situation for Malaya.

25. But according to an article in *The Guardian*, white women in Kenya 'still play bridge in the morning and tennis in the afternoon' (*Guardian Women* June 29 1981).

26. I first went to Rhodesia as an infant in 1918. My father, a mining geologist, had settled there in 1907, but returned to Britain for the duration of the 1914-18 war. I left in 1945, but return frequently on short visits to the country.

COLONIAL WIVES: VILLAINS OR VICTIMS?

Beverley Gartrell

> The form taken by women's oppression is not only historically specific, but also class specific. Within any stratified society it is clear that some women are more oppressed than others, and indeed some women may themselves be engaged in oppression (Bujra 1978: 27).

Introduction

Few women have been described so negatively as the British *memsahib*, referred to in one recent history as 'the most noxious figure in the annals of British imperialism' (Miller 1977: 46). Now that Britain's colonial empire has disappeared, recent historical studies are re-evaluating 'yesterday's rulers' of the empire, but women are almost invariably neglected in these accounts.[1] Even memoirs written by former colonial officials themselves often pay scant attention to the presence of their wives. The major written accounts of these women thus remain the novels set in colonial situations, and the version of the *memsahib* conveyed by novelists is often savagely negative.[2] Officials' wives are portrayed as narrowly intolerant, more prejudiced and vindictive towards the colonized than their men, abusive to servants, usually bored, viciously gossipy, prone to extra-marital affairs destructive to peaceful social relations, and cruelly insensitive to women of the colonized races.

In this paper I intend to bypass these fictional portrayals and look instead at the social situation of officials' wives, what was expected of them and how they tried to cope. It is a reconnaissance paper intended to open problems for discussion rather than to provide definitive answers. Attention to the role of colonial wives seems useful on three grounds. First, this case provides an extreme example of the difficulty of grasping the 'position of women' without placing them historically in a given cultural and class situation. Second, the invisibility of officials' wives in scholarly accounts of the colonial period makes for a distorted and incomplete picture of the social relations through which domination was maintained. The *memsahib* needs to be made visible and audible again if we are to understand that historical situation as it was, not as it has been fictionalized. Third, the colonial service shared certain characteristics with other organizations of the same generic type that are still with us, such as the military and diplomatic services, and even perhaps the higher levels of corporations. Some of these are examined in other papers in this volume.

Sources used here include interviews with colonial officials who served in Uganda, and some of their wives,[3] as well as published materials. One rich ethnographic document has been drawn on heavily: Emily Bradley, an experienced official's wife, in 1950 published a book of advice to young colonial officials' wives just setting out for Africa. She sets out clearly and wittily the normative expectations such women would encounter, mixing practical suggestions with ideological inculcation in the characteristic manner I experienced myself in Uganda. For I have also drawn on six years' experience in Uganda as the wife of a Canadian aid official based in Entebbe. When I arrived, a year after independence, many British official families remained; the old British social patterns were crumbling but were still discernible. This analysis applies specifically to Uganda, but we are probably dealing with generic cultural patterns of colonial structures, which showed specific adaptations according to circumstance and tradition within each colony.

Colonial service as organizational type

Colonial service shares some features with other organizations: the corporation, the military and diplomatic services among them.[4] In all of these, a predominantly male body of employees is hierarchically organized; at the 'officer' level, the total person of the employee, including his moral character, is assumed to be relevant to job performance; a high degree of loyalty to the organization is expected and is supported by an appropriate ideology; employees are subject to frequent transfers determined by the needs of the organization, rather than those of the employee. In the case of the colonial, military and diplomatic services, officers are also expected to see themselves at all times as representatives of their country. To varying degrees, ritualized social activities are considered to be part of the 'job'.

In all these organizations wives are personal dependents of their husbands, and are ranked *solely* in terms of the status held by their husbands in the organization. Their own personal attributes or prior achievements are irrelevant in determining this derived status. We thus can picture, in Eichler's terms (1973: 46), a shadow social pyramid in which women are lower in status than their husbands, but higher in status than men who are lower ranking than their husbands, *irrespective of the women's personal qualifications*. This status ranking permeates social relations among organization wives (cf. Callan 1975). Among a highly mobile population, it has the same kind of usefulness as age-set categories have among nomadic pastoralists: a newly-transferred wife can immediately know to which women she must defer, and over which others she can claim precedence, by establishing the organizational relations of their husbands to her husband.

These organizations also pose a common paradox: the wives of employees have no formal ties to the organization, yet the organization's senior members are not only seen as holding some power over them, but often claim authority to control or at least guide them.[5] Their behaviour may be regarded, formally or informally, as relevant to superiors' decisions on husbands' careers. These claims necessitate further ideological support to justify the extension of authority to those not formally members of the organization. Despite these generic similarities, the specific situation and purpose of each organization will affect actual social process and especially the content of the supporting ideologies.

Women and colonial service: Uganda

To start, we need to recite some well-known, even trite, points. First, the British colonial service was an organization adapted for ruling British colonies at minimal cost. The fundamental disagreements over the purposes of that rule are not directly relevant to this paper. Second, British rule led to the formation of racially-exclusive enclaves. It has been argued that in the Uganda Protectorate racial stratification, class divisions and access to real power are not isomorphic (Gartrell 1979). But this paper deals primarily with social status, so complexities of control of wealth and resources in Uganda can be set aside.

Until very late in the colonial period, Europeans - men and women - held higher social status than Indians or Africans, and within the European category officials as a group had higher status than non-official Europeans. The latter were mostly missionaries with related medical and educational staff, and businessmen who, along with some Indians, manned the institutions linking peasant production to world markets. The colonial state closely regulated the economy and was itself a major appropriator of peasant surplus (Gartrell, op.cit.). The life-style of the officials and their families was directly underwritten by this appropriation. The officials, of course, did not see the situation in these terms. A deeply-held ideology of service and 'trusteeship' provided a normative framework, often implicit, justifying their presence and allowing them to take their privileges and relative comfort for granted.[6] But this ideology of service pertained to the work of men. It did not, in itself, provide a rationale for the presence of wives.

Remarkably few Europeans were required to run the colonial economy of Uganda. The 1948 census shows 3,448 men, women and children, 0.06 percent of the total population. The European staff of the colonial administration - from Governor down to secretaries - totalled only 724.[7] They ran a colony roughly the size of England and Wales, with an African population of about five million. Thus we are dealing with tiny communities of whites, scattered over the colony, with concentrations only at Kampala, the commercial centre, and Entebbe, the administrative capital. The proportion of European to African population is not unusual for colonies with this type of economy. Armed force was available to back up British rule, but in amounts disproportionate to the population dominated. In case of serious disturbances, extra troops had to be brought to Uganda from Kenya.

In this situation the style of the ruling officials was itself a tool of domination. The impressive dignity and awesomeness of the District Commissioner was the 'front line' of rule.[8] More broadly, maintenance of a mystique of European superiority was believed to be essential to the maintenance of domination.

Political domination, very small numbers, physical vulnerability of the European category, combined with specifically British beliefs and attitudes, had several implications for officials' wives. First, this situation provided a rationale for the paradox of the organization claiming the right to control persons who were not formally members. A wife's lapse from conformity to accepted norms, especially in relation to Africans, or any behaviour seen as undignified if observed by Africans, could bring the reproach of 'letting the side down', weakening the prestige and hence threatening the position of Europeans as a group.[9] In serious cases it could be suggested that a wife who failed to 'fit in' would be better off living at home in Britain. While the more extreme sanctions may have been used rarely, knowledge of their availability would nevertheless have helped to induce conformity. The political significance of 'dignity' in a colonial situation thus provided a rationale for social controls, over both men and women, of an order different from those needed over the officers of a business firm or even of the military.

Women's contribution to the colonial system

But why should wives have been present in the colonies? Wives' fares, and the provision of housing more or less adequate for them, cost penny-pinching colonial administrations money.[10] Wives were not necessary for the physical care and feeding of officials; these tasks could be carried out by well-trained house servants. In the early years of colonial conquest in many areas it was not unusual for British men to establish sexual liaisons with local women (e.g. for India see Ballhatchet 1980). But once colonial rule was firmly established the presence of British wives was encouraged, in the belief that the services they provided offset the monetary costs of their presence. There were, of course, the nurturant and restorative functions widely ascribed to wives, who were expected to provide solace for the stresses of organizational life and to send their men back ready to work with renewed vigour. This function may have been especially important in situations of cultural isolation; on some one-man out-stations the wife was, as Bradley puts it, the only person with whom a man could discuss the day's doings in his own idiom (1950: 114). The companionship, the reduction of loneliness, the greater comfort of a home supervised by a woman, were expected to reduce turnover and increase officers' efficiency in jobs where experience was seen as essential before a man could be of much use.

But the presence of wives did very much more. They were representatives of the home culture, and of its moral standards. Their function, in this regard, was to assist in maintenance of the 'dignity' seen as politically essential. They helped to maintain 'civilized standards' in general, and specifically with regard to sexuality. In British thought, uninhibited sexual liaisons on the part of the male officials with women of the 'subject races' could lead to embarrassments, reduction of 'dignity' and political difficulties. The severity of the norms against such liaisons seems to have varied from one colony to another, and to have changed over time.[11] In Uganda such liaisons appear to have been frowned on, although they undoubtedly occurred. It was not 'immorality' that posed problems, for officers who chose to marry African women were, in Uganda at least, expected to resign immediately from colonial service.[12] The underlying cause for concern appears rather to have been political. First, once rule was stabilized, sexual liaisons could reduce the essential 'dignity' and social distance from the ruled. Second, continued involvement with an African woman was seen as a threat to the impartiality expected of an officer in his handling of the 'native races'.[13]

Thus the presence of white wives provided socially legitimate sexual relationships; it also provided a vocal group with a vested interest in maintaining norms against politically threatening male sexual transgressions. Women became agents of the external moral order - as Smith (1973) has suggested - *even against their own men*, specifically with regard to sexuality and generally in the maintenance of behaviour defined as essential to 'dignity'. The presence of a few 'ladies' in the enclave helped to keep all men 'up to the mark' and to prevent the erosion of standards involved in 'going native'. This function, although carried on outside the offices and represented on no organizational chart, was nevertheless politically relevant to the British style of colonial domination. To other colonial rulers with differing attitudes to sexuality, dignity, social distance and power, the presence of European women may have been less significant.

The politics of sexuality, in reverse, led to the conviction that white women in the colonies must be carefully protected from the sexually threatening African male.[14] In Uganda, this conviction persisted despite little confirming evidence. One police officer with twenty years' experience in Uganda wrote that ' ... the good behavior of the Uganda African towards white women was proverbial.' (Harwich 1961: 9). Nevertheless, this sexual fear helped, with other factors, to restrict women's independent activities beyond the white enclaves.

In addition to their customary nurturant and restorative functions, colonial wives were expected to maintain a certain 'style of life'. Only a minority of Government employees was actually drawn from the upper-middle-class; nevertheless the majority was expected to conform to the style set by this element, concentrated especially in the Administrative

Service. It took considerable skill and good management for the wife of a junior officer to live and entertain as expected, yet not overspend her husband's modest salary (cf. Bradley 1950, Chap.11). However luxurious their standard of living seems to us now compared to that of the peasants whose work supported the system, they perceived their salaries as small in comparison to those obtainable at home, the expected patterns of entertaining, and especially the post-war inflation of prices in Uganda. Nor could a couple safely economize by living quietly. Speaking of budgeting, Bradley said,

> Your club subscription is also a priority. It not only enables you to play games, but you and your husband are expected to be 'good mixers' and young people who sulk in their tents earn some justified disapproval. The part you play in the life of the community is as much the subject of scrutiny by your elders as the quality of your husband's work in the office or in the district (1950: 125-6).

The ideal wife was a gracious hostess at whose house people gathered after games, for drinks and, for the men, shop talk. Compromises were reached here, and failures of communication that had interfered with work earlier in the office were repaired. Sources of tension inherent in the structure, especially between administrative and technical staff, were reduced by this informal socializing.[15]

> There has been a great deal of criticism of the apparently undue importance attached to an officer's wife. But on calm reflection it must be conceded that in a mixed society, each section of which is gravely responsible to the other, it is important for an official to demonstrate not only that he can administer but that his worldly acumen is at least as sound as his professional ability. In this his task is made infinitely easier if his table is graced by a wife possessing some measure of tact, charm and a pleasing appearance. Many inter-departmental difficulties and personal misunderstandings have been smoothed out over a cup of tea or a glass of port after a well served meal that might otherwise have been detrimental to the service or damaging to a career (Harwich 1961: 5-6).

Another duty of wives was provision of hospitality for European travellers. In Uganda during the war years, the flying boat service using Entebbe as a way-station often experienced delays. The most important travellers went to Government House, while others were billeted on senior officials. Up-country, touring officers stayed with junior members of their department. In the postwar years the construction of the Entebbe Hotel, a chain of up-country rest houses and changes in travel allowances eased this burden considerably.

Yet another duty was adornment of official dinners, garden parties, and receptions. Wives were expected to turn up appropriately attired - gloves and hats at garden parties and airport welcomes, despite the heat - and were slotted into the ceremonial in the order of precedence of their husbands' rank. Much has been written about these rituals; they were, in British official thought, another of the tools of domination, creating an impression of majesty through pomp and circumstance (cf. Kirk-Greene

1978: 227). Whether these affairs ever impressed any 'natives' is moot, but they did provide opportunities for the rulers to dress up and impress one another. My evidence suggests that a number of women disliked the rigidity and pomp, yet dutifully played their parts. Others seem to have taken the rituals very seriously. Many commentators have noted the almost obsessive concern shown by some women over questions of ritual precedence.

As one's husband moved up in the hierarchy, new responsibilities were taken on. One very important task was the welcoming and socialization of newly-arrived wives, and transmission of the unwritten norms of behaviour. The conventional wisdom and attitudes to servants, and Africans in general, were passed on along with advice about cockroaches and why everything had to be ironed and how to handle the water filters. Awareness of the sexual fear, and of the over-riding importance of 'dignity', was transmitted together with advice on spraying the drains.[16] Few newly-arrived wives had had independent experience of Africa against which they could test these assumptions. For most, this early socialization would discourage any inclinations they had had for venturing beyond customary behaviour, and would provide them with categories and attitudes which would continue to structure their perceptions of the African world beyond the enclave. As Berman has pointed out with regard to the training of officials by similar processes of subtle example and informal experience (1974: 32), knowledge acquired in such a manner reinforces resistance to change. Senior wives were thus an important link in the perpetuation of the colonial social system.

Wives were also useful to the administration as a reserve pool of labour. In the small out-stations, many a wife pitched in to lend a hand in the office when work piled up, without pay. During World War II in Uganda, wives were drawn on in large numbers to help out, as reduced numbers of officers tried to cope with vastly increased duties (Gartrell 1979, Chap.VI). To some wives, part-time or full-time paid work offered valuable help for stretched budgets, and a relief from coffee parties. Such jobs were, of course, on temporary terms. Nurses were perhaps the most fortunate, for their skills were easily transferable and usually in demand. Many other women with professional training had to be content with routine work.

> What I am sure I need not impress upon you is your duty to do what you can for the good of the community, and therefore 'the good of the cause.' ... If one of the lordly ones [senior officials] is freed by you from some of the routine drudgeries of the office and can give his mind and his time to the creative side of his job, to travelling, or those contacts of which I have said so much, your contribution to the overall picture may be greater than if you were, say, weighing babies or district visiting on your own. You may thus find yourself a silent partner to *two* of His Majesty's pro-consuls, and *what more does a right-minded woman ask of life*? (Bradley 1950: 166-168) (second emphasis added).
>
> You are also unlikely to be given anything but a very junior post, probably

172 *Gartrell*

clerical. Any administrative or executive talent or experience you may have, if you exercise it at all, must be hidden under a bushel as big and dark as a tar barrel ... I need not remind you that you are even more unlikely to receive equal pay for equal work than you would be in England ... nor will you be let off any of your duties as an official's wife and hostess. If you are too tired at the end of the day to go out or to entertain your husband's friends and colleagues it will be a loss, and the subject of some criticism (op.cit.: 169).

From the point of view of the employer, use of wives as a reserve labour pool had many advantages: transport costs already paid in any case, no additional housing costs, employees' willingness to accept low pay and lack of job security and, as Bradley notes, to be 'put upon' in other ways, readily available in times of high demand and easily discardable at no cost to the employer in slack periods. The very structure of the situation ensured that government, as the main employer, could hire and fire as it wished often competent women whose skills, in a wider market, could have brought them much higher pay.[17] Official attitudes, the susceptibility to transfer, and the expectations of her as a wife and hostess made it impossible for an official's wife, no matter how well trained, to build an independent career. The best she could hope for was temporary paid work.

To summarize, the role of the ideal colonial wife involved several contributions to the British colonial system. British wives were custodians of the health and psychological welfare of the officials, representatives of the external moral order of the distant home civilization, sanctions against politically harmful sexual liaisons, facilitators of tension-reducing informal socializing, unpaid innkeepers, instruments for social reproduction of the system through socialization of the new cohorts who would in time replace them. In times of need, they provided a readily available pool of labour. Interestingly, all of these functions except that of sanction against harmful sexual liaison are explicitly recognized, and expressed in less pompous language, by Bradley. Her counsel is one of acceptance through understanding. She was forthright that colonial service was a man's world; the wife had a duty to keep her man well fed and healthy, and herself happy and satisfied, not for her own sake but because her boredom or unhappiness would detract from the efficiency of his work (1950: *passim,* esp.p.112). One must be a 'silent partner'.

According to this gospel, you must be serene, reposeful and silent, but also chatty and stimulating. You must be happy to be alone, yet glad to put everything aside and be at anyone's disposal. You must be interested in the work, and yet a refuge from it, knowing nothing and yet everything about it. You may shed the light of your charming personality on the company, but more often sink into a shadowy corner, still, anonymous and non-existent, concerned that these creatures are fed and refreshed, with everything arranged so that your triumphs are unnoticed and you are utterly taken for granted. You may be witty, but you must never be unkind, a repository of gossip and a spreader of none, fascinated by roads and drains and court cases all about a goat, indifferent to nothing but your own concerns. Does this seem like an echo from an older world of 'women and children last?' The colonies are still remote in time and space from the world you know in which husband and wife both have jobs, and both share the domestic duties in the time that is left over from wage-earning, as many of your friends in England are now doing. Your husband is 'the master', the work is his life. You really are going to a man's world in which you will be very much the lesser half of this imperial partnership (op.cit.: 120).

Don't imagine that your husband will rise up and call you blessed. Not a bit of it. He will take it all for granted, like all the other contributions to his purr of general well-being (op.cit.: 51).

Bradley, writing in 1950, realized that the war years had changed the conception of women at home. But an earlier conception had been imported to the colonies in the mental baggage of both men and women, and survived there as long as British rule, unaffected by trends at home. The elements of this cultural definition of woman's role as helpmate, subordinating herself and her interests to her husband and his work, were drawn from upper-middle-class home culture. But the intensity and longevity of this conception in the colonies can best be understood, I suggest, in relation to the extreme structural conditions of colonial service.

Smith says,

The situation of women cannot be understood without relating it to the family. Nor can the structure and organization of the family be understood without grasping how it is determined by the organization of the productive enterprise. It is the mode of production characteristic of a society which determines the existence of its members (1973: 5).

In this case we are dealing not with the mode of production characteristic of a society, but with the organization of work in one part: the specialized form of bureaucracy adapted for governing a peasantized people, for facilitating peasant production and the flow of goods to world markets, while appropriating part of the surplus to support itself. Obtaining and running colonies was defined as a male activity. For this task an unusually high degree of staff mobility was needed. The job stress created by isolation, climate, maintaining domination over people of other cultures, and structural strains within the organization, was extreme; therefore the need for 'sub-contracted' nurturant and restorative services for workers was also great. Thus the structure itself required that the 'sub-contracted' services be handled by women who did not themselves aspire to independent careers that could conflict with the mobility of, and reduce services to, the male worker. But the function of the ruling administration in colonial production did not in itself entail that the supporting women come from the ruling population. Indeed, in the early stages of British colonization, colonized women frequently were taken as mistresses and occasionally wives. It seems that specifically British ideological elements - their theories of how to maintain domination, racial exclusiveness, preference for social distance and so on - made it worth the cost of importing their own women as soon as conditions permitted. Unfortunately for the colonial service, the selection of women depended on the marital choices made by its members; there was no recruitment specialist with a penetrating and objective eye to screen candidates for suitability. The custom of class endogamy helped to ensure that at least some proportion of the wives going out had already internalized the definition of woman as self-denying helpmate. For the maintenance of the system of work relations characteristic of the British colonial administration required that it be internalized *by both men and women*. The publication of Bradley's book in 1950 is symptomatic of an emerging problem; before women's aspirations had begun to stir as a result of their wartime experiences in Britain, such a book explicitly setting out normative expectations and advising wives on how to cope would have been thought quite unnecessary.

The conditions of colonial life

The heavy normative expectations, high pressures for conformity and frequent changes of posting were, overall, greater than those placed on corporate or diplomatic wives, while the conditions of living were often incomparably harsher. In this section we shall look more closely at these conditions, and in the following section, the patterns of response that women developed.

Women who married into the colonial service obviously had to leave behind the daily support of kin and friends, the usual range of entertainment and cultural facilities, and the comfortable familiarity of the home environment. One woman said during an interview,

> ...I missed good music, books, going to plays, you know, the sort of ordinary day to day life of saying hello to someone on the bus ... The paper man coming, the postman knocking on the door, dropping into the village shops and having a gossip with all sorts of different groups of people ... but I found in Uganda we were all the same.

In an article of advice to new wives, a District Commissioner's wife wrote:

> It is essential for any young woman marrying into H.M.Colonial Service to have some interest or hobby to occupy her spare time ... I remember being perfectly miserable in a lonely out-station; there the sole [sic] Europeans were a doctor who drank heavily and took drugs, the District Commissioner, who was the doctor's drinking companion, and ourselves.
> There was no woman to chat with and I was used to a host of girl friends and a very busy life ...
> I took to wandering down to the Boma [Governmental Headquarters building] ... at sundown to watch the Police Askari lowering the Union Jack and another sounding the Retreat, a melancholy sound, on his bugle. I got a thrill out of this and tried to imagine I was helping to hold up the Flag in a British outpost of Empire.
> You want more than this to keep your spirits up during the first hard years of adjustment ... (Watney 1954: 38-39).

These quotations strikingly reflect the implicit assumption that rewarding social relations would be limited to the white enclave. Having lived in small colonial towns with an ethnically diverse population, these women could nevertheless say 'we were all the same' and 'there was no woman to chat with' because the cultural categories of the colonial system blocked perception of any possibility of companionship except among women of their own race and background. Language difficulties, especially in earlier years, would have inhibited friendship with Indian or African women. But the more fundamental inhibition was the 'We Europeans / others' dichotomy characteristic of British colonial attitudes.

Isolation, lack of cultural facilities and poor housing were most common in the early stages of an official's career, when he and his wife were likely to be posted to 'up-country' administrative stations. A three-roomed building with grass or tin roof and no running water was home for many young wives, although in Uganda, by the 1950s, housing standards on most stations were greatly improved. As development programmes led to increased staffing, stations were manned by three or four British officials, and wives. While often grateful for more company, some women found new stresses in the necessity of maintaining a veneer of sociability when thrown into close and continuous contact with companions whom one had not chosen, and with whom one might have little in common. On these stations the District Commissioner's wife, if he had one, was *senior* and expected to 'give the lead' to other women; however, status distinctions were de-emphasized and everyone was expected to 'muck in' and share in enclave activities and mutual entertaining.[18] Under these conditions deep friendships were formed, as were deep antagonisms. Both were apt to be disrupted by transfers.

Career progress for the husband usually meant moves to larger stations, and eventually to the administrative capital, Entebbe. Here, in a beautiful garden settlement, officials ran the affairs of the Protectorate, then joined their wives for golf at the European Club overlooking Lake Victoria. In contrast to the informality of up-country stations, protocol ruled in Entebbe; in the 1930s, people even arranged themselves at Sunday church services in order of precedence. Several informants commented that the 'official' atmosphere and concern with precedence was probably greater than in most British colonial capitals, for it was undiluted by the presence of businessmen and other 'unofficial' whites, who lived in Kampala.[19] The demands of protocol could be daunting to new arrivals. One man recollected:

> You take three visiting cards - two for you and one for your wife or something - and you must make absolutely certain that you call at a time that the person you're calling on is bound to be out, otherwise it's embarrassing for both of you. You wear a hat and a suit and your wife wears a hat and gloves. So in the heat of the day having carefully discovered at what time the Secretary for African Affairs (my boss) would certainly be on the golf course and his wife would certainly be in the Botanical Gardens, because they would know they were going to be called on - that's how the grapevine operates - so, choosing that time, we walked, because we didn't have a car, in the heat of the sun with hot sweaty shirts, hats and gloves, peered round the hedge to see if they were out, and they weren't. Something had gone wrong. But they

were obviously getting into their car to go out, so we hid in the ditch - suit, hats, gloves, high-heeled shoes, silk stockings and all. Then the car drove away and we stepped up, knocked, and said, 'Oh dear, what a pity they are out,' and left three cards. I am not sure we thought it was odd. There were those on whom you had to call, those on whom you could if you wanted to and those on whom you didn't need to. And if you got it wrong, heaven help you. (personal communication)

One English wife, frank about her lower middle-class origins, told me she had been 'absolutely petrified' by the other wives with whom she had first had to deal. The 'senior lady' at her first station had been a well-known 'horror' (see below). But many women found the severity of expectations offset by real warmth, friendliness and concern to welcome newcomers - as long as they showed themselves willing to adapt to prevailing norms.

Life in the colonies did offer these women one compensation that had become rare for most of their sisters at home: a leisured life with many servants. A new wife first had to learn to cope with subordinates of different culture, when both sides often had imperfect knowledge of a common language. Once the knack of management had been acquired, the resulting leisure was a boon to some, a threat to others. I made no systematic observations of the 'servant problem' - that never-ending topic of conversation in the tropics - but I gained the strong impression that some women *needed* inefficient service, and acted to ensure it, thus filling their time with the necessity of close supervision. Women busy with jobs, volunteer work or other outside activities, like experienced bachelors, seemed to attract responsible staff needing minimal direction.

What activities were available to fill this time? Decorating the home, a source of self-expression for most middle-class wives, could provide only a limited outlet. Standardized bungalows and the graceless, uniform, hard furniture issued by colonial public works departments set severe limits on creativity. Fine possessions did not long survive frequent moves over rough roads, or tropical mildew and ants. Despite the mobility, building a garden was an important outlet for many women, who learned to console themselves with the thought that other families would enjoy the fruits of their work.

Motherhood could fill a great deal of time, especially if one subscribed to the belief that competent African *ayahs* (nursemaids) were not available. But this deep source of gratification was also fraught with anxiety over health problems not experienced in temperate climates. Culturally appropriate schooling was not available for European children in most colonies. Therefore at a tender age children were sent home to boarding school, but needed care during holidays. As one woman told me, 'It was a constant conflict. I never knew where my duty lay - at home looking after the children during the holidays, or with my husband. We worked out a sort of compromise, but I always felt split.'[20]

Some women found personal satisfaction and filled part of their leisure time by good works: starting baby clinics for Africans, teaching literacy classes, Red Cross work. The organization of such charitable activities was influenced by the hierarchical character of enclave social life. Lady Surridge, describing her years as a junior wife in Tanganyika Territory in the inter-war period, recalls a desire to start programs that would reach out to African women, but she had felt unable as a junior wife to break with prevalent patterns, when the senior women had not 'given a lead'.[21] In post-war years governmental policy put more emphasis on welfare and development, and the leadership of strong-willed Governors' wives such as Lady Cohen in Uganda and Lady Twining in Tanganyika,[22] along with such senior women as Lady Surridge, set a new example. No quantitative information is available, but it seems likely that only a minority of women spent much time on such volunteer welfare services and inter-racial women's groups.

One might expect that these wives, many of them well-educated, could find much satisfaction in exploring the world around them by taking an interest in either African people or the natural environment. Some British officials, despite heavy work loads, developed rewarding avocations in amateur ethnography, history, languages, archaeology or natural history, and their publications often remain useful contributions to knowledge. However, serious enquiry by the leisured wives was rare. Part of the explanation undoubtedly lies in the sexual fear that restricted women's unaccompanied movement beyond the white enclave. But the prevalent definition of a wife's role did not include independent intellectual enquiry, even as a hobby. Learning was, perhaps, regarded as unfeminine. Bradley, a woman of considerable intellectual acumen, urged that some hobbies be developed, but still wrote of ' ... your sewing machine and his typewriter;' ' ... your knitting and his books' (op.cit.: 27). Hobbies should not be taken too seriously lest they interfere with the husband's needs.

So, aside from sewing, reading, and painting perhaps, women were expected to fill time left over from domestic management with the athletic activities believed essential to health, and the endless round of coffee parties, bridge games, Sunday lunches, picnics, dinners, amateur theatricals and so on at which the same small body of Europeans met day after day. But all these activities were subject to disruption when the administration ordered the husband to a new post. Younger officials often moved once a year, although more frequent moves were not unheard of. In addition, tours of duty of 24 to 30 months were interspersed with long leaves - four to six months - in Britain. Women with school-age children often split their year between Britain and the colony. This mobility was taken for granted; no one expressed concern for the effects of stress on colonial families. Yet recent research has shown that frequent moves contribute to depression in wives (Seidenberg 1973; Weismann and Paykel 1972). Vandervelde (1979) emphasizes the heavy stress on American corporate wives of moving on average every *five* years. Although colonial wives had to move much more frequently, the institutionalized procedures for welcoming and incorporating newcomers may have mitigated the strains somewhat. Thus the stress of frequent mobility was added to that of restricted facilities, remoteness from kin and friends, a 'foreign' environment, and heavy role-demands, with little outlet for autonomous activities.

Patterns of coping

It is too late for sociological investigation to produce quantitative information on different styles of coping with these conditions. In this section I rely on my own participant-observation and on discussions with many former officials' wives to give an impressionistic account. I suggest that, contrary to the picture presented by novelists, many wives were able to cope while remaining pleasant and well-balanced people. Their inner resources were sufficient to absorb the stresses, at a personal cost only they knew. Some conspicuously enjoyed their lives, and came close to living up to the role-demands outlined above. These I call the 'successes'. Other women were quietly unhappy, yet managed to fulfil their main obligations without causing family and neighbours conspicuous pain. At the other extreme were those women who acquired a reputation as 'horrors': some bullied their servants, terrorized junior wives, feuded with their neighbours, and generally made life unpleasant for all around them.

The 'successful' women fall into two types: 'participants' and 'domestics'. The 'participants' were often highly intelligent women who chose to sublimate their own interests and to identify themselves with their husbands' work. They were able to turn to advantage the interpenetration of 'work' and 'play' characteristic of colonial enclave life. They performed the usual obligations of hostess, listened carefully to the shop-talk, and often had a shrewd understanding of social processes involved. This style of coping-by-sharing is that recommended by Bradley, which she followed herself. But the wife alone could not adopt this style if married to a man unwilling to share his work with her, or unwilling to trust her tact and discretion.

My own department head's wife was an exemplary case. As the young wife of a technical officer, she had happily spent long periods living in tent camps in the bush with two small children. When her husband was promoted to head of the department, based in Entebbe, she set herself the task of assisting him to restore morale to a demoralized department, and to welcome and integrate the diverse aid personnel, as well as the few African professional staff joining the department in the immediate post-independence years. Her hospitality was warm, open and frequent. Her servants were treated with kindness and respect. She lived up to Bradley's norm: often witty, never unkind. Her shrewd understanding of the tensions within the department was hidden behind a vivacious smile and an ample supply of tact. Despite our differences in status and political philosophy we became friends, which would have been impossible in the more rigid pre-independence days. To my amazement, this paragon of efficiency and graciousness confessed, late one night, that she envied me because I had kept up my own work, albeit at that stage part-time and subordinate to my domestic responsibilities. Sitting in the dark, she spoke of her longing for some means of expression independent of her children, her husband, her 'senior lady' role that she filled so well. She had tried writing children's stories, but without success. At times she despaired of ever finding an *activity of her very own*, to fill that inner need. This confession was never referred to again.

'Participants' had the knack of treating what to others would be stressful discomfort, as adventure. The 'domestic' style of successful coping differed in that women confined their interests to the more usual 'feminine' spheres of home-making and child-rearing, without developing strong interests in their husbands' work. Compatible charitable or missionary activities were sometimes added. In my observation, most of these wives were active in church work. However, my knowledge of them is too external to enable me to discuss the relation of their religious faith to their capacity to create homes that were havens of peace for families and friends. The social identity ascribed to me, of an 'intellectual' and researcher, inhibited easy rapport with them, both while I lived in Entebbe and later while carrying out interviews.

While these women in their contrasting ways actively enjoyed their years in Africa, others managed to meet the main role-demands but were frank about their unhappiness. For example, one described her life as long arid stretches of doing flowers and formal entertaining, which she felt to be artificial.

> I found it much more of a man's life than a woman's life. He had this job that he was utterly absorbed in ... And of course there were endless opportunities for games which my husband was very keen on, very involved in ... It was a very worthwhile job for a man to do, terribly absorbing, absolutely overwhelmingly absorbing, but I found for a woman and an ordinary sort of suburban housewife ... there wasn't anything to do. I simply could not get excited about doing flowers or the Uganda Council of Women ... The housework was all done for me but it was a constant battle of chasing the servants.

Volunteer activities, so gratifying to some, brought scorn:

> some of the things I did, like the Uganda Council of Women, were so trivial and so ridiculous. One of the most amusing things about the Uganda Council of Women was that they built a headquarters in Kampala ... The whole idea of the Uganda Council of Women was to bring all the races together ... you know, running down to each other's houses ... The first thing we came up against was that we had to build three loos because the Indians wouldn't use the Europeans' loo and the Africans wouldn't use the Europeans' loo and the Europeans wouldn't use anybody's loo except their own.
>
> The Uganda Council of Women was supposed to help bring the races together. We would all go and demonstrate our crafts and we would be terribly patronizing to the other two races, show them how to bring up their children in the correct British fashion and sort of chatter ... generally sort of chivvy people.

One successfully adapted wife told me about another:

> She was my neighbour for several years. Even after he'd been promoted to
> Entebbe, she could not seem to get the knack of dealing with servants, and
> was always coming through the hedge to ask me to help with some new
> domestic crisis. The only thing she was really interested in was horses - and
> jumping ... After a while she started spending a lot more time in England
> with the children. (personal communication)

The ranks of these quietly unhappy women graded into the 'horrors':
those women who compensated for their misery by 'acting out' in various
ways. Real-life models for the bitter, status-obsessed, intolerant bullies
featured in many novels of colonial life certainly existed. I cannot describe
these women from intimate personal knowledge, for when I lived in the
enclave I avoided them.

It is important here to distinguish between the evaluations made by
those living within the culture we are examining, and those of critical
outsiders. Officials and their 'successful' wives would, I think, recognize
the typical novelistic *memsahib* as a reasonably accurate portrayal of a
certain type, which they themselves disliked and regarded as a failure.
During interviews, terms ranging from 'out of her depth' to 'difficult' to
'a horror' were used to convey subtly or openly the reputations earned by
some of these women. The grosser forms of bullying, such as losing one's
temper at servants, were not regarded as 'good form'. Even-tempered
paternalism, in the kitchen as in the office, was the approved style of
control. Alcoholism, vicious gossip, bullying of junior wives, feuding
with neighbours, or a reputation for extra-marital affairs, created tensions
within isolated enclaves which were disruptive to work. People used to
dread the transfer of such a woman to their community.

The perspective of the external observer

So far, 'success' has been treated as ability to cope with the demands
imposed by the norms of the colonial enclave sub-culture, expressed so
clearly in Bradley (1950). In essence these demands could be summarized
as 'being concerned with everyone's needs but your own', while
remaining a happy, well-balanced and giving person. The oppressiveness
of this definition of the women's role needs no further comment.

But all too often, in the colonial context, 'everyone' referred implicitly
only to other white people within the enclave.[23] Even the 'successful'
women are vulnerable to the accusation, frequently made, that British
wives were even more ethnocentric, more concerned to maintain a rigid
colour bar, and more concerned with status and protocol, than their
husbands (cf. Kuklick 1979: 122). Because research was rarely carried out
in colonial enclaves, solid evidence of gender difference on these points is
lacking. But the reports of many observers, both inside and outside,
cannot be lightly dismissed, and in addition we can see that the differing
conditions of life of men and women could well have generated somewhat

different attitudes and behaviour. Let us deal first with women's apparent obsession with precedence and protocol, often a subject of condescending scorn even among officials. Stories abound of long feuds among women started because of a hapless *aide-de-camp*'s error in dinner-party seating, or a mistake in order of precedence at some public ritual.[24] Most women clearly did take these matters much more seriously than most men, although some men too became upset at such symbolic slights. These people were living in a highly artificial society where the bureaucratic hierarchy of the work-place pervaded almost all public social relations, and determined allocation of measurable rewards: salaries, housing, furniture allotments, precedence. However, for many men the biggest rewards came from their work, from a sense of achievement on the job. Thus symbolic recognition of, say, a promotion by a more prestigious seat at a Governor's dinner party provided public recognition of achievement, over and above that already derived from the work itself. But for the wife, who had few direct opportunities for autonomous achievement in her own right, the dinner party placement became a symbolic compensation for her deprivations. One woman, after telling me of the frequent transfers, long separations and other difficulties entailed by her husband's career, said, 'But the first time I was senior lady, and the Governor took me in to dinner, made it all worth while'. Such rare and derivative symbolic rewards were all the achievement that the colonial system allowed to the wives who served it. That women who in other circumstances were more level-headed, fought bitterly for what they regarded as their due, highlights the artificiality of the social system rather than any pettiness inherent in women.

Allegations that the presence of wives had harmful effects on race relations take two forms. First, it was often said within the Colonial Service that officials had much closer relations with the colonized before wives and the organized social life of the enclaves absorbed their time. Kuklick (1979: 122-129) has effectively disposed of this view, arguing that it was not so much the presence of women but larger numbers of Europeans and greater ease of road travel that reduced the close contact of the early days of foot safari. Further, she points out, the greater frequency of sexual contacts of those early days is hardly a valid index of egalitarian social relations.

The second form alleges that after patterns of enclave life became firmly established, wives were more restrictive, more insistent on maintaining a rigid colour bar, and in general more ethnocentric than were their men. While, as in the first version, there may be an element of scapegoating in this view, there is probably some basis for this allegation. We saw above that wives were valued by senior authorities for their ability to maintain morale by creating the culturally familiar patterns of home life in the tropics. This attempt to perpetuate the familiar had as it obverse the exclusion of the threateningly unfamiliar, the foreign. The concern for health - one's own, one's husband's, and above all one's children's - contributed to anxiety about the unfamiliar, and unwillingness to venture beyond the comforting safety of the enclave. All of this was reinforced by sexual anxiety. The 'policing' of the sexual boundaries between the races was, we saw above, part of wives' political function in British colonies, and a function enthusiastically carried out by women secure in their own definitions of morality and hierarchy. Women's range of contacts with Africans was often very much narrower than that of their working husbands. Residential segregation and the formal, artificial chit-chat of such official inter-racial affairs as Governor's garden parties kept opportunities for easy contact to a minimum. Thus the fear of the unfamiliar remained greater for wives than for their men. Whether through fear or other factors, many women remained profoundly ignorant of, and uninterested in, the life of those beyond the enclave, and even resentful of its penetrations. The very heaviness of the role-demands may have contributed to this narrowness. To be successful wife, mother, home manager, hostess, mentor and guide to junior wives, participant in enclave entertainments, with perhaps a little volunteer work added on, could easily fill one's days.

But if women did tend to police the racial boundaries more sternly than men, this was a difference of degree only. We must not forget that both men and women came from a culture that emphasized hierarchy and exclusiveness; in the colonies, the criteria were merely altered to bureaucratic position and race, instead of social status. It is folly to think that race relations in British colonies would have been easy if only British wives had not been present, for social distance was central to the British style of domination.

Conclusions

The structure of colonial society, and the narrowness of enclave life, certainly brought out much behaviour in women that we now find unattractive. I have attempted to demonstrate two main points here: first, that the negative stereotype of the British *memsahib* conveyed in literature is based on an extreme type that was disapproved of even within colonial society. Those women who lived 'successful' lives by the criteria of that society remain largely unrepresented in colonial literature. Second, given the very heavy role-demands and lack of gratifications, we should not be surprised that some women acted out their resentments and became 'horrors' to some degree. What is surprising is that so many women were able to summon the inner resources to cope with the demands, and to live 'successful' lives within the constraints of their situation. I have argued that this situation was even more constricted and oppressive than for other women of their social class at home. Paradoxically, this additional constriction is directly related to their social function as part of a colonial system of oppression. For these women simultaneously enjoyed the immense privileges accorded to colonizers.

With regard to broader questions, it would be difficult for feminist theorists to maintain that in a colonial situation there could be a 'sisterhood of the oppressed'. In such a situation, the forms of oppression of women were so specific to each stratum that attempts by women to reach across the social barriers between colonizer and colonized inevitably had a degree of artificiality. Among the privileged colonizers, wives suffered from constrictions and forms of oppression specific to that element. These rather subtle constrictions need to be understood, I suggest, to grasp better the manner in which they fulfilled their function as part of a colonial system, a form of oppression different in kind and greater in magnitude.[25]

Notes

This paper is a revised version of one given to the Canadian Association of African Studies annual meeting, Guelph, Ontario, May 1980. My thanks to Arlene McLaren, Philip Stigger and Ian Whitaker for their helpful criticism of earlier drafts, and to Barbara Butler for her skilled help in manuscript preparation.

  1. Kirk-Greene's paper (1978) on British colonial Governors is a partial exception. He acknowledges the presence of Governors' wives in five scattered references and one short section. The rather negative comments of the first paragraph of this section are balanced by more positive statements in the second. Many memoirs give an impression of a wife as a ghostly presence in the background looking after the housekeeping. Conspicuous exceptions that convey a sense of the wife as active participant include Cairns 1959 and K. Bradley 1966 (husband of Emily Bradley, quoted often in this paper.)

  2. Some leading examples include the portrayal of European wives in Forster's *A Passage to India*, first published in 1924, and Orwell's depiction of Mrs Lackersteen and her niece in *Burmese Days* (1949). In conclusion, Orwell describes the niece as follows: 'Her servants live in terror of her, though she speaks no Burmese. She has an exhaustive knowledge of the Civil List, gives charming little dinner parties and knows how to put the wives of subordinate officials in their places - in short, she fills with complete success the position for which Nature designed her from the first, that of a *burra memsahib*' (op.cit.: 287). Further study is needed of the topic.

  3. These interviews were done in 1974-75, in Great Britain. The main focus was on the effect of officials' ideology on development policy in Uganda; material on the situation of officials' wives was gathered as a sideline. Further information on the approaches used and the sample interviewed is given in Gartrell (1979). Interviews ranged in length from one hour to four days. In many cases I was invited to stay, or was asked to share a meal; conversation with wives outside the formal interview setting was especially fruitful. I am deeply grateful to those who so hospitably shared something of their past lives with me, and to the Canada Council for the pre-doctoral fellowships that supported the research.

  4. Smith (1973) on the position of women in relation to the corporation, and Callan (1975) on diplomats' wives have been especially helpful in this section.

  5. Callan (1975) discusses this paradox at length.

  6. The complexities of this ideology, and the extent of variations among individuals, are discussed in much greater detail in Gartrell (1979).

  7. The influx of technicians and specialists in the 1950s raised the European population in 1959 to about 10,800, or 0.16 percent of the total population. The census data do not indicate how many officials' wives were resident. Figures are drawn from the *Uganda Non-African Population Censuses*, 1948 and 1959, in E.A.

Statistical Dept. (1953 and 1960), and Gartrell (1979: Table 7.5, 269).

8. Berman's discussion of 'prefectoral field administration' (1974: 27-31) has been very helpful to my own analysis.

9. This need to maintain dignity was mentioned by some informants as justification for maintenance of the colour bar at the European clubs. One said, 'We *had* to have some place that was just our own, with no Africans watching us. We really needed a place where we could let go, get drunk, make fools of ourselves without letting down the British raj.' On the discipline of maintaining 'privacy' and 'dignity', see also Kirkwood, this volume.

10. Officials were directly employed by each colonial administration, and conditions of service differed somewhat from colony to colony. For Uganda, wives' passages to and from the colony were fully paid by the colonial administration after 1937 (Jeffries 1938: 116). Jeffries writes that the principle of free passages for wives was widely accepted at that time, although some individual colonies, including Kenya and Tanganyika, were still providing assisted passages only (ibid: 116-117). Free or subsidized semi-furnished houses were provided for officers in most colonies.

11. Kuklick (1979: 122-3) says that in Ghana liaisons with native women were officially prohibited as early as 1909, when an official circular threatened 'disgrace and official ruin' to men who persisted.

12. Evidence on this point for Uganda comes from explicit statements of the norm during interviews with senior officials, in the context of discussions of two known cases where men did resign on such a marriage.

13. A former official, who had served in a colony somewhat more permissive than Uganda, expressed this point colloquially; 'If you dip your wick selectively, that's o.k. But if you start dipping it at large, you create a political problem. Your job is to manage Africans, not to be managed by them. You don't give anybody an opportunity to get a handle on you'. The political problems consequent on a young official's liaison with a Somali woman form a central *motif* of Hanley's novel, *The Consul at Sunset*, based on his own experience of the extreme conditions of the British occupation of Italian Somaliland during World War II. This novel is especially revealing on attitudes to women, both European and Somali.

14. The most detailed study of this topic to date is Inglis (1975) on Papua New Guinea. I know of no counterpart yet for British African colonies. My information is based in part on the informal advice given by well-meaning senior wives to new arrivals in Uganda. This fear was probably a factor contributing to the limitations placed on the employment of women in colonial service, a topic outside the scope of the present paper. An interview with one of the first women community development officers to serve in Uganda was instructive on the attitudes expressed by senior men in the provincial administration to the idea of women moving about in the villages by themselves. See also Kirkwood (this volume).

15. An interesting picture of the social life of an up-country station, and of the manner in which its few Europeans went about entertaining one another, can be gleaned from Dobson's novel, *District Commissioner*. Dobson had been an administrative official in Tanganyika. Tanner (1963), another former official, has given a more disenchanted account of life in such small Tanganyika communities.

16. Bradley says, 'Your senior lady will indeed probably mother you as much as you will allow her to do, and perhaps a little more. She will know when you are ill, and come and nurse you, and take over care of the baby, and feed your husband and order your household and keep your servants up to scratch until you are better, all without hesitation. It is to her that you will turn when you are puzzled or troubled about anything that crops up. She will know the local custom about servants and their wages, their food, and their maintenance when you are away. She will advise you about how and when and where to order your bulk

stores, and the sources of fresh local produce. She will give you seedlings and cuttings and slips from her garden, and probably a generous share of its produce until yours is established. It is all part of the colonial tradition, taken as a matter of course. The kindness far outweighs any tiresomeness you may feel that your private afairs are public property' (1950: 151). Bradley's book is in many ways a reduction to writing of the advice of an experienced senior lady, of somewhat more liberal views than many. Senior ladies had functions other than socialization, not discussed here.

17. Not all wives were permitted to take jobs. I know of one case where a bored wife wanted to take a part-time clerical job, but was forbidden by her husband's superior. Inflation at that time made it increasingly hard for junior officers to stay within their budgets. She was told her husband was sufficiently senior that there was no financial need for her to work, and jobs available must be left for wives needing the money: an example of senior members of an organization claiming control over those not directly members of it.

18. See Dobson (1954) and Tanner (1963).

19. The only 'unofficial' European who lived in Entebbe was the bank manager. For a short time, the post was held by a man married to the romantic novelist, Marjorie Warby. Her book *Senior Lady* (1944) is said by informants to be a remarkably accurate picture of social life in the capital.

20. Bradley (1950, Chap.17) discusses the conflicts involved at length.

21. Transcript of interview with Lady Roy Surridge, Manuscript Collection, Colonial Records Project, Rhodes House Library, Oxford. Quoted by permission of Lady Surridge.

22. Helen Mary Twining was the wife of Sir Edward Twining, who ended colonial service as Governor of Tanganyika. She had been a medical doctor before her marriage in 1928. She held temporary appointments as medical officer in northern Uganda and Mauritius, broken by periods in England with her children, and terminated each time by his transfers. Sir Edward's biographer makes no mention of her practicing during his gubernatorial appointment, but she continued wherever he was serving to take a keen interest in medical affairs and women's and children's welfare. In Tanganyika she organized the Red Cross and 'gave a lead' to women to get involved in volunteer work. On his elevation to a K.C.M.G., Sir Edward wrote, 'May who is very happy about it cannot get accustomed to being called Lady Twining and answers the phone with "Dr.Twining speaking."' (Bates 1972: 200). From then on her derived title took precedence over her achieved one.

23. This stricture does not apply to Bradley (1950). Her chapters on race relations are vivid illustration of the type of liberalism characteristic of some British officials in the post-war period: a firm belief in the superiority of one's own culture, combined with a willingness to accept as friends people of the 'native races' who could conform to the practices of that culture. Among women, a practical manifestation of this outlook was instruction of the wives of rising young African officials in the intricacies of British entertaining styles. It is easy from today's perspective to be condescending about this, but we must recognize the courage of those who often suffered sanctions for breaking the earlier patterns of racial exclusivity. In Uganda, attempts to open membership in the European clubs to educated Africans failed, right up to independence, even when led by senior people; the struggle over this issue left bitter memories in some informants. See also Tanner (1963).

24. A classic incident is described in the memoirs of Uganda's first Governor, Sir Hesketh Bell (n.d.: 123). See also Kirk-Greene (1978) and many others.

25. Jamieson (1981) has put forward a similar argument with regard to the divisions between white and Indian women in Canada.

MEMSAHIBS IN COLONIAL MALAYA:
A STUDY OF EUROPEAN WIVES IN A
BRITISH COLONY AND PROTECTORATE
1900-1940

Janice N. Brownfoot

Introduction: a Stereotype and its Sources

Colonialism of the British pattern was not only a socio-economic and political force but also a living environment in which various races were brought into physical proximity and symbiotic relationship. European women, particularly wives, played prominent and decisive roles in this cultural and racial interchange, and had extensive and permanent effects on it. Analysis of the functions and influence of the wives throws new light on the history of white communities in colonial areas and reveals new perspectives on the relationships between white and indigenous societies. As a result knowledge about the history of colonialism can be broadened and assumptions concerning its significance and effects may be redefined.

Published evidence and existing stereotypes of the wives would hardly lead one to such conclusions. The *memsahibs'* place in the British Empire experience has seldom been seriously studied, and conventional images of them are frequently unflattering. During the colonial period European men most commonly perceived the wives as a group: 'the ladies' or the *memsahibs*, who played passive roles and were acted upon, rather than having any positively effective or active functions. They have also been presented as objects of humour or ridicule, blamed for the presumed progressive loss of white prestige after the turn of the century, sometimes maligned for supposedly widening the gap between the races, and also criticized for behaviour considered inappropriate in a race said to be superior. 'All the *mems* did in Malaya was play bridge and fornicate', one technical officer has stated (T.S. in interview with Mrs Corrie, February 1981). As with all myths and stereotypes there is a degree of truth in these representations, but the reality was far more complex.

The need for scholarly research into this topic was crystallized for me after watching some television dramas based on W. Somerset Maugham's stories set in the Malaya of the 1920s. It is partly due to Maugham that certain stereotypical images of the *memsahibs* still survive, but it is also partly due to him that in the inter-war era Malaya became 'fashionable', resulting in a flurry of publications including guide-books, travellers' accounts and popular literature. Thus were created some of the enduring pictures of whisky-swilling planters, and bored, empty-headed, flirtatious *mems*. Such sources, together with other contemporary literature, tend to confirm and reinforce the long-standing images of popular mythology that parallel closely those of the *memsahibs* in novels about India, portraying distinctive, but seldom attractive, character types.

A Note on Sources and Method

The material used here forms part of my wider research on white female society in colonial Malaya during the nineteenth and twentieth centuries.[1] Discovering the story of the *memsahibs* and presenting it from their own perspective has posed novel and fascinating challenges. Locating and gaining access to relevant source materials has been difficult, as much invaluable evidence (for example diaries, photographs and letters) was lost, looted or destroyed during the Japanese bombing and occupation of the region from late 1941 until 1945. Few authentic records by women remain from the early days; the evidence that does exist is geographically scattered, fragmentary and often contradictory. Many types of material have been consulted, making this a necessarily multi-disciplinary endeavour.[2]

To challenge the unbalanced images drawn by men and to enable the women to tell their own story, I collected first-hand evidence from extensive oral interviews and questionnaires with a range of former Malayan residents, male as well as female. Such evidence itself raises many problems owing to divergent opinions, contradictory information and a clear-cut dichotomy between men's views about the women and the women's views about themselves. The diversity of the evidence has shown that the exceptions are just as important as the generalities. I generalize in this paper, then, where there has been an acceptable majority of emphasis, or an overwhelming ideological consensus, even where there were some exceptions.[3]

Historical Background

In sketching the historical background to this study three main periods of European involvement can be usefully distinguished. The first is the era from the 1780s to the late 1880s when Europeans moved into the region and established domination and control. The second can be dated from around 1890 to the end of World War I, which formed an important watershed. The numbers of Europeans resident during this period increased rapidly, numerous commercial enterprises were established and expanded, rubber and tin boomed, and administrative control was extended and consolidated in the hands of the nascent Malayan Civil Service. Finally, there is the brief but crucially important inter-war period, characterized by economic slumps and booms, technological change, and the alternate influxes and outpourings of numbers of Europeans as the country's economic fortunes fluctuated, until, in December 1941, the opening of the Pacific War marked the beginning of the end of white colonialism. The bulk of this paper is concerned, of necessity. with the last two periods, mainly the latter.

While Singapore was colonized by commerce the Malay States were initially colonized primarily by Government servants who claimed to be acting in the best interests of the Malay population. They, like most Victorians, believed in the value of progress and of the spread of Western civilization. As in Rhodesia (see Kirkwood, this volume), the primary occupations of many of the early Europeans were in agriculture and mining, but in the Straits Settlements and subsequently in the main towns of the Peninsula and of Borneo business activities, service industries and professional occupations soon became far more important in numbers employed, although not in terms of revenue raised. European involvement thus brought many more commercial people relative to civil servants than in other parts of the Empire under the political status of colony and protectorate, not that of settler dominion.

Europeans nonetheless lived in circumstances generally similar to those of their contemporaries throughout the British Empire, the closest parallel being India. Some similarities are described in this volume by Gartrell (for Uganda) and Kirkwood (for Rhodesia). However, most Europeans living there thought Malaya special, if not unique; certainly there were differences from other dependencies deriving from Malaya's particular geography and colonial situation. Resident Europeans developed a very real sense of Malayan identity, although few ever viewed themselves as settlers. Indeed, they were commonly described as 'birds of passage', 'pale strangers', so that even the many who fell in love with the country were influenced by 'a ridiculous convention [which] invariably persuades them to describe this vivid, happy and satisfying period of their lives as "exile"' (Ransom 1969: 132). The most important causal factor here was the belief that Malaya's hot wet climate made it environmentally unsuitable for permanent white settlement.

Wives were expected to conform to such perceptions about long-term European involvement in the area, and were accorded functions appropriate to the circumstances. For example, they did not sever their ties with the Mother Country unlike settlers in Rhodesia (Kirkwood, this volume); on the contrary they maintained and reinforced links with 'Home' while also developing a sense of identity with and roots in Malaya. They had to adapt to a lifestyle that was at once pioneering (in some parts even up to the Second War) and provincial, exotic and conformist, in which Europeans were big fish in a small pond, but were also considered by some observers to be 'second-rate people in a first-rate country'.

Wives as a distinct group

The European community always made up less than 1 percent of the total population; but from 1901 it experienced fairly steady, generally consistent, internal growth (particularly in the two decades to 1921) with a considerable increase in the total number of females. It was also demographically unbalanced and unnatural, consisting largely of adults between the ages of twenty and fifty, with many more men than women, and very few children over the age of seven. Most adult females were wives or widows, the majority engaged in household duties. The male attitude towards the importance of this occupation was summed up by a leader concerning the census in the *Straits Times* of 2 March 1911 which stated baldly 'No entry need be made for women engaged in domestic duties at home' – an incidental illustration of the researcher's difficulties.

There were also some single women in Malaya who were potential or prospective wives, many of them consciously seeking husbands. Single working women who went out on their own initiative, mostly as teachers or nurses, never formed more than a small percentage of the total female group, but in company with the 'fishing fleet' which, as in India, arrived annually on holiday in search of husbands, they constituted an informal marriage market. Although there were always a few who, for various reasons, never married, single women were generally under considerable pressure to become wives so that they would fit into the established community hierarchy.

Since the European community as a whole identified itself first and foremost by skin colour, this feature clearly divided the European wives from their Asian and Eurasian counterparts, apart from the few Eurasian women who might have 'passed' as white. (There was in fact very little 'passing' in the South African sense in Malaya, as the Eurasians tended to form their own united, endogamous and separate community.) European wives also felt a sense of Malayan identity *vis-à-vis* their contemporaries in other parts of the Empire and in metropolitan society simply by virtue of their geographical segregation, and the particular socio-economic and political circumstances in which they lived reinforced this physical separateness. The functions and contributions of wives also helped create for them a corporate identity since marriage itself pre-determined their roles, which in turn were reinforced by the special characteristics attributed to women generally and to wives in particular.

The 'Civilizing Mission' and the Significance of Marriage

The Victorians believed that white women carried with them to colonial territories as part of their personal 'baggage' civilizing influences thought to be beneficial to white men, the European communities and the British Empire. In an alien, seemingly decadent tropical world of heat, luxuriant vegetation, diseases and 'strange, heathen customs', the community's bungalows and clubs were oases of European civilization to which wives and families brought normality, giving their menfolk also a sense of stability and purpose. In the twentieth century the importance of this civilizing mission remained.

The significance of the mission was irrevocably bound to the assumption of white supremacy. Convinced that they were imperial rulers because it was their destiny as an inherently superior race, whites believed that they must maintain their prestige and a privileged position amongst the subject races which they ruled. Western civilization and standards must be defended and the community must remain united and white. Wives were intrinsic to this maintenance and defence. By producing pure-bred children, recreating metropolitan domestic and social life, and enforcing a social distance between Asian subjects and their colonial rulers, wives were to underline the European sense of a common Caucasianism, while also establishing more decorous, orderly, conformist communities than those of pioneering conditions. When, at the end of the nineteenth century, it appeared that European prestige was declining, the importation of wives seemed to many a logical solution for halting this decline.

In fact the characteristics of conventionality and morality commonly attributed to wives - and often mocked - were virtues useful to colonialism. The anonymous, presumably male, author of the 1907 *Guide to Singapore* (p. 6) waxing lyrical about the daintily-clad European lady whom one could see out strolling in Singapore town, comments that

> One reflects with pride ... that such as she are the mothers of the proud sons who impose the restraints and excitements of Empire upon the millions of these dark races of the earth.

Evidence indicates that men actually took greater care of themselves, their language and their surroundings in the presence of wives. Informants such as Miss Lillian Newton (see note 7) lived in Singapore from 1895 until 1925, and Dr Cicely Williams (interview, September 1975) who went out in 1938, have confirmed that European men were sartorially more correct, better behaved and more polite with *mems* present. According to Miss Newton, and others, wives stabilized both the community and its standards and in so doing helped prevent white men from going 'troppo' (mental) or 'native', or becoming alcoholics, behaviour which 'let the side down' and compromised white prestige. If a man had begun a degenerative decline, however, popular opinion endorsed the belief that his best means of salvation was to go 'Home' and find a suitable European wife. Somerset Maugham's story 'Before the Party' illustrates the point clearly.

Yet despite the pre-eminence attributed to them in the maintenance of 'civilized' standards, and although the desirability and advantages of marriage were not questioned, wives were not wholeheartedly approved of. Most white men's attitudes to wives were distinctly ambivalent, and have been succinctly summed up by a married Army officer: *mems* were, he has stated, 'necessary nuisances' (interview with Colonel Hayes-Palmer, February 1981). It is not difficult to understand this viewpoint when we consider what marriage involved, and its effects; some brief comments are therefore in order.

The Circumstances and Effects of Marriage

As a ruling elite all Europeans were expected to maintain high standards of living. 'Poor whitism' was feared and condemned for the unedifying image it created of the white man. A man had necessarily to expend a large proportion of his salary to maintain such living standards; a wife, and any subsequent family, pushed expenditure considerably higher, but when money was available marriage was popular. 'Now that everybody has been making a small fortune in rubber', wrote government cadet Alan Baker to his mother from Malacca, 'there is the inevitable mania for matrimony.' (letter of 20 October 1910). The Western image of the 'ideal' wife, devoted to home and family, professionally unambitious and 'economically unproductive', prevailed in Malaya even in the inter-war period; Europeans there, as in India, were slow to recognize 'the modern advance in the intellectual and social position of women' (Diver 1909: 25). As a result of this ideal and of the considerable restrictions imposed by the 'marriage bar', together with the limited opportunities available, very few wives took salaried work outside the home in the decades before the Second World War. Their husbands would not allow it. Thus as Ward-Jackson affirms, quoting the Bucknill Report of 1919, 'Marriage necessarily entails in Malaya a very much greater proportionate increase in expenses than it does in Great Britain' (1920: 16).

Since the possession of a wife was both significant and costly, it is not surprising to find that most employers put restrictions on when their employees could acquire one, by maintaining what cartoonist Denis Santry called in 1920 the 'curious habit of forbidding their employees to marry until they earn a certain salary.' (1920: 46). This could seldom be attained before the age of thirty, at least until the inter-war years.[4] But there was also a general belief that men should be able to marry younger to help normalize the white community's sex ratio, and to alleviate many of the social problems – including those of Asian mistresses, prostitution and venereal disease – which were thought to result from artificially delaying marriage in healthy young men. In common with accepted practice throughout the Empire, and until he could afford a white *mem*, a man often maintained an Asian mistress. Usually known as a 'keep' or more euphemistically as a 'bed-book' or 'bed-dictionary', she might be Malay, Chinese, Indian, Eurasian, Japanese or Siamese. But very few men ever married their 'keeps' or any other Asian women. Despite rosy myths to the contrary, antagonism to inter-racial marriage had always been greater than acceptance, even in the pioneering days of the nineteenth century. By the turn of the twentieth century a man found that marriage to a white wife was necessary for his promotion prospects, for social acceptability and to assist in maintaining the separateness and colonial ethos of the ruling white community. A European who married an Asian woman at the very least prejudiced his future career and was likely to be dismissed or sent home. Very few took the chance.

Once a *mem* was attained, the 'keep' was usually rejected, often simply told to go, but sometimes pensioned off, depending on the scruples of the individual. If there were any children from the relationship they might be provided for, but were sometimes simply abandoned. Evidence on this subject is understandably difficult to obtain, but Mrs Mary Hodgkin records the case of one child, the daughter of an English planter and a Malay mother, whom the father had 'left high and dry because he has got him an English wife! - [so] no one wants her'. As he would do nothing for the girl, Miss Josephine Foss, Headmistress of Pudu Girls' English School in Kuala Lumpur, paid for her to go to boarding school in Singapore (Hodgkin, letters of 20 January and 18 March 1932).

The exalted, pedestal status which European wives enjoyed was underlined by the preferential manner in which they were treated by contrast with Asian and Eurasian women. European women, whether married or single, were part of the elite simply by virtue of their race, irrespective of their class origins and social backgrounds. All such women enjoyed a 'scarcity' value, but single women were a particularly highly prized resource; each could afford to be discriminating about a marriage partner, having a statistical choice from about six bachelors. Being female was enough, irrespective of attractive looks, bright personality or intellectual abilities, although the woman who possessed these multiplied her choices of a husband. Once a white woman married she took her status from her husband and, as men defined the position and functions of wives, the obligations and duties expected of her altered accordingly. Even the honorific changed: wives as a group were called '*Memsahibs*', a generic title borrowed from India, while each individual wife was called '*mem*' by servants, other subordinates and most adult whites; a single woman was generally called 'Missie' whatever her age.

The general effects of marriage were similar for all wives, although they varied in detail. A wife was not a leader but a supporter whose duties were to 'pack and follow' wherever her husband and his work led, and to 'fit in'. The rules for wives as men delineated them were summed up by one *mem* as 'Everybody does this, nobody does that' (Keith 1954: 51). Since their social position in their own community and in the eyes of the Asian communities derived from their marital status, few wives disputed (at least openly) their accorded place or the roles and advantages which went with this, despite its numerous restrictions on their freedom of action. Indeed, notwithstanding the constraints and the negative male attitudes, the majority of *mems* would probably have agreed that the advantages they enjoyed in Malaya made the country what one businessman's wife has called 'a paradise on earth' (Mrs V. Kitserow; interview August 1973).

Informants have agreed that the greatest of these advantages was the high standard of living. By going to Malaya many wives had, like their husbands, improved their social and economic position. Some of these *mems* are described in Somerset Maugham's short stories, while Maugham himself, writing in 1929 about planters' wives in *A Writer's Notebook* (1967 ed: 217) has recorded the somewhat spiteful comment that at home most of them 'instead of having a house with plenty of servants and a motor car, would ... be serving behind a counter.' Mrs Hodgkin, remarking in 1932 on the wonderful wedding presents given to one couple, says of the wife how funny it was to see 'that common little woman owning things that one would only see in a real aristocrat's old home in England.' (Hodgkin, letter of 12 February 1932).

Wives in rural areas

We now look briefly at the living conditions of two groups of wives. Urban dwellers often referred condescendingly to those living 'up-country', 'out-station' or 'in the Ulu' (jungle), while country-dwellers maintained that urbanites, particularly those in Singapore, lived in artificial environments, knew little or nothing of the Asian scene, and were out of touch with the realities of a *truly pioneering* existence where the real individualists and the few eccentrics of European society were to be found. However in really isolated locations European social relations could be problematical. According to Malayan civil servant Victor Purcell, trivial frictions might develop over 'whether Mrs X had received her mail before Mrs Y'. He argues, with scant evidence, that in these conditions 'the centre of all emotion and potential trouble was, naturally, the European ladies ... ' (Purcell 1965: 182, 183, 192). Yet totally isolated wives, like those of the managers of tobacco estates in Sabah in the 1920s, may well have appreciated some opportunities for friction and trouble. The life was 'a loneliness of soul and mind. You longed for your own kind to chat with' (interview with Mrs Florence White, May 1972; see also Kirkwood, this volume).

Even in 1927 fortitude and a sense of humour were necessary, as Mrs Alice Berry Hart's account of life in the Malayan rubber reveals. During her first week of housekeeping in her flimsy rat-infested home, she 'felt desperately that we had everything in our bungalow except the essentials - no running water, no sinks, no proper ice-box.' There were other frustrations: the cooking arrangements were primitive and cockroaches invaded the food, while drinking water had to be double filtered and boiled and furniture disinfected weekly. Yet there were compensations to living on the estate, not least of which was the triumph she felt 'in maintaining a household routine in spite of difficulties.' (A.B[erry] H[art], 1927: 598-99, 600-1, 606). For many, difficulties remained, even in the 1930s. Mrs Hodgkin, writing in September 1931 of a rubber estate area at Kapar about forty miles from Kuala Lumpur, was convinced that 'It must be terrible. The outlook is mud, the atmosphere is steam and the fauna is mosquitoes.' (letter of 25 September 1931). Another estate she visited had elephants, tigers and crocodiles on it, and two months earlier 'the man with the wages for the coolies was held up by bandits!!!!' (letter of 24 December 1931).

During the inter-war years some estate wives remained isolated, particularly if transport was a problem. In the early days of the twentieth century wives frequently used to journey to each other or the nearest town by bullock-cart. By the 1920s most planters owned a car, but a wife's access to this was dependent on estate requirements. Although white women could ride horses, bicycle, or walk alone anywhere in Malaya in complete personal safety, distances were normally too great to enable easy social mixing, and some women were understandably fearful of snakes, tigers and other jungle creatures. Overall, therefore, planters' wives led fairly restricted social lives. To be involved in the more formal social round of the government *mems*, they had to go and write their names in 'The Book' at Government House or the Residency - according to one informant few planters' wives bothered to do so.

Government Officers' Wives
Social life for Government wives was indeed more formal than it was for wives of planters: it was also mobile and nomadic, with periodic transfers around the country as their husbands were posted, sometimes out-station, sometimes in a capital town. Seldom would a couple stay in any house longer than two years without a break. 'You have to take the life as you find it and be ready to flit at the first order. Make your career a home, and not a bungalow.' (Baker, letter of 26 June 1913). The career could be exciting: one Government surveyor's wife, resident in Malaya since before the 1914-18 war, had experienced a life 'of many adventures mostly featuring tigers and crocodiles' (Hodgkin, letter of 24 July 1931). As her husband became more senior a wife's living conditions usually got 'posher', with more modern conveniences as she moved to urban areas. The housing experiences of one *mem*, who went to Malaya in 1925 as a nursing sister and married a Government agricultural officer in 1927, are typical. The house in which she and her husband first lived out-station in the state of Pahang had only a Shanghai jar and dipper for bathing, and 'thunder boxes' (buckets in boxed seats) for sanitation, which were emptied daily by prisoners from the local jail under armed guard. Often left alone for days in the open, unlocked house, Mrs Jolly (questionnaire 1974: 6) has emphasized that she never felt insecure. By 1934 she was living in Singapore in a modern, two-storey house which had electric fans, stove and hot-water heater, a long bath and a septic tank with flush toilet.

The Contributions and Functions of Wives
Although there were differences of detail in the lifestyles of the *mems*, the great majority of them were, and anticipated being, home-makers and

mothers: occupations which not only directed their roles both inside and outside domesticity, thus reinforcing their sense of a corporate identity, but also determined their particular contributions and functions in the colonial situation. Although the circumstances and details changed these were *essentially* the same, whether the period under study is the 1830s or the 1930s, and to them we now turn.

Home management

The typical masculine opinion was that a European housewife in Malaya had 'only one duty, to have an interview with Cookie once a day.' (Scott 1939: 14). On marriage, however, most husbands were relieved to transfer the responsibility for home management to their wives, realizing perhaps, albeit unconsciously, the subtle irritations but profound significance of domestic organization for the individual couple and the community. Efficient, competent home management was part of a wife's 'civilizing mission', and in times of economic stringency her talents at making ends meet could be crucial. During the world slump of 1929-34, for example, Mrs Dorothy Downe recalls that a desperate English planter whom she knew took work for $30 per month (approximately £3.10.0d at the then rate of exchange) which his Russian wife supplemented by growing vegetables, breeding chickens and making her own sugar from coconut flowers: her husband's admiration for her was unstinting (interview with Mrs D. Downe, January 1972). In the same slump conditions, Mrs Hodgkin discovered that doing her own shopping and catering had 'made a tremendous difference to the budget which is hopeful as well as being fun' - although her Cookie strongly objected to this innovation (Hodgkin, letter of 17 August 1932).

A *mem* had to ensure that bungalow and contents were regularly inspected for insects, snakes and vermin, even when living in towns: furnishings such as cushions and cushion covers regularly needed replacing as a result of 'cockroaches having had nibbles' out of them (Hodgkin, letter of 6 May 1932). Until the 1920s, with virtually no modern sanitation anywhere, the *toti* or night-soil coolie visited European bungalows daily to empty the sanitary buckets, a form of sewage disposal which many Europeans found 'inconceivably disgusting' (Peet 1960: 29). But unlike their Rhodesian contemporaries (see Kirkwood, this volume) Malayan Europeans did not have to make an excursion down the garden to visit the lavatory, as each bedroom in a bungalow had its own bathroom with individual sanitary arrangements attached, consisting of one or two commodes and, much later, flushing toilets.

Most *mems* lived in rented, furnished accommodation. Everyone had 'barrack furniture' (Baker, letter of 12 August 1913), but most couples added their own ornaments and pictures for individuality. There were, however, fashion trends in interior decoration. In late 1931, when everyone else had adopted the Chinese style, the Hodgkins kept theirs English: 'The house looks ripping after Mary's efforts with the curtains and cushions', enthused husband Ernest (Mary Hodgkin, letter of 1st October 1931 and Ernest Hodgkin, letter of 31 July 1931). But other *mems'* attempts to achieve individuality were thwarted. When Mrs Alice Smith, an American who arrived in late 1937, altered and renovated all the company-issued furniture in her KL bungalow her satisfaction was short-lived: 'The neighbouring *mems* came and saw and admired and went home and the next week all the furniture in all the houses had suffered a like fate.' (Smith, personal recollections sent to J.B., c. 1952: 10).

Relations between servants and mistress were perhaps the most important factor for successful home management and the maintenance of European health and well-being in the tropics. 'Your servants were more important to you than your friends', declared one *mem* (Smith, personal recollections 1952: 2). Servants were usually considered essential - if a wife tried to do her own housework she would quickly become 'physically exhausted and dripping with sweat' (interview with Mrs Buckeridge, June 1976) - but some wives would have agreed with the *mem* who claimed that servants were 'maintained by husbands to frustrate their brides.' (Keith 1954: 50). With Kirkwood (this volume) we can ask: were servants liberators or tyrants? The question is an important one, not least because the mistress-servant relationship was reciprocal. An efficient, reliable staff made housekeeping easy, but limited a wife's involvement in it. As in other colonial territories, most servants in Malaya were male and they knew intimately both their employers' personalities and their residential quarters; information which enabled them to wield power in various overt and subtle ways. For example, custom and circumstances (notably wood fires and kerosene tin 'stoves') meant that *mems* relied particularly on their servants' assistance for cooking and budgeting. 'Cookies' customarily cheated their employers on the side. Everyone knew this went on, so a new *mem* could glean from older residents 'much advice, and tips as to the cookie's favourite ways of making money out of one.' Mrs Hodgkin quickly discovered that hers was making a '1/2 cent per egg out of us' (letter of 24 July 1931). To exert any control at all over servants competence in bazaar Malay was essential, and even then they could simply refuse to co-operate. One wife whose household supplies seemed to vanish at an alarming rate found that questioning her Chinese servants was of little help:

> They do not know where these things go to - they go - that is all. Helplessly, I survey their stolid yellow faces knowing that neither now, nor henceforth, shall I get any satisfactory answers. Truly the great stone wall of China is symbolic. ('D.K.', July 1926: 90)

Mems also had responsibility for the welfare of the staff and their families, in whom a kindly, humane interest needed to be shown to win and keep their respect and co-operation. Mrs Ensor, a rubber planter's wife during the inter-war period, remembers that with her five servants, their wives and children, she was responsible for the well-being of 22 people. 'I felt honoured [she has written] when they allowed me to doctor - bind up cuts and sores, etc. - [and] once I found myself setting a broken arm, the doctor, whom they flatly refused to allow to touch the child, standing beside me telling me what to do' (1973: 17).

Where servant-mistress relationships were good, bonds of mutual loyalty and affection would develop, and then servants commonly stayed for years.[5] Unfortunately, we know little about servants' feelings towards Europeans, as documented evidence is scant. However, an anecdote told by one *mem* implies her servant's gratitude and devotion. During the 1920s when there was a glut of labour willing to be servants, Mrs Cynthia Koek engaged in Singapore an inexperienced young boy in his first job. She trained him from scratch, giving him also an hour's English lesson every day. Consequently

> after the Japanese War ... he spoke such good English that the British made him the Head Cook of the Mountbatten Club (he was also a wonderful cook). He did so well, [but] he was very kind and he wanted to come back to us. [However] I said 'You stay with the Military, you'll do much better'.

Nevertheless, as the Koeks had been interned in Changi Prison and came out with nothing, this former servant regularly brought them dehydrated food and other necessities, and in later years continued to visit them, after he had opened his own restaurant (interview with Mrs C. Koek, June 1976).

As there was clear-cut occupational specialization by race among servants, most Europeans in fact employed a multi-racial staff. However, we know very little about servants' relationships with, and attitudes to, one another; to my knowledge, no serious research has been done on this dimension of the colonial Malayan race-relations experience. From the European perspective servants were a primary point of contact with the Asian communities, but not the only one, and not all Europeans gained in understanding from this racial interchange. At least one *mem* (who was born in Malaya in 1914, then returned in 1932 after education abroad, and married a planter in 1935) has admitted that, for her, servants 'didn't seem to exist, they were sort of background, there for my benefit. What I missed and how I regret it now'. (Mrs Talou, personal communication to J.B., 20 August 1973). Space does not allow further discussion of the race-relations aspect, but in the sources considered so far I have not yet come across evidence of any 'brown or yellow peril' incidents (cf. Kirkwood, this volume).

Marital and Family Relations

Successful marriages were important, not only for the individual couple but also for the smooth functioning of the whole European community. Given that wives were generally expected to play essentially supportive roles within established precedents, perhaps the most successful marriages were those in which the wife conformed to the community's and her husband's expectations, which were by no means undemanding.

European men believed that a wife's reaction to the climate was a determining factor for a successful marriage. The majority of men, including doctors, presumed that white women suffered more from the climatic conditions than did white males.[6] The men's opinions have not been corroborated by the majority of *mems*. Even before the 1914-18 War, when women wore many layers of garments (including long tweed skirts and long-sleeved blouses with stiff, starched collars over steel-boned stays) evidence suggests that few suffered any more from the climate than did their menfolk.[7] Indeed, the energy of the white women of Sandakan (Sabah) at the turn of the century for riding, dancing and tennis might, as one of them, Dorothy Cator (1905: 16) drily commented, 'have made some people a little sceptical as to whether our health was really in such a precarious condition as it was etiquette to think.'

White men wanted European wives in Malaya so that they could have a more 'normal' family life, and as motherhood was regarded as part of their married career few wives remained childless. For most, child-bearing was a desirable duty along with its Imperial significance. For the majority of European wives and children family life was pleasant, happy, enriching and united until the time came for schooling. Although most *mems* employed *amahs* or *ayahs* (children's nurses) to assist with child care, these servants usually did the chores and the baby-sitting, which left mothers free to teach, socialize and enjoy their children. However, Asian nurses were a mixed blessing as Ida Bryson wrote to her friend in 1928: 'You can have very little idea of the enormous grip which the average *amah* or *ayah* gets on a child even with the mother about most of the time.' (Bryson, letter of 21 April 1928). Once they were seven years old the majority of children were sent overseas for education partly as a result of the universal belief that the tropical environment was socially and climatically damaging to children after this age. Most mothers then faced years of separation from their children. Dubbed 'the tragedy of the East', because of its effect in breaking up the family, this practice also created a considerable dilemma for wives, who suffered divided loyalties as conflict arose between wifehood and motherhood (see also Macmillan, this volume). Which she chose depended on whom the individual wife cared about most. Although she missed her son deeply, Mrs Ida Bryson (letter of 11 January 1930) was adamant that she would rather be with her husband; but some women chose to be 'good mothers' rather than 'good wives'. If, however, a wife cared about her husband and her marriage, there was an informal rule that she should not stay overseas with the children too long, because if *she* did not look after her husband some other woman would, possibly an Asian.

Social Life and Voluntary Work

By the early twentieth century the social significance of wives was paramount and they directed much of the community's social life which, as in the nineteenth century, emulated that of the metropolitan countries and of colonial India. Wives were much occupied in organizing and attending social activities, which gave husbands after-work relaxation and helped to bind the white community into a more tightly cohesive whole. By maintaining standards of etiquette and a variety of social proprieties and ceremonial, wives helped reinforce the community's separate enclave identity amongst the vast Asian majority. A social hierarchy, evident from the earliest days of European settlement, was maintained up to the Second World War and emphasized the importance of precedence. Among its manifestations were the customs of 'signing the books' at the residence of the senior Government official (e.g. at Government House or the District Officer's Residence) and of paying courtesy calls with cards. By the 1930s 'calling' consisted simply 'of popping cards in a letter-box at the end of the drive and scuttling for shelter!' (Hodgkin, letter of 16 July 1931; see also Gartrell, this volume). Nevertheless a bachelor would be warned to 'call' correctly because

> unless he pays his calls in the proper manner leaving his little cards at the houses of the ladies he wishes to know, he will not get far in the social world and will run the risk of being 'cut' at the club, not only by the ladies, but by their husbands. (Pearce 1932: 50)

Much social life was institutionalized in clubs. Initially male establishments dating from the earliest days of European settlement, clubs were primarily of two types: general and sporting. From the late nineteenth century white women were included as 'honorary members' and were discriminated against in various ways. Playing little or no role in club management, they could not initiate policy nor alter the rules. They were often forbidden entry to male preserves such as the bar and were frequently restricted to specific areas of the club-house, either in a room set aside for them, as at the Penang Club between the wars, or demarcated by lines on the floor. In the 1920s the European Club at Klang had an end specially reserved for *mems* with bathroom attached and weekly papers like the *Sketch* and *Tatler* supplied, while in the same decade, according to one planter's wife, the men of a planting club near KL had a special section built on for the *mems* which they nicknamed 'The Cowshed' (interview with Mrs M. Riches, January 1973).

During the inter-war years, some wives were engaged in running all-female organizations concerned mainly with charitable and voluntary welfare work, most of which had been founded prior to 1914.[8] Despite the small numbers of European women involved and of Asian women reached, these organizations were important at various levels. Their establishment reflected women's perceptions of shared feminine interests, which cut across both the white community hierarchy and the colour line. Informants have agreed that although voluntary work was not regarded as a social obligation for a white woman, many had a social conscience and 'thought they should do something or ... wanted to do something' (interview with Mrs K. Cansdell, January 1974). Welfare and charity interests were believed also to have therapeutic effects because, argued one doctor, they 'take us ... out of ourselves, away from introspection and real or imaginary troubles or worries' (Black 1932: 105).

European women had, however, faced much opposition from their menfolk in establishing voluntary work for Asians, being often accused of unwanted, patronizing interference. Those who wished to take an interest in the world around them found it was simply 'Not Done', and that instead they were encouraged to create a separate white domestic and social circle. By the 1930s, concern about burgeoning problems in the British Empire led to a somewhat belated suggestion that wives' social-work talents could be mobilized for the good of the Empire and its subject peoples because (argued Professor Ernest Barker in an article published in January 1932: 56) 'when women understand one another, the battle is won, and the way is easy for men'. His co-author (now Dame) Freya Stark, pointing out (p.59) that 'the intolerance, narrow-mindedness and stupidity of the average official's wife' had been repeatedly impressed upon her, records that such wives had not only been unfairly slandered but were one of the Empire's greatest assets. If it were made fashionable for white wives to embrace wider horizons by undertaking social work, she suggests, it would liberate them and also be a means of conciliation between British and native peoples. In Malaya *mems* had been engaged in social work for many years on their own initiative, rather than that of their menfolk, and the effects of this were wider than predicted.[9]

Mems played, for example, a major role in the development of the Young Women's Christian Association and the Girl Guides Movement in Malaya in the early twentieth century. These were at once both conservative and progressive forces: conservative because they emphasized the importance of traditional domestic duties and feminine skills, progressive because they introduced Asian women to new ideas, principles and customs. By bringing Asian women out of the home and expanding their horizons, these organizations were not only initiating important social change but had, quite unintentionally, a subversive effect on colonialism. Indeed they were viewed with disfavour if not suspicion by many European men, for, although they may have been 'maternalistic', they provided numbers of Asian women with leadership training, imbued them with self-confidence and exposed them to Western methods and values, thus helping to undermine the myth of white superiority. When Malaya achieved Independence in 1957, these self-same Asian women were ready to fill positions vacated by the Europeans, providing a variety of skills and organizing competence vital to the new nation. It can be argued that, rather than being enemies of Malayan nationalism, white women stimulated and advanced its development - albeit unwittingly.[10]

European wives were involved in, or made significant contributions to, many other pursuits, notably in the fields of literature and journalism.

Such is their importance that these two aspects merit a paper to themselves, but some brief comments may be made. The publications of wives present us with rather different pictures of Malaya from those of male writers, and confirm the point that women and men frequently viewed European - and Asian - society in that country from separate perspectives. On the subject of European–Asian relations, for example, the novels and/or short stories of such writers as Mrs le Fevre ('Sianu'), Sylvia Brett (the Ranee Sylvia of Sarawak) and Jessie Davidson consistently show more sympathetic, positive and affectionate attitudes towards the various resident Asian races than do many of their contemporary male counterparts. Most male novelists fall into the Maugham mould in which Asians simply provide exotic background to the main plot or theme of the story, and rarely appear centre stage. By comparison the three women writers mentioned, and others, often highlight Asian characters; their views on race relations favour and promote more equal mixing between European and Asian than the colonial ethos and British policy would allow or accept.[11]

Factors Dividing Wives

So far we have considered the *memsahibs* as a distinctive group with certain common characteristics that gave them a basic corporate identity. However, there were also significant barriers dividing them, of which the four most important are discussed below. Of lesser importance were divisions between those who were mothers and those who were not, and the varying religious and denominational affiliations.

Male occupational divisions

The community's most basic occupational division was between Officials and Unofficials, the former generally remaining apart from the latter - 'they had to keep a bit of "class"' (interview with H. J. Grummitt, July 1977). The Government Service was further divided into cadets and non-cadets. Cadets, of whom there were 250 in 1929, were the administrators who formed the Malayan Civil Service or 'Heaven-born' while non-cadets staffed Education, Police and the Technical Services (Public Works Department, Forestry, and so forth). Internally each of these sections or departments was ranked hierarchically, the actual order of positions being listed in Government gazettes. The occupations of the Unofficials covered all private enterprise, non-governmental careers including planting, mining, commerce and education, and were also internally ranked.

As might be expected, most Europeans mixed both professionally and socially within their particular employment category and at the same level. A wife generally took her status from her husband's occupation and her position in the hierarchy from his level of seniority, so that she was automatically 'promoted' with him. Usually a wife also followed her husband's pattern of social mixing, at least when with him, because 'men set the patterns of who mixed with whom' (interview with Mr and Mrs B. Buckeridge, June 1976). Similar 'pecking orders' existed in Government, the Armed Forces and in the Unofficial occupations. For example, in each area the wife of the senior Government official was the senior woman, and the rest of the Government wives were ranked under her according to the positions of their husbands in the official gazette. Usually called the *'Mem Besar'* (literally 'Big Woman' i.e. First Lady) and whether married to the Governor, a Resident or a District Officer, these wives were expected to take the lead, attend all official events, perform various ceremonial functions such as declaring open fetes and new buildings, and generally set an example right down the scale to the newest, commonly the youngest, Government *mem*. Among planters the wife of the manager was in the same pre-eminent position, and the wife of the most junior assistant was at the bottom of the scale.

Although wives of all ranks and occupations often mixed in women-only pursuits, a number of informants have agreed that MCS wives were frequently 'stand-offish and snobbish' compared with other Government service *mems* and the wives of Unofficials. One planter's wife has commented 'The fact that I didn't know any Government people is significant - they did not mix greatly with 'trade', except on official levels or [in] things like golf' (Mrs Hazel Mitchell, questionnaire, 1975: 2) while another has asserted that most snobbery came from the 'Heaven Born's' wives, 'who, on the whole, had nothing to be snobby about.' (Mrs J. Bunney, questionnaire, 1973: 2, 6; and interview with her, August 1973). Their exalted position went perhaps to their heads: many a Government *mem* reputedly thought 'that she has a mission in life which is to set an example ... as from the high-born, to those other vain creatures whose husbands are merely merchants, or lawyers, or even more lowly still, planters or journalists.' (Wilson 1928: 320).

One employment grouping which most observers had difficulty fitting into the community hierarchy was that of the missionaries, particularly the non-Anglicans. The order of the hierarchy itself (Government officials; the professional classes; rubber planters and miners; and lastly merchants and their assistants) is revealing evidence of the transfer to Malaya of British class values and social presumptions, particularly when it is remembered that the two bottom groups were primarily responsible for the financial and economic success of the colonial venture. For this very reason, many Europeans from these occupations resented the attitudes of the 'Heaven-Born' and the Military who, like their Indian Civil Service counterparts, had appropriated the position at the top of the structure and who, as one planter's wife has complained, 'were paid by the revenue from rubber and tin' (Mrs J. Herring, questionnaire, 1972: 2).

Social origins and nationality

Although social origins within and between the main categories varied, the men were more socially homogeneous than were the women, among whom there were greater divergencies across the class spectrum. The limited evidence available from interviews, questionnaires and letters suggests that the majority of wives came from what can be described as broadly middle-class backgrounds, but there were also representatives of the working classes and the aristocracy. However, most working-class wives, such as those married to railway drivers or to 'other ranks' in the Armed Forces, were absorbed into the middle-class majority, partly as a result of their improved lifestyle and position. There was in KL in 1932, for example, 'a priceless Cockney of the Cockneyest - wife of the Sargeant in the Volunteers - She is a really terrible but most amusing person, used to barrack loife - naow in a reel bungalow with 'er own boy an' all [sic] - Cripes!!' (Hodgkin, letter of 8 June 1932). At the other extreme some Government wives were members of the British aristocracy although they were not necessarily respected for their rank and titles. One titled Governor's wife, for example, has been described as 'quite nice looking but has the most awful voice'; at a Guiders' Association Annual General Meeting she had 'asked the most stupid questions which no woman of intelligence would have asked' (Hodgkin, letter of 18 March 1932). Indeed, education could be an important factor in underlining a *mem's* status. By the inter-war period, numbers of *mems* were university graduates or had other tertiary qualifications. Apart from trained teachers, nurses and doctors, one new bride of 1932 was a botanist with a Cambridge B.Sc. (who had been researching for her doctorate until she went to Malaya), while an older contemporary, Mrs Savage Bailey, had trained at the Slade and in Antwerp (Hodgkin, letter of 5 August 1932).

Nationality was an important divisive factor between wives. There was little social mixing between British and European nationalities; even among the broadly 'British' groups many non-English wives felt that the English *mems* looked down on them, despite a commonly-held opinion that English wives were the least adaptable to Malayan conditions. One Scottish *mem*, wife of a tin mining engineer, who went out in 1937, thought rural Highland Scotswomen were particularly suited to Asian country life (Mrs E. MacLeod, questionnaire, 1973: 6), while an Australian planter's wife who first arrived in 1917 has similarly suggested that Australian women adjusted much better than Englishwomen being more adaptable, able to improvise, and treating their servants more sympathetically (interview with Mrs A. Philson, January 1973). Conversely, Englishwomen have claimed that Australians and Americans were generally 'too egalitarian' and 'too casual'. The divisive influence of English attitudes of superiority and national separateness was forcefully criticized by one English *mem*, Dorothy Cator:

> Every country, whether white or black, has some manners and customs peculiar to itself, but we English refuse to recognise this well-known fact. We pride ourselves on standing first among the nations of the world, and instead of being careful for that very reason to show our superiority by special courtesy, we force our insularism where it is not wanted and ride rough-shod

over many ways which may not agree with ours. This characteristic often makes us intolerably offensive to other Europeans, and to coloured races ungenerous and cruel ... (1905: 62)

Working women (married and single) and non-working wives

The division between working women, both single and married, and non-working wives, was an important one, although numbers of women went to Malaya single and subsequently became *mems*. From the 1890s career opportunities opened up in nursing and teaching, both for the Government and in mission enterprises. The Colonial Nursing Service offered security, a pension from 45 and, in Malaya, better conditions than many other colonial territories. One Nursing Sister, Janet Steele, who went out in 1937, recalls the advantages of living in a small Peninsula town, sharing a bungalow and three servants with only one colleague, working a straight 8-hour shift and enjoying numerous social pursuits: 'Life was *never* boring' she has emphasized (Sister J.Steele (Mrs Bunney) questionnaire, 1973: 6, and interview, August 1973). Similarly, a school-mistress who arrived in Singapore in 1928 to teach at a Methodist Girls' School found her work-load, extra-curricular activities and social functions meant that life was 'very demanding but exciting and satisfying in many ways ... We had no time to be bored' (Mrs A. Lyne, questionnaire, 1972: 6). A very few white women went as children's nurses or governesses but were put in a difficult social position as members of the domestic staff amongst Asian servants while also being members of the ruling group.[12]

Inevitably most single working women married. Once married, a *mem* was commonly most interested 'in running the house and garden, reading, sewing and visiting friends' and engaging in social activities such as amateur dramatics and in Church work (Mrs A. Lyne, questionnaire, 1972: 6). Moreover, the 'marriage bar' came into operation, supported by the convention that European women were harmed by doing much work in the tropics and reinforced by the attitudes of most husbands that having a working wife would reflect adversely on their own position and social status. The restricting effects of these factors were greater for wives in Malaya than for those in the metropolitan countries because of the prevailing male hostility to *mems* engaging in voluntary social work. They also help account for the apparent irony that, with servants to look after house and children, so few wives were allowed, or went, to work. Many men assumed, therefore, that wives were merely 'married dolls' (Sidney 1926: 91) who idled their time away uselessly and who lived sedentary, empty lives pining for their children overseas and longing for leave. The comments of the Reverend Nigel Williams reveal the typical male opinion. He recalls that he

> once met the wife of a doctor in Tapah, a country town, who: did not read, could not sew, played no musical instrument but the gramaphone [sic], played a poor game of golf and an appalling hand at bridge; she must have

found life difficult; I don't know what became of her. (personal communication to J. B., January 1973)

Having put so many limitations on the *mems*, European men then criticized them either for inactivity or for indulging in bridge and gossip. Richard Sidney suggested (ibid) that more wives should take employment because those who earned their living always seemed happier and healthier than the rest: but he offers no advice as to how *mems* were to overcome existing prejudices against their employment, nor where they were to find the jobs. Apparently the blame, the problem and the solution lay with the wives.

If a wife were widowed the situation could change dramatically, because if she chose to stay in Malaya she was usually obliged to earn an income. Before the First World War widows commonly took in lodgers, opened and ran boarding houses or did typing or sewing at home. One enterprising, talented tailoress, Mrs Beale, was long employed as Court Dressmaker by Robinsons, a famous Singapore store, and charged expensive fees in comparison with local Chinese and Indian tailors. During the 1920s and 30s it became increasingly common for a widow to take employment outside the home. Some returned to teaching or nursing, others became private secretaries and a few opened shops or boutiques. One doctor's widow, Mrs Rattray, ran a public house at Cameron Highlands during the 1930s until the Japanese Occupation, while another began a European preparatory school at Frasers Hill in 1933. Mrs Arnold Savage Bailey (mother of British actress Dulcie Gray) whose husband was tragically killed in a boating accident in Singapore in 1936, took a three months' crash course and became Librarian of Raffles Library; she was subsequently presumed drowned on one of the last boats out of Singapore in 1942 (Denison 1973: 63).

Wives who married 'out'

A tiny though very important percentage of white women married Asian or Eurasian men, and were commonly ostracized by the European community as a result. As white women were the zenith of European prestige, the woman who married out was 'letting the side down' in an irredeemable manner. Exceptions were made only when the woman concerned married an important, prestigious Asian such as a member of one of the Malay Royal families or aristocracies. In October 1930, for example, Sultan Ibrahim of Johore married Mrs Helen Brockie Wilson who had divorced her doctor husband in order to marry him. A report in *British Malaya* (November 1930: 198) records that thousands had gathered outside the Register Office in London to cheer 'such a genuine and delightful love match.' As the wife of a very rich, powerful husband, the Sultanah Helena had to be publicly treated by all whites with deference and respect.

Helena was an educated and socially acceptable woman, a very different type from the popular image most Europeans held of white women who 'married out'. It was commonly believed that these women came from the lower strata of British (or European) society – perhaps being barmaids or landladies' daughters – who met their husbands while the latter were studying in the UK and, attracted by the promise of riches and Oriental exoticism, married and went East. In popular mythology the story usually continues with the break-up of the marriage after the wife experiences hostility from her husband's family, is perhaps treated more like a chattel than with the queen-like adoration which she had anticipated, and so discovers that life out East is not what she has expected.[13]

Some women who married Asians certainly did fit this pattern, but mention must also be made of those European wives who had happy, successful, long-lasting marriages to their Asian husbands, suffering the racialist opprobrium of sections of the British community with courage, forebearance and fortitude. Most immersed themselves in the Asian group into which they had married, and usually limited their contact with Europeans, perhaps only to women's organizations such as the YWCA and the Girl Guides, because many found white women generally less racially prejudiced than white men.[14] This male racial antagonism, particularly in its aversion to mixed marriage, played a vital role in white/Asian relations, but can only be briefly commented on here. It derived partly from a belief that white women were sexually desirable to Asian men and so must be protected from them. Not only did a section of white women not want such protection but (from the Asian perspective) the general opinion of some elderly Asian men interviewed is that white *mems* were unattractive, dowdy, insipid and smelt unpleasant. However, some have admitted that they desired sexual experiences with white women who, as a result of images created by Hollywood, they believed were all sexually advanced and liberated: yet few had ever seriously considered marrying a European wife.[15]

Conclusion

This paper has presented an interpretive account of the lives and experiences of *memsahibs* in colonial Malaya with the intention of illustrating the characteristics of wifehood common to this particular group of wives and of suggesting the effects which the *mems* had jointly and individually on the local and the Imperial situation. Although their complex position has necessarily been briefly sketched, some valid conclusions may be drawn.

The lives of Malayan *mems* followed the same broad pattern as those of their counterparts elsewhere. Some details nonetheless were unique to the Malayan colonial experience. Malayan *mems* formed a distinctive group within a white community which itself, by the early twentieth century, had special characteristics resulting from Malaya's geographical and climatic conditions, her economic wealth, the nature of her Asian population and the specific socio-political features of British colonial rule.

The wives' presence did not guarantee a permanent white settler society, which was not envisaged, but it was essential to the continuation of British colonial rule and to the maintenance of the myth of white superiority. The racial and social distinctness of the European community depended on white men marrying European wives who, with male approval, helped to maintain a separate white enclave.

This colonial world was also male-dominated, and its survival necessitated male control of the *memsahibs*. Its continuation seemingly depended as much on the *mems* acquiescing to the demands of their menfolk as on Asian subjects remaining submissive and controllable. Since the *mems* were in Malaya because European men required their presence, it is understandable that men defined their roles and, through marriage, laid on them a variety of constraints which regulated their impact and largely restricted their activities to the European community. White men's determination to seclude wives in this way derived also from their sense of proprietory ownership, their code of chivalry and from specifically English male ideals of the period concerning uncontaminated whiteness. Masculine attitudes to wives were ambivalent and contradictory as men sought both to control and to protect. Men limited the *mems* to marital and social life, and then criticized them for being limited. By making wives responsible through their *civilizing influence* for the white community's prestige, men maintained a double standard and blamed the *mems* for any reputed loss of white status. These responsibilities gave the *mems* some power but were also onerous. As it was assumed that Asians were constantly observing them, wives had to be consistently circumspect in their dress and behaviour: 'I would love to return [to Malaya], not as a *Mem*, but able to meet and see who and what I wanted to, in fact to do as I liked' one wife has wistfully recorded (Talou, personal communication to J.B., August 1973). *Memsahibs* were marked as economically 'unproductive' killjoys, but could also be accused of 'letting the side down' and were made the scapegoats for processes of change unacceptable to European men.

Most male portrayals of the *mems* differ, sometimes dramatically, from the wives' own stories; for behind the stereotypes lies a different, more complex, reality. The *mems'* experiences and influence were broader and more significant than has previously been recognized, and were not always what men desired or anticipated. In Malaya, as elsewhere, the white women who had the most freedom to organize their own modes of life were those without husbands, whether single or widowed. But, as this study has also illustrated, even wives with husbands present were able on occasion to break through the constraints of marriage, particularly in their social and voluntary welfare interests. At one level wives upheld the mores and customs believed essential to the maintenance of European supremacy, but at other levels they introduced Asians to modernizing ideas and techniques which challenged the dominant assumptions. Realizing that

they shared with Asian women a harmony of interests in a common
'woman's world', some *mems* formed friendships with their Asian sisters
which, if not absolutely equal, at least permitted informal mutual
education and some understanding. In these ways, wives helped
undermine the European male world and its ethos. By exerting power and
influence through traditionally feminine domestic, maternal and charitable
duties, the *mems* reinforced the enclave identity of the white community
yet unwittingly introduced subversive processes which helped to threaten
the colonial system. Indeed as individuals and as a group they influenced
decisively the character of racial and cultural interchange in colonial
Malaya, and helped to determine the form and outcome of that episode in
the history of the region.

Notes

1. In this paper the term 'Malaya' is used to cover former British colonial
possessions in the geographical areas previously known as the Straits Settlements
(Malacca, Penang and Singapore) and the Malay Peninsula - which are now
divided into West Malaysia and Singapore - and in the two States of Borneo now
known as Sabah and Sarawak, East Malaysia. Where it has been necessary to refer
to them separately, the modern titles of these geo-political units have been used.
Abbreviations used are KL for Kuala Lumpur, MCS for Malayan Civil Service.

2. In comparison with the writings of settler women in Rhodesia available to
Kirkwood (this volume) very few women who lived in colonial Malaya published
memoirs of their lives and experiences. For this paper and in my wider research,
sources include official publications, magazines and newspapers, contemporary
materials, fiction, missionary archives, and written and oral reminiscences,
together with other historical works. Owing to exigencies of space very few of
these have received bibliographic reference here. The material briefly presented has
been summarized from a much more detailed treatment, with full documentation,
in my forthcoming thesis 'White Female Society in Malaysia and Singapore in the
Twentieth Century' (cf. also Butcher 1979 and Allen 1983).

3. Many of the comments made in this paper summarize answers given in
interviews and questionnaires. Among those who responded were a few who
wished to remain anonymous, although the majority were willing to be identified.
Therefore I have given false initials to the former where necessary, but have
openly named the latter. Although this has resulted in two differing procedures it
provides authenticity. Following the advice of various scholars the great majority
of the interviews have not been taped but are in hand-written form. I have also
freely attributed, and have quoted from primary source materials including
memoirs, reminiscences and typescripts, many by women and many written for,
or lent to, me, as well as from personal letters which I have been permitted to use.
All of these are in my possession as either originals or photocopies. I am
particularly indebted to Mrs Mary Hodgkin who has lent me the letters which she
wrote home to her family during the 1930s and has permitted me to quote
extensively from them. The above materials have been referenced as follows:

For questionnaires: Name/Initials, questionnaire, date completed.
For interviews: interview with - Name/Initials and date of conducting it. To
date 226 interviews have been completed (134 female, 92 male). The great
majority of interviewees have been Europeans, but about 50 have been Asians
and Eurasians.
For letters sent to me: Name/Initials, personal communication to JB, date.
For letters to others: Name/Initials, letter of (date).
For memoirs, reminiscences, etc: Name/Initials, Memoirs sent to JB, date.

4. Many companies imposed these restrictions partly to ensure that employee loyalty to the individual company would be well established before allowing the possibly conflicting demands of a wife. (Contrast Butcher 1979, Chs. 4 and 6).

5. A number of *mems* have written tributes about their servants. There are numerous stories concerning servants who were waiting to greet and work again for their European employers following the end of the Japanese Occupation.

6. There was much medical debate concerning the fitness or otherwise of white women for tropical conditions. See discussion in Butcher 1979, especially Chapters 3, 4 and 6, and Chapter 3 of my thesis, for an alternative approach.

7. This point has been made by two white women who lived in Singapore from the mid-1890s and who have remembered very clearly the Victorian and Edwardian clothes worn by their mothers and later by themselves. Mrs Dorothy Downe was born in Singapore on 28 May 1894, the daughter of missionaries - her evidence is contained in an interview conducted with her in January 1972 and her questionnaire of 1974, p. 2. Miss Lillian Newton lived in Singapore from 1895 until 1925 and her information is to be found in a number of interviews with and personal communications to me between 1972 and 1977, as well as in her memoirs 'More Exquisite When Past', typescript, n.d., Royal Commonwealth Society Library, London.

8. When engaged in welfare work and other women-only pursuits *mems* frequently overcame or simply ignored the community's status and occupational divisions discussed below. This issue is considered in depth in Chapters 4 and 5 of my thesis and in a paper awaiting publication: Janice N. Brownfoot, 'Community Relations and Women's Organizations - European Women and the Asian Communities in Colonial Malaysia c. 1900-1957', presented at the Association of Historians of Asia Conference, Kuala Lumpur, Malaysia, 25-29 August 1980.

9. The points raised here are discussed in my thesis and in my 1980 paper listed above, and are based on a wide variety of sources both oral and written.

10. For information on Guiding and many other matters I am indebted to Ibu Zain who was interviewed on my behalf, partly for this essay, during October and November 1982 by Ms Jenifah Dadameah of Muar, Johore, Malaysia. It has been argued that Malayan nationalism was little developed until during and after the Second World War, although Independence was granted in 1957. However, British understanding of Malay nationalist feeling was apparently limited, and knowledge was perfunctory. Interview with Ibu Zain, 1982; and see the analysis by W. Roff (1967).

11. White women in colonial Malayan literature are discussed in Chapter 7 of my thesis.

12. It should also be noted that there were always a few white prostitutes working in the area, particularly in Singapore, although it is understandably impossible to determine precise figures. Their presence was unwelcome to the Colonial Government but the concern about them was not so much that they were prostitutes as that their behaviour would bring dishonour to white prestige.

13. Examples of marriages between white women and Asian men breaking up owing to these factors have been mentioned by a number of informants, but verification has been almost impossible. The myth itself is nevertheless more important in this context.

14. This point is in direct contradiction to many commonly-held male views concerning white women and their attitudes to non-white races, including those expressed by informants. Of course exceptions can be found, but those women who married Asians and continued to mix with white women have mentioned that overall they found the women more accepting, tolerant and understanding of their mixed marriage than they did white men - especially English men. White men have admitted in interviews with me that the fact that a white woman could

find an Asian man attractive and desirable enough to marry him constituted a very wounding blow to their egos, quite apart from the concern which they had that such actions would adversely affect white prestige and community solidarity.

15. Interviews have been conducted with Chinese, Eurasian, Indian and Malay men from a broad cross-section of educational and occupational backgrounds. On this subject perhaps the most helpful have been those with Datuk Shabuddin Y. K. Cheng, August 1976; Mr Chan Chen Swee, May 1976; Mr Khoo Boon Miang, May 1976; and Mr Tan Peng Gee, May 1976.

BIBLIOGRAPHY

Allen, C. (ed) 1983. *Tales from the South China Seas*. London; André Deutsch/BBC.

Allen, Dorothy 1960. *Sunlight and Shadow*. Oxford; O.U.P.

Annan, N. 1955. 'The Intellectual Aristocracy'; in J.H. Plumb (ed.) *Studies in Social History*. London; Longmans Green & Co.

—. 1966. 'Introduction' to Grant, M., *Cambridge*. London; Weidenfeld & Nicholson.

Ardener, E. 'Introductory Essay' to Ardener (ed.) 1971 *Social Anthropology and Language*. London; Tavistock.

—. 1971a. 'The New Anthropology and its Critics'. *Man* (N.S.) 6: 449-467.

Ardener, S. (ed.) 1975. *Perceiving Women*. London; Dent: New York; Wiley.

—. 'Introduction' to Ardener, S. (ed.) 1975.

—. (ed.) 1978. *Defining Females*. London; Croom Helm: New York; Wiley.

—. (ed.) 1981. *Women and Space; ground rules and social maps*. London; Croom Helm: New York; St. Martin's Press.

—. 1983. 'A Note on Gender Iconography: the Vagina'. Paper presented at the A.S.A. Decennial Conference, July 1983.

Atkinson, J.A. 1982. 'Anthropology' (Review Essay). *Signs: Journal of Women in Culture and Society* 8,2; 236-258.

Austen, Jane 1813. *Pride and Prejudice*.

—. 1818. *Persuasion*. (O.U.P. edn.)

Ayer, A.J. 1977. *Part of My Life*. Oxford; O.U.P.

Baker, Alan C. 1910-1920. *Letters to Mother from Malaya*. S.O.A.S; pp. ms II/12-22.

Balfour, Alice 1895. *Twelve Hundred Miles in an Ox Wagon*. London; Edward Arnold.

Ball, Oona H. 1923. *Sidney Ball: Memories and Impressions of 'An Ideal Don'*. London; Methuen.

Ballhatchet, Kenneth 1980. *Race, Sex and Class under the Raj*. London; Weidenfeld & Nicholson.

Bamfield, Veronica 1974. *On the Strength: the Story of the British Army Wife*. London & Tonbridge; Charles Knight & Co.

Barker, Professor E. and Stark, Freya. 'Women and the Service of the Empire'. *Contemporary Review*, January 1932; pp. 54-61.

Barr, Pat 1976. *The Memsahibs; the Women of Victorian India*. London; Secker & Warburg.

Bates, Sir Darrell 1972. *A Gust of Plumes*. London; Hodder & Stoughton.

Batey, Mavis 1982. *Oxford Gardens*. Amersham; Avebury.

Beadle, Muriel 1961. *These Ruins are Inhabited*. New York; Doubleday: (1963) London; Hale.

Beeton, Isabella Mary (1894 edn.) *Everyday Cookery and Housekeeping Book*. London; Ward, Lock & Bowden.

Bell, Sir Hesketh n.d. *Glimpses of a Governor's Life: from diaries, letters and memoranda*. London; Sampson Low, Marston & Co.

Bent, J. Theodore 1892. *The Ruined Cities of Mashonaland*. London; Longmans Green & Co.

Berger, P.L. and Kellner, H. 1964. 'Marriage and the Construction of Reality.' Reprinted 1971 in Anderson, M. (ed.) *The Sociology of the Family*. Harmondsworth; Penguin.

Berman, Bruce D. 1974. *Administration and Politics in Colonial Kenya*. Ph.D. Dissertation, Yale University, University Microfilms, Ann Arbor, Michigan.

B[erry] H[art], Alice. 'Housekeeping and Life in the Malayan Rubber'. *Blackwoods Magazine*, CCXXI, MCCCXXXIX, May 1927, pp. 598-613.

Black, Kenneth, Professor 1932. 'Health and Climate with Special Reference to Malaya.' *The Malayan Medical Journal*, 7, pp. 99-107.

Blackstone, Tessa 1976. 'The Education of Girls Today.' in Mitchell, J. & Oakley, A. (eds.) *The Rights and Wrongs of Women*. London; Penguin.

Blair, Juliet. 'Private Parts in Public Places: the Case of Actresses.' in Ardener, S. (ed.) 1981.

Bobbit, Mary Reed 1960. *Dearest Love to All: Life and Letters of Lady Jebb*. London; Faber & Faber.

Boggie, Jeannie 1938. *Experiences of Rhodesia's Pioneer Women*. Bulawayo; Philpott & Collins.

—. 1959. *A Husband and a Farm in Rhodesia*. Published privately in Rhodesia.

Bottomley, A.K. and Coleman, C. A. 1980. 'Police Effectiveness and the Public: The Limitations of Official Crime Rates.' in Clarke, R.V.G. & Hough, J.M. (eds.) *The Effectiveness of Policing*. London; Gower.

Bourdieu, P. 1977. *Introduction to a Theory of Practice*. Cambridge; C.U.P.

Bradley, Emily G. 1950. *Dearest Priscilla: letters to the wife of a colonial officer*. London; Parrish.

Bradley, Kenneth 1966. *Once a District Officer*. London; Macmillan.

Brett, the Hon. Sylvia Leonora (the Ranee Sylvia Brooke of Sarawak) 1920. *Toys*: a novel. Published by the Author.

—. 1935. *The Merry Matrons*: a play. Kuching, Sarawak; Government Printing Office.

—. 1941. *A Star Fell*. London; T. Werner Laurie.

Bridger, H. 1980. 'Cross-cultural Aspects of Organisation as Experienced in Expatriate Family Moves.' in Johnstad, T. (ed.) *Group Dynamism and Society: a Multinational Approach*. Cambridge, Mass. Oelgeschlager, Gunn 2 Hain for E.I.T., Copenhagen.

British Malaya: later called *Malaysia*. Journal of the British Association of Malaya.

British Medical Association 1977. *Getting Married*.

Brown, Rosemary. 'The Real Kitchen Cabinet.' *Daily Mail*, November 1981.

Brownfoot, Janice N. 'Community Relations and Women's Organisations - European Women and the Asian Communities in Colonial Malaysia c. 1900-1957.' Paper delivered at the Eighth Conference, International Association of Historians of Asia, Kuala Lumpur, Malaysia, 25-29 August 1980.

—. 'White Female Society in Malaysia and Singapore in the Twentieth Century.' Forthcoming thesis, School of Oriental and African Studies, London, Department of History.

Brownmiller, S. 1975. *Against Our Will: Men, Women and Rape*. New York; Simon & Schuster.

Bryson, Mrs Ida. Letters home from British Malaya, 1927-1941. Photocopies in the possession of Janice N. Brownfoot.

Bujra, Janet 1978. 'Introductory: female solidarity and the sexual division of labour.' in Caplan, Patricia & Bujra, Janet (eds.) *Women United, Women Divided*. London; Tavistock.

Burgess, Anthony (selector) 1969. *Maugham's Malaysian Stories*. Singapore; Heinemann Educational.

Burke, Barbara [Oona H. Ball] 1907. *Barbara Goes to Oxford*. London; Methuen.

Butcher, John G. 1979. *The British in Malaya 1880-1941*. Kuala Lumpur; O.U.P.

Butler, Mrs A.G. MS *Memoirs*. Bodleian Library, Oxford [courtesy of C. Colvin].

Butler, S. 1903. *The Way of All Flesh*. London; Grants Richards.

Cairns, J. C. 1959. *Bush and boma*. London; John Murray.

Callan, H. 'The Premiss of Dedicaton: Notes toward an Ethnography of Diplomats' Wives.' in Ardener, S. (ed.) 1975.

Carpenter, Humphrey 1977. *J.R.R. Tolkein: The Authorised Biography*. London; Unwin.

Cary, Robert 1973. *Countess Billie*. Zimbabwe; Galaxie Press.

Cator, Dorothy 1905. *Everyday Life Among the Headhunters and Other Experiences from East to West.* London; Longmans, Green & Co,
Cohen, A. 1974. *Two Dimensional Man.* London; Routledge & Kegan Paul.
Comer, Lee 1974. *Wedlocked Women.* Leeds; Feminist Books.
Conran, Shirley 1975. *Superwoman.* London; Sidgwick & Jackson.
—. 1979. *London; Superwoman in Action.* Sidgwick & Jackson.
Crick, M. 1976. *Explorations in Language and Meaning.* London; Malaby.
D.K. 'A Woman's Life in an Up-Country Bungalow.' *British Malaya* 1, 3, July 1926, pp.89-92.
Davidson, Jessie A. 1927. *Dawn - A Romance of Malaya.* London; Andrew Melrose.
—. 1927. *Fetters of Love.* London; Andrew Melrose.
Davies, Hunter. Article in *Good Housekeeping Magazine*, October 1980.
Delamont, S. and Duffin, L. (eds.) 1978. *The Nineteenth Century Woman.* London; Croom Helm.
Denison, Michael 1973. *Overtures and Beginners.* London; Gollancz.
de Waal, D. C. 1896. *With Rhodes in Mashonaland.* Capetown; J.C. Juta & Co
Dillard, Heath 1976. 'Women in Reconquest Castile.' in Stuard, S. Mosher (ed.) *Women in Medieval Society.* Philadelphia; Univ. of Pennsylvania Press.
Dingwall, Robert 1980. 'Ethics and Ethnography.' *Sociological Review,* 28, 4: pp. 871-891.
Diver, Maud 1909. *The Englishwoman in India.* Edinburgh & London; Blackwood & Sons.
Dobson, Kenneth 1954. *District Commissioner.* London; Museum Press.
Douglas, Mary 1966. *Purity and Danger.* London; Routledge & Kegan Paul.
—. 1978. 'Cultural Bias'. R.A.I. Occasional Paper 35. Reprinted in Douglas, M. 1982, *In the Active Voice.* London; Routledge & Kegan Paul.
The Draconian series. The Dragon School, Oxford.
Duffin, L. 'The Conspicuous Consumptive: Woman as an Invalid.' in Delamont, S. & Duffin, L. 1978.
East African Statistical Dept. 1953. *Report on the Census of the Non-native Populaton in Uganda Protectorate.* 25th February, 1948, Nairobi.
Eichler, Margrit 1973. 'Women as Personal Dependents.' in Stephenson, Marylee (ed.) *Women in Canada.* Toronto; New Press.
Eliot, George 1872. *Middlemarch.* Edinburgh.
Engel, Arthur 1975. 'The Emerging Concept of the Academic Profession.' in Stone, L. (ed.) *The University in Society.* Princeton; Princeton Univ. Press.
Ensor, Mrs. 'Malaya as I remember It.' Memoirs written early in 1973 and sent by her son-in-law to Janice N. Brownfoot.
Entebbe 1960. *Non-African populaton census,* 1959.
Ewen, S. 1976. *Captains of Consciousness.* U.S.; McGraw Hill.
Faber, Geoffrey 1933. *Oxford Apostles.* London; Faber & Faber.
Farquhar, June 1974. *The Mukamba Tree.* Bulawayo; Books of Zimbabwe.
Finch, J. 1980. 'Devising conventional performances: the case of clergymen's wives.' *Sociological Review* 28, 4: 851-70.
—. 1983. *Married to the Job: Wives' Incorporation in Men's Work.* London; George Allen & Unwin.
Forster, E.M. 1936. *A Passage to India.* London; Penguin edn.
Foucault, M. 1977. *Discipline and Punish.* London; Allen Lane Penguin Books.
Friedan, Betty 1981. *The Second Stage.* London (1982); Michael Joseph.
G.E.R.T.R.U.D.E. 1978. (trans. Maryon Macdonald). 'A Postface to a Few Prefaces.' *Journal of the Anthropological Society of Oxford* IX, 2: 133-142. Orig. publ. in *Cahier d'Etudes Africain,* Paris.
Gartrell, Beverley 1979. *The Ruling Ideas of a Ruling Elite: British colonial officials in Uganda.* Ph.D. Dissertation, City University of New York. University Microfilms, Ann Arbor, Michigan.
Geertz, C. 1975. *The Interpretation of Culture.* London; Hutchinson.

Gifford, Margaret Jeune 1932. *Pages from the Diary of an Oxford Lady 1843-1862.* [Margaret Dyre Jeune]. Oxford; Blackwells.

Goffman, E. 1961. *Asylums.* Harmondsworth (1968); Pelican.

Goldberg, L. C. *et al* 1965. 'Local-Cosmopolitan: Unidimensional or Multidimensional.' *American Journal of Sociology* 1965, pp. 704-717.

Goody, J. 1982. *Cooking, Cuisine and Class.* Cambridge; C.U.P.

Grant, M. 1966. *Cambridge.* London; Weidenfeld & Nicholson.

Green, Vivian H. H. 1974. *A History of Oxford University.* London; Batsford.

—. 1979. *The Commonwealth of Lincoln College 1427-1977.* Oxford; O.U.P.

Greer, Germaine 1970. *The Female Eunuch.* London; McGibbon & Kee.

Guide to Singapore (anonymous). Singapore; n.d. but c. 1907.

Halsey, A.H. (ed.) 1976. *Traditions of Social Policy.* Oxford; Blackwell.

Hamilton, Nigel 1981. *Monty; the Making of a General, 1887-1942.* London; Hamish Hamilton.

Hanley, Gerald 1951. *The Consul at Sunset.* London; Collins.

Harrison, Brian. 'Miss Butler's Oxford Survey.' in Halsey, A. H. (ed.) 1976.

Harwich, Christopher 1961. *Red Dust: Memories of the Uganda Police 1935-1955.* London; Vincent Stuart.

Hayter, William 1977. *Spooner: A Biography.* London; W.H. Allen.

Heald, Madeline 1979. *Down Memory Lane with some Early Rhodesian Women.* Bulawayo; Books of Zimbabwe.

Hebdidge, D. 1979. *Subculture: The Meaning of Style.* London; Methuen.

Heilbrun, C.G. 1979. *Reinventing Womanhood.* London; Gollancz.

Helfrich, M.L. 1965. *The Social Role of the Executive's Wife.* Bureau of Business Research, Ohio State University.

Hertz, Robert 1960. *Death and the Right Hand.* London; Cohen & West.

Hochschild, A. 'The Role of the Ambassador's Wife: an Exploratory Study.' *Journal of Marriage and the Family* 1969, pp. 73-87.

Hodder-Williams, R. 1978. 'Politics from the Marandellas Grassroots.' Paper delivered at the Annual Conference of the African Studies Association of the United Kingdom, September 1978.

Hodgkin, E.C. (ed.) 1979. *Smith, Arthur Lionel Forster. 1880-1972. Chapters of Biography.* Printed for Private Circulation.

Hodgkin, Mrs Mary. Letters Home from Malaya to Relatives and Friends, 1931-1940. Photocopies in the possession of Janice N. Brownfoot.

Hole, Hugh Marshall 1928. *Old Rhodesian Days.* London; Macmillan & Co.

Humphrey Ward, Mrs 1918. *A Writer's Recollections.* London; Collins.

Ifeka-Moller, C. 'Female Militancy and Colonial Revolt.' in Ardener, S. (ed.) 1975.

Inglis, Amirah 1974. *The White Woman's Protective Ordinance: Sexual Anxiety and Politics in Papua.* London; Sussex Univ. Press.

Interviews; texts recorded by Janice N. Brownfoot with 226 respondents.

Jacques, C.H. 1977. *A Dragon Century 1877-1977.* Oxford; Blackwells.

Jamieson, Kathleen 1981. 'Sisters under the skin: an exploration of the implications of feminist-materialist perspective research.' *Canadian Ethnic Studies* 13, I: 130-143.

Jeffries, Charles 1938. *The Colonial Empire and its Civil Service.* Cambridge; C.U.P.

Johnson, Joseph 1886. *Noble Women of our Time.* London; Nelson.

Kanter, Rosabeth Moss 1977. *Men and Women of the Corporation.* New York; Basic Books.

Keith, Agnes Newton. 'Home in Borneo.' *Straits Times Annual* 1954; pp. 46-52

'Kingsway' School *Prospectus,* ?1925 & 1981. Printed privately.

Kipling, Rudyard 1891. *Plain Tales from the Hills.* London; Macmillan.

—. 1892. *Barrack Room Ballads.* London; Methuen.

Kirk-Greene, Anthony H.M. 1978. 'On governorship and governors in British Africa.' in Gann & Duignan (ed.) *African Proconsuls.* New York; Free Press.

Kirkwood, Deborah 1977 (MS). 'North Oxford Wives.' Paper presented at the Oxford Women's Social Anthropology Seminar.

Kitahara, M. Comment published in Hertz, Martin F. (ed.) 1982. *Diplomacy: the Role of the Wife (a Symposium)*. Institute for the Study of Diplomacy, Edmund A. Walsh School of Foreign Service, Georgetown University.

Kuklick, Henrika 1979. *The Imperial Bureaucrat: the Colonial Administrative Service in the Gold Coast, 1920-1939*. Stanford, California; Stanford University, Hoover Institution Press.

Leach, Sir Edmund 1982. *Social Anthropology*. Glasgow; Fontana (Fontana Masterguides.)

Leavis, Q.D. 'Henry Sidgwick's Cambridge.' *Scrutiny* XV, I, December 1947.

Le Fèvre, Mrs B. (pen name 'Sianu'). *Short Stories About Malaya*. in British Association of Malaya Collection, Royal Commonwealth Society Library, London.

Leonard, A.G. 1896. *How We Made Rhodesia*. London; Kegan Paul, Trench, Trubner & Co.

Lessing, Doris 1950. *The Grass is Singing*. London; Michael Joseph.

—. 1952. *Martha Quest*. London; MacGibbon & Kee.

Lévi-Strauss, C.L. 1968. 'Social Structures of Central and Eastern Brazil' and 'Do Dual Organisations Exist?' in *Structural Anthropology*. London; Allen Lane Penguin Press.

Lewis, Mary Blackwood 1897-1901. 'Letters about Mashonaland'. Published in *Rhodesiana*: publication of the Rhodesia African Society, No.5, 1960.

Luke, S. 1974. *Power: A Radical View*. London; Macmillan.

McCabe, S. and Sutcliffe, F. 1978. *Defining Crime: a Study of Police Decisions*. Oxford; Blackwell.

McCall, C.J. and Simmeons, J.L. 1966. *Identities and Interactions*. London; Collier-Macmillan.

Macdonald, Sheila 1927. *Sally in Rhodesia*. London; Heath Cranton Ltd.

Mackenzie, John 1871. *Ten Years North of the Orange River*. Edinburgh; Edmonston & Douglas.

MacLean, Joy 1975. *The Guardians*. Bulawayo; Books of Zimbabwe.

McWilliams Tullberg, R. 1975. *Women at Cambridge*. London; Gollancz.

Mallet, C. E. 1924-7. *A History of the University of Oxford*, vols. I-III. London; Methuen.

Mark, R. 1978. *In the Office of Constable*. London; Collins.

Marshall, M. Paley 1947. *What I Remember*. Cambridge; C.U.P.

Maugham, W. Somerset. *Complete Short Stories of W. Somerset Maugham*. (3 Vols.) London; Heinemann 1957.

—. *A Writer's Notebook*. Harmondsworth; Penguin 1967; (first published 1949; Heinemann.)

Mayer, Iona. 'The Patriarchal Image: Routine Dissociation in Gusii Families.' *African Studies* 34, 4, 1975.

Miller, Charles H. 1977. *Khyber: British India's Northwest Frontier*. New York; Macmillan.

Miller, E. J. 'Some Reflections on the Role of the Diplomatic Wife: a Working Note.' *Diplomatic Service Wives' Association Bulletin*, July 1977.

—. 'The Role of the Wife of the Head of Mission.' *Diplomatic Service Wives' Association Magazine*, Spring 1981, pp. 13-23.

Mitchison, Rowy. 'An Oxford Family.' in Hodgkin (ed.) 1979.

Mitford, Nancy. 'The English Aristocracy.' *Encounter*; September 1955.

National Council of Women of Southern Rhodesia 1953. *Women in Central Africa*. Salisbury; The Mercantile Publishing House.

Needham, Rodney (ed.) 1973. *Right and Left: Essays on Dual Symbolic Classification*. Chicago; Univ. of Chicago Press.

Newton, Lillian. n.d. 'More Exquisite When Past.' Typed Mss; original in the Royal Commonwealth Society Library, London.

Nicholson, Patricia J. 1980. *'Goodbye Sailor': the Importance of Friendship in Family Mobility and Separation.* Inverness; Northpress Ltd.

Okely, Judith. 'Privileged, Schooled and Finished: Boarding Education for Girls.' in Ardener, S. (ed.) 1978.

Olivier, S.P. 1957. *Many Treks Made Rhodesia.* Capetown; Howard B. Timmins. (First published in Afrikaans under the title *Die Pioniertrekke na Gazaland.*)

Oman, Carola 1976. *An Oxford Childhood.* London; Hodder & Stoughton.

Orwell, George 1949. *Burmese Days.* London; Secker & Warburg.

Packer, Joy 1975. *Deep as the Sea.* London; Eyre Methuen.

Page, Gertrude 1907. *Love in the Wilderness.* London; Hurst & Blackett.

—. 1908. *The Edge o'Beyond.* London; Hurst & Blackett.

—. 1910. *Jill's Rhodesian Philosophy, or the Dam Farm.* London; Hurst & Blackett.

Pahl, J.M. and R.E. 1971. *Managers and their Wives.* Harmondsworth; Pelican.

Pearce, J. Cyprian. 'Humours of Calling in Malaya.' *British Malaya* 7,2, (June 1932) pp. 50-51.

Peet, G.L. 'When We Were Young.' *Straits Times Annual* 1960, pp. 27-32.

Pocock, D. *The Idea of a Personal Anthropology.* A.S.A. Conference Paper, 1973.

—. 1975. *Understanding Social Anthropology.* Teach Yourself Books; London; Hodder & Stoughton.

Police Review; 13/12/81; 21/11/80; 17/10/80; 19/9/80; 7/3/80.

Police Magazine; February 1981.

Pratt, Fanny. Unpublished letters 1842-1865; in the possession of Mona Macmillan.

Profiles of Rhodesia's Women 1976. National Federation of Business and Professional Women of Rhodesia. Salisbury; private publication.

Purcell, Victor W.W.B. 1965. *Memoirs of a Malayan Official.* London; Cassell.

Questionnaires; completed by 149 respondents and returned to Janice N. Brownfoot.

Quiggin, M.A. in Phillips, A. 1979. *A Newnham Anthology.* Cambridge; C.U.P.

Ransom, Ronald. 'Highways and Byways.' *Straits Times Annual* 1969; pp. 132, 134, 136.

Raverat, G. 1952. *Period Piece: a Cambridge Childhood.* London; Faber & Faber.

Report of the Committee appointed to Inquire into the Cost of Living 1913. Salisbury; Government Printer.

Report on Employment of Native Female Domestic Labour in European Households in Southern Rhodesia 1932. Sallsbury; Government Printer.

Report of the Malayan Public Services Salaries Commission; Sir John Bucknill, President. (Known also as the Bucknill Report.) Singapore, 1919; Foreign & Commonwealth Office Library, London.

Richards, Hylda 1952. *Next Year Will be Better.* South Africa; Hodder & Stoughton Ltd.

Rivière, P.G. 1971. 'Marriage: a Reassessment.' in Needham, R. (ed.) *Rethinking Kinship and Marriage* (A.S.A. II). London; Tavistock.

Rodgers, Annie 1938. *Degrees by Degrees.* Oxford; O.U.P.

Roe, Philippa J. 1982. *The British Army as a Subculture.* Unpublished dissertation, Oxford Polytechnic.

Roff, William B. 1967. *The Origins of Malay Nationalism.* New Haven; Yale Univ. Press.

Rogers, Barbara 1980. *The Domestication of Women.* London; Tavistock.

Rosaldo, M.Z. 1974. 'A Theoretical Overview.' in Rosaldo, M.Z. & Lamphere, L. (eds.) *Woman, Culture and Society.* California; Stanford Univ. Press.

Rothblatt, S. 1968. *The Revolution of the Dons.* Cambridge; C.U.P.

Runcie, Rosalind. 'Clergy Wives are People Too.' *The Times,* 7 August 1982.

Sampson, A. 1975. *The Seven Sisters: the Great Oil Companies and the World they Made.* London; Hodder & Stoughton.

Sandford, Elizabeth 1831. *Woman in her Social and Domestic Character.* London; Longman, Rees, Orme, Brown & Green.
—. 1836. *Female Improvement.* London; Longman, Rees, Orme, Brown & Green.
Santry, Denis and Wilson, Claude 1920. *Salubrious Singapore.* Singapore; Kelly & Walsh.
Sciama, L. 'The Problem of Privacy in Mediterranean Anthropology.' in Ardener, S. (ed.) 1981.
Scott, John H. MacCullum 1939. *Eastern Journey.* London; Gifford.
Seidenberg, Robert 1973. *Corporate Wives - Corporate Casualties.* New York; American Management Association.
Selassie, T. B. 1981. '"Centre" and "Periphery" in history: the Use of Warriors and Women in Traditional Ethiopia.' *Journal of the Anthropological Society of Oxford,* XII, 1.
Sidney, R.J.H. 1926. *Malay Land.* London; Cecil Palmer.
Sloan, Agnes. 'The Black Woman.' in *Southern Rhodesia Native Affairs Department Annual* (NADA) 1923. Salisbury; Government Printer.
Smith, Mrs Alice (now Mrs Hartley). 'Personal Recollections.' Typescript of notes for a talk given in the U.S.A., c. 1952; photocopy in the possession of Janice N. Brownfoot.
Smith, Dorothy E. 1973. 'Women, the family and corporate capitalism.' Republished 1977 in Stephenson, M. (ed.) *Women in Canada.* Don Mills, Ontario; General Publishing.
Soldier Magazine; correspondence 1978.
Southern Rhodesia Native Affairs Department Annual (NADA) 1923. Salisbury; Government Printer.
Southern Rhodesia Yearbook 1952. Salisbury; Rhodesia Printing and Publishing Co. Ltd.
Southgate, P. 1980. *Women in the Police.* London; H.M.S.O.
Spender, Dale 1980. *Man Made Language.* London; Routledge & Kegan Paul.
Spooner, William. *Diary* MS. New College Archives, Oxford.
Steer, David 1980. *Uncovering Crime; The Police Role.* London; H.M.S.O.
Stockley, Cynthia 1903. *Virginia of the Rhodesians.* London; Hutchinson & Co.
Stone, L. (ed.) 1975. *The University in Society.* Princeton; Princeton University Press.
Strachey, Lady 1898 [1928 edn.] *Memoirs of a Highland Lady* [Elizabeth Grant]. London; Murray.
Sullivan, P.K. 'The Role of Women in the Police Service - the Effects of the Sex Discrimination Act. A Comparison of Respective Positions.' *Police Journal* Vol. LII (4) October 1979; pp. 336-343.
Sullivan, W.M. 'Toward Unsnarling the Foreign Service 'Wife Problem''. *Foreign Service Journal,* April 1977.
Tanner, R.E.S. 1963. 'Who goes home? A post-mortem on small European communities in Tanganyika.' *Transition* 8 & 9.
Tanser, G.H. 1974. *A Sequence of Time, The Story of Salisbury, Rhodesia.* Salisbury; Pioneer Head.
Tawse Jollie, Ethel 1924. *The Real Rhodesia.* London; Hutchinson.
Taylor, B. 'The Outdoor Trail to Management Training.' *Shell World*; Jan/Feb 1981.
Taylor, Mary 1865-70. 'The First Duty of Women.' One of a series of articles for women in the *Victorian Magazine.*
Thackeray, W.M. 1847-48. *Vanity Fair.* 1863 edn., London; Bradbury & Evans.
Tisdall, E.E.P. 1963. *Mrs Duberly's Campaigns.* London; Jarrolds.
Tredgold, Robert 1968. *The Rhodesia that was my Life.* London; George Allen & Unwin Ltd.
Trevelyan, G.M. 1943. *Trinity College. A Historical Sketch.* Cambridge; C.U.P. (1972 edn.)

Trinity College, Cambridge *Annual Record* 1981-82. (The Master's Commemoration Speech.)

Turner, Victor 1969. *The Ritual Process: Structure and Anti-Structure.* Harmondsworth; Penguin.

—. 1974. *Dramas, Fields and Metaphors.* New York; Cornell Univ. Press.

Vandervelde, Maryanne 1979. *The Changing Life of the Corporate Wife.* New York; Warner Books.

Warby, Marjorie 1944. *Senior Lady.* London; Collins.

Ward-Jackson, C. 1920. *Rubber Planting: A Book for the Prospective Estate Assistant in British Malaya.* Kuala Lumpur; Incorporated Society of Planters.

Watney, B. 'To colonial wives.' *Health Horizon,* Winter 1954; pp. 37-42.

Weinrich, A.K.H. 1973. 'Social Stratification and Change among African Women in a Rhodesian Provincial Town.' Paper delivered at the First Congress of the Association for Sociologists in Southern Africa.

Weissman, Myrna and Paykel, Eugene 1972. 'Moving and Depression in Women.' *Transitions/Society* 9, 9: 24-28.

Whitaker, B. 1979. *The Police in Society.* London; Methuen.

White, A.S. 1965. *The British Council: the First 25 Years 1934-1959.* London; the British Council.

Whyte, W.H. 'The Wives of Management.' *Fortune,* October/November 1951.

Wilson, W. Arthur. 'Mems and Mannerisms.' *British Malaya* 2, 12 (April 1928); pp. 317-320.

Winstanley, D.A. 1947. *Later Victorian Cambridge.* Cambridge; C.U.P.

Young, M. 1979a. 'Pigs 'n Prigs: A Mode of Thought, Practice and Experience.' *Working Papers in Social Anthropology,* University of Durham, No.3.

—. 1979b. 'Ladies of the Blue Light - Female Social and Physical Space within the Police - and the Sex Discrimination Act.' Paper presented at the First Durham University Workshop on 'Women in Society'.

—. 1980. 'The Mythology of Crime; Classification, Practice and the Symbols of Evil.' Unpublished seminar paper, Durham University.

NAME INDEX

See also Bibliography, pp. 211-218

SUBJECT INDEX

B840448

Southern Methodist Univ.   fond
HQ 759.I47 1984
The Incorporated wife /

3 2177 00236 7116

DATE DUE

Interlibrary Loan		
4 Weeks Use		
No Renewals		
DTM		
# 342882		
11-1-00		
T=251		
GAYLORD		PRINTED IN U.S.A.